TRACING YOUR COALMINING ANCESTORS

FAMILY HISTORY FROM PEN & SWORD

Birth, Marriage and Death Records
David Annal and Audrey Collins

Tracing Your Channel Islands Ancestors
Marie-Louise Backhurst

Tracing Your Yorkshire Ancestors
Rachel Bellerby

The Great War Handbook
Geoff Bridger

Tracing Your Royal Marine Ancestors
Richard Brooks and Matthew Little

Your Rural Ancestors
Jonathan Brown

Tracing Your Pauper Ancestors
Robert Burlison

Tracing Your Huguenot Ancestors
Kathy Chater

Tracing Your East End Ancestors
Jane Cox

Tracing Your Labour Movement Ancestors
Mark Crail

Tracing Your Ancestors
Simon Fowler

Tracing Your Army Ancestors
Simon Fowler

A Guide to Military History on the Internet
Simon Fowler

Tracing Your Northern Ancestors
Keith Gregson

Your Irish Ancestors
Ian Maxwell

Tracing Your Northern Irish Ancestors
Ian Maxwell

Tracing Your Scottish Ancestors
Ian Maxwell

Tracing Your London Ancestors
Jonathan Oates

Tracing Family History on the Internet
Christopher Patton

*Tracing Your Prisoner of War Ancestors:
The First World War*
Sarah Paterson

Tracing Your Tank Ancestors
Janice Tait and David Fletcher

Great War Lives
Paul Reed

Tracing Your Air Force Ancestors
Phil Tomaselli

*Tracing Your Second World War
Ancestors*
Phil Tomaselli

Tracing Your Secret Service Ancestors
Phil Tomaselli

Tracing Your Criminal Ancestors
Stephen Wade

Tracing Your Legal Ancestors
Stephen Wade

Tracing Your Police Ancestors
Stephen Wade

Tracing Your Jewish Ancestors
Rosemary Wenzerul

Fishing and Fishermen
Martin Wilcox

Tracing Your Canal Ancestors
Sue Wilkes

TRACING YOUR COALMINING ANCESTORS

A Guide for Family Historians

Brian Elliott

Pen & Sword
FAMILY HISTORY

First published in Great Britain in 2014 by
PEN & SWORD FAMILY HISTORY
An imprint of
Pen & Sword Books Ltd
47 Church Street
Barnsley
South Yorkshire
S70 2AS

ISBN 978-1-84884-239-7

Typeset by Concept, Huddersfield, West Yorkshire.
Printed and bound in England by CPI Group (UK) Ltd, Croydon, CR0 4YY.

Pen & Sword Books Ltd incorporates the imprints of
Pen & Sword Archaeology, Atlas, Aviation, Battleground, Discovery,
Family History, History, Maritime, Military, Naval, Politics, Railways, Select,
Social History, Transport, True Crime, Claymore Press, Frontline Books,
Leo Cooper, Praetorian Press, Remember When, Seaforth Publishing
and Wharncliffe.

For a complete list of Pen & Sword titles please contact
PEN & SWORD BOOKS LIMITED
47 Church Street, Barnsley, South Yorkshire, S70 2AS, England
E-mail: enquiries@pen-and-sword.co.uk
Website: www.pen-and-sword.co.uk

CONTENTS

Acknowledgements   ix
'A day I shall never forget'   xi
Glossary   xiii
Introduction   1

PART 1: THE MINER IN CONTEXT   7
Chapter 1: Discovering the Working Life of your Miner-Ancestor 8
Getting set on   11
Homes and transport   13
First days: working at the pit top   14
First days: working underground   16
Pony drivers   19
Job variety and progression   22
Colliers   23
Bathing and women's work in the home   26
Officials: deputies and overmen   28
Under-managers and managers   30
Mining engineers   31
Pit sinkers   33
Engine winders   35
Pay   35
Further reading   38

Chapter 2: Accidents, Disasters and Disease   39
Everyday accidents and dreadful disasters   39
Occupational diseases and ailments   43
Research guide: 45
    Burial registers   45
    Civil registration   45
    HM Inspectors' reports   45
    Accessing annual mines inspector's and disaster reports   55
    Newspapers and periodicals   56
    Where to find newspapers   63

Internet sources   65

Other useful sources   65

Was your mining relative or ancestor in the mines rescue service?   73

Did your coalmining relative or ancestor receive a bravery or
gallantry award?   75

Further reading, video and film   80

Chapter 3: Rights and Strikes: Associations and Unions   82

Union development c.1780-present   85

Strikes and lock-outs   86

    Notable strikes and lock-outs   87

Demonstrations and galas   89

Banners   90

Miners' leaders   91

Women   92

Research guide   93

Further reading   94

Chapter 4: Women and Child Miners   96

'Invisible' female miners   99

Women pit-top workers   100

Women and children working underground   106

The Children's Employment Commission (Mines) and its two Reports
1840–42   108

Further reading   116

Chapter 5: Coalfields and Miners at War   118

First World War, 1914–18   118

Spanish Civil War, 1936–39   131

Second World War: 'We'll do the fighting if you get the coal'   132

Selective sources and further reading   138

Chapter 6: Using the Census   140

Incomers and Miner-Households: a case study of Treeton, near
Rotherham in south Yorkshire (1891)   140

Further Treeton sources   151

Chapter 7: Making Use of Objects and Ephemera   152

Pit checks   152

Early union badges   154

Later union, strike and commemorative badges   155

Safety lamps   156

Ceramics and glassware   157

Small metalware	159
Ephemera	160
Awards	163
Clothing and equipment	164
Chapter 8: Collieries and Coalfields	165
Coalfields post-1947	165
Lists of coal mines	166
Printed maps and plans	169
Further reading	170
Colliery names	170
PART 2: WHERE TO FIND INFORMATION	171
Chapter 9: Regional Sources	172
SCOTLAND	174
The coalfields of Scotland	174
ENGLAND	184
Northumberland & Durham coalfield	184
Cumberland coalfield	192
Yorkshire (& Nottinghamshire/Derbyshire) coalfields	194
Lancashire and Cheshire coalfields	204
Midlands coalfields	210
Bristol and Somerset/Forest of Dean (Gloucestershire) coalfields	219
Kent coalfield	224
WALES	225
North Wales coalfield	226
South Wales coalfield	228
Chapter 10: National Sources	238
SCOTLAND	238
National Mining Museum	238
National Records of Scotland	239
National Library of Scotland	241
Scottish Screen Archive	241
National Museums Scotland	242
RCAHMS	242
Scottish Genealogy Society	242
Online sources	243
ENGLAND (& UK-wide)	244
National Mining Museum	244
British Library	244

Coal Authority   245
Institution of Mechanical Engineers   246
Iron Mountain   246
The National Archives   247
NUM   247
Working Class Movement Library   248
Online sources   248
WALES   252
National Museum Wales   252
Big Pit National Coal Museum   252
National Waterfront Museum   252
National Museum Cardiff   253
National Library of Wales   253
National Screen & Sound Archive   254
Online sources   254

Index   256

ACKNOWLEDGEMENTS

Many individuals and organisations deserve my thanks for their help during the course of the five years of research and writing of this book. Special thanks are due to Rupert Harding and Simon Fowler at Pen & Sword Books for their patience and support and to Susan Last for copy-editing the text. Thanks also to Ian Helliwell for typesetting and design. The curators and librarians at our three excellent national mining museums have been extremely kind and helpful. Grateful thanks are due to Ceri Thompson at the Big Pit, who has responded to numerous queries on both Welsh mining and mining in general; and also to Robert Prothero-Jones at the National Waterfront Museum. I am indebted to staff at all of the national organisations consulted for supplying and/or directing me to information, and special thanks are due to the British Library's staff at Colindale when I was working on newspaper sources during the early stages of research. Author Geoffrey Howse deserves thanks for his kindness and hospitality when I was at work in London.

For the research section, several hundred regional librarians, information officers and archivists responded to my requests for information about mining sources via letter, telephone, email and website enquiry form; and many read and approved relevant entries, though any errors and omissions remain my own. Many thanks to them.

I am grateful to the Masters and Fellows of Trinity College, Cambridge for permission to quote from the Munby archive; and also to the Gallery of Costume, Platt Hall (Manchester City Galleries) for permission to use a Clayton image from their collection. Thanks are also due to the Big Pit/ Museum of Wales for permission to use extracted material from their *GLO* magazine. Most of the illustrations used in this book are largely from my own picture collection unless otherwise credited. My friend, Ian Winstanley, founder of the online Coal Mining History Resource Centre, has been a constant source of support whenever needed; as have many family history societies and family historians that I have met at meetings and events over many years; indeed, several of them were even kind enough to supply case studies relating to their mining ancestors. Michelle Hassall and her son Tommie Hassall were kind enough to allow me to reproduce an extract from the award-winning essay, 'A day I shall never forget'. Aspects of my work

'Shag's Main'. Impromptu outcropping such as this 1912 example was also common during subsequent strikes and lock-outs: Midhope, Sheffield.

on military, census and other related family history information received much appreciated specialist help from Jayne Daley and Andrew and Fiona Featherstone.

Great thanks go out to the many miners and mining family members whom I have met and interviewed over many years. Without their help the book would not have materialised in its present form. And finally a huge thank you to my wife, Angela Elliott, for putting up with me and my seemingly never-ending shift-work in my study over such a long period of time.

'A DAY I SHALL NEVER FORGET'

[Extracted from an essay written in 2007 by 11-year-old Tommie Hassall after he had visited – with his granddad – derelict mining cottages in a former South Yorkshire pit village.]

Aflat cap hung on the back of the door which led upstairs and beneath it lying on the floor was a shiny tin with a handle. 'That's a snap tin,' explained granddad. 'Is that because it snaps together?' I asked. 'No, snap, food, that's what they put in it!' For a moment I thought I could hear the sound of picks chiselling at the coal underground. I remembered watching a mineworkers' procession with my mum to mark twenty years after the last miners' strike. I didn't really understand then. It didn't seem dark like the mines must have been. I just remember the vibrant colour of silk banners being held by groups of men swaying in a soft light and the sound of a band. I felt I had lingered in the room too long, there was something still and private here, something intimate and alive. The soul had

Banners, bands and marchers during the 2004 Yorkshire miners' gala that Tommie witnessed in Barnsley.

been ripped from the heart of the village but locked in this abandoned cottage were memories and a way of life that would remain forever. I needed to go outside and I felt I had intruded on the past. Granddad followed, we pushed the door and made it secure. The light hurt my eyes for a moment, like a miner when he first comes out from underground and I knew that I had taken something from the past with me. This was a day I would never forget.

The full essay won Tommie the Simon Beaufoy [children's] Short Story Competition, established in honour of the award-winning screenwriter, whose films include *The Full Monty, Slumdog Millionaire* and *Salmon Fishing in the Yemen*.

The onsetter signals to the winding engineman for the cage to be raised up the shaft. The miners about to ascend to light include boys barely tall enough to reach the safety bar: Denby, Derbyshire, c.1910.

GLOSSARY

Job-related

Agent	The chief official of a large colliery or group of collieries or Group Manager after nationalisation.
Back-overman	An **Overman** in charge of the back-shift of workers in a coal mine, i.e. men in charge of repair and maintenance.
Banksman	Man employed in charge of signals and **cage**-loading at the top of the shaft. Collects **checks** from the men and liaises with the **winder**.
'Big-hitter'	A modern and unofficial term used in some areas to describe a highly-paid miner employed – often on contract work – for example making **headings.**
Blacksmith	Colliery blacksmiths sharpened miners' picks and repaired and maintained metal items, as well as shoeing horses and ponies. Also see **Farrier**.
Block-layer	or **Roadman** or **Plate-layer**. A man employed in laying and maintaining rail tracks underground.
Breaksman	See **Winding Engineman**.
Bummer	The man in charge of a group of men on a **longwall** face.
Buttyman	Before nationalisation a person who has an agreement with the colliery owner or manager to independently employ and pay a small group of miners. Also see **Sub-contractor**.
Coalmaster	Old name for a colliery owner, especially in the eighteenth century and earlier.
Coalminer	or **Miner**. Generic term for a person who works underground at a coal mine.
Checkweighman	A man chosen by the miners to monitor and check that the amount of coal that each man or team had extracted was correctly weighed at the surface, an essential requirement under the piecework system.
Collier	or **Hewer**. A skilled and experienced miner who extracts the coal from a seam at a **coalface** and sets supports for safety. Sometimes the word is used in a generic sense, especially in newspapers. Also see **Getter**.
Corporal	A person responsible for a group of haulage hands. Known as a '**Doggy**' in Lancashire and Staffordshire.
Cutterman	A miner responsible for operating a coal-cutting machine.

Dataller	A day-wage worker, usually an underground general labourer.
Deputy	or **Fireman**. A qualified underground official responsible for the safety and operation of men in a **district** of a mine.
Dinter	A man employed on floor excavation on underground **headings** and roadways.
Discharge note	A certificate given to each worker who satisfactorily completed his contract of service at one colliery and which had to be produced before he could be engaged at another. Suspended in 1896.
'Doggy'	See **Corporal**.
Door trapper	A boy (or girl) working underground responsible for opening and closing ventilation doors.
Drawer	The Lancashire (mainly) version of a **Hurrier, Putter, Trammer** or **Hurrier**.
Faceworker	A modern term for a **miner** who regularly works at the **coalface**.
Farrier	A person responsible for the stables of horses above and below ground. Traditionally shoes horses.
Filler	A man working with a **collier** to manually load coal into tubs or on to conveyor belts.
Fireman	See **Deputy**.
Fitter	A qualified man responsible for the repair and maintenance of underground machinery and equipment.
'Gaffer'	Used especially post-1947 (nationalisation) for a manager or other senior official.
Getter	A man employed in breaking down or detaching coal after it has been 'holed' or undercut. Also see **Collier, Getter** and **Hewer**.
Gummer(man)	Person employed to remove the small coal and dirt from a worked area such as a hand-got or mechanised coalface.
Hanger-on	or **Hooker-on**. The man employed to hang **corves** or **tubs** on to the rope/cage in the pit bottom or at levels via an **endless rope haulage** system.
Haulier	See **Pony Driver**.
Hewer	See **Collier**.
Hitcher	See **Onsetter**.
Holer	A man employed to manually undercut the coal prior to extraction or shotfiring. Also see **Collier** and **Getter**.
Hooker-on	See **Hanger-on**.
Hurrier	See **Putter**.
Hutch Runner	Scottish version of a **Drawer, Hurrier, Putter** or **Trammer**.
Jigger	Underground haulage engine operator.
'King Edward'	A term used in humour, especially in Yorkshire, to describe a miner who spends too much time working underground, doing overtime etc.

Linesman	A man responsible for laying out survey lines underground.
Manager	A qualified person in charge of a coal mine, answerable to the Inspector of Mines.
Master Sinker	See **Sinker**.
Miner	See **Coalminer**.
'Nipper'	A boy miner, especially in Yorkshire.
Official	An experienced and qualified **Deputy** or **Overman**.
Onsetter	or **Hitcher**. Person in charge of the shaft signals and loading/unloading of men and tubs or skips in and out of the **cage** in the **pit bottom**.
Ostler	The person in charge of the underground stables and horses. Also known as a **Stableman**. Also see **Farrier**.
Overlooker	See **Overman** and **Back-overman**.
Overman	An underground **official** intermediate between a **Deputy** and an **undermanager,** usually responsible for more than one **district** of a coal mine. Also known as an **Overlooker** in some coalfield areas.
Paddy mail driver	Underground worker responsible for the safe operation of of a **man-riding** vehicle or paddy train, taking miners to their places of work.
Platelayer	See **Blocklayer**.
Picker	A man, woman or boy who picks dirt and debris from the coal on the pit-top picking tables/**screens**.
'Pit-brow lassie'	A female miner working on pit-top jobs, including **tiplers**, most notably in Wigan and Lancashire.
Pitman	Generic term for a **coalminer**; more specifically a man who examines or inspects the shafts or was in charge of the pumps in the shaft.
Pony driver	or **Pony-putter**. A boy or young miner responsible for moving empty or full tubs with the help of a pony or horse. A general **Haulier**.
'Powder Monkey'	A person who assists a **shotfirer**.
'Prop Bobby'	A miner who checks that props are sound and that they are are in the right place.
Putter	or **Trammer** or **Drawer** or **Hurrier.** A man or boy (and before 1842 a girl or woman) employed in pushing or pulling full and empty tubs (or **sledges**, or **corves**) along underground roadways by hand.
Roadman	See **Block-layer**.
Ripper	A skilled underground miner who enlarges and supports the roofs or **roadways**.
Shotfirer	A suitably qualified person (appointed by the **colliery manager**) who fires shots of explosives in a heading, stone drift or district. Often a prerequisite to becoming a **Deputy**.

Sinker	A specialist miner, part of a team, employed for the sinking of shafts from the surface to the pit bottom, a Master Sinker in charge.
Stableman	See **Ostler**.
Stallman	A **Collier** who works in a stall or face.
Stone Duster	A man employed to distribute stone dust along the roadways in order to reduce inflammability.
Sub-contractor	See **Buttyman**.
Timberman	A person responsible for preparing and conveying wooden props to the coalface and roadways.
Trammer	See **Putter**.
Under-manager	An intermediary between the colliery manager and officials, responsible for the underground operation of the mine; and deputizing for the manager in his absence. Known as '**Under-Viewers**' in the nineteenth century.
Under-Viewer	See **Under-manager** and **Viewer**.
Viewer	Nineteenth-century name for a mine manager.
Winding Engineman	or **Breaksman**. A skilled man in charge of the steam or electric **winding engine** at a colliery, particularly its operation.

Miner-related

Allowances	Extra pay allocated for extreme work, e.g. wet conditions.
Backshift	The afternoon or evening shift, used for pre-production preparation, including repairs and maintenance. Also see **Shift**.
Bait	See **Piece** and **Snap**.
Bannickers	Short work trousers worn just below the knee.
Beat Knee	(or elbow or hand) A common occupational ailment. Bursitis (painful swelling of the knee) caused by kneeling and crawling.
Bond	The legal agreement by which the miner was bound to his master/employer for a set period, usually a year (especially in Northumberland and Durham, and Scotland).
Bull Week	Two weeks of intense and/or prolonged work so as to earn as much as possible before Christmas.
Check	A numbered brass (usually) token issued to prove the presence of a miner in the pit. Normally hung in the lamp room. Also known as a **Tally**.
Clogs	Sturdy leather footwear with wooden soles and attached iron grips or studs.
Contraband	Illegal materials (especially combustible) found or confiscated before going underground.
Drawers	Miners' shorts or knickers worn when working in hot conditions.
Dudley	Metal, 'clock-shaped' drinking water container carried by a miner underground. Capacity of 2, 4 pints or more.
Hand-got	Coal extracted manually, mainly by pick, wedge and shovel.

Hoggers	A footless stocking, usually worsted.
Holing	Manually undercutting a coal seam, the miner often laying on his side to do the work: 'to hole'.
Jack	Tin drinking water bottle with a cork stopper.
Mandrel	See **Mandril**.
Mandril	or **Mandrel**. A miner's pick (Welsh).
Man-riding	Miner riding on an underground rail via a moving tub or set of tubs or on a moving conveyor belt.
Miner's phthisis	See **Silicosis**.
Moleskin	Hard-wearing and warm material often used for miners' trousers.
Nystagmus	Painful miners' disease characterized by oscillation of the eyeballs.
Piece	See **Snap**.
Pneumoconiosis	Respiratory disease caused by the long-term inhalation of dust in mines. Also known as 'black lung disease'. Also see **Silicosis**.
Price List	Piecework pay-rates agreed by the miners/unions and the management/owners, published in the form of a small booklet, usually for a particular colliery.
Shift	A set period of work, usually expressed as 'days' (morning/early afternoon); 'afters' (afternoon/early evening) and 'nights' (evenings/early mornings). Also see **Backshift**.
Silicosis	A disease of the lungs caused by prolonged inhalation of silica dust. Also known as **miner's phthisis** and 'black spit'; and is a form of **pneumoconiosis**.
Sliding scale	Variable miners' pay-rate according to the selling price of coal.
Snap	A miner's portable meal/snack, often contained in a tin. Also known as his **Bait** and **Piece** in Scottish and northern coalfields.
Stint	An amount of work by one man in a **shift**.
Tally	See **Check**.
'Tipple Tin'	Small, usually round and numbered, metal container used to contain a miner's pay and issued i.e. tipped out, on pay-day.
Tommy Box	A small container, usually metal, used to store a miner's lunch. Also see **snap**.
Tommy Shop	A shop owned by a colliery owner or **butty** where pay credits or tokens were exchanged for goods under the **Truck System**.
'Trammer's Scab'	Bruised and rubbed vertebrae as a result of the miner catching his backbone along a low roof during **tramming**.
Truck System	Payment of wages in kind.
Vesting Day	Official date for the nationalisation of coal mines: 1 January 1947.
'Yorks'	Leather straps tied around each trouser leg below the knee. Allegedly to keep the trouser bottoms dry; or keep them out of boots; or stop vermin crawling up the leg – or all three!

Colliery-related

Adit	A tunnel driven into a hillside for working the coal and/or transport and/or drainage. Also see **Drift**.
Afterdamp	Deadly mixture of non-inflammable gasses after an underground **firedamp** explosion.
Blackdamp	Suffocating gas heavier than air, which may also be poisonous. Also known as **Chokedamp**.
Blower	A sudden outburst of gas from the coal seam or surrounding rock, say from a crack of fault.
Box-hole	Underground cabin used as an office.
Cage	A colliery carriage or lift for ascending and descending a shaft. Can be single or multi-deck. Also known as a **Chair**.
Chokedamp	See **Blackdamp**.
Chocks	A system of timber or steel roof supports (known as **Cogs** in some regions) for use at the coalface. Hydraulic steel versions are the most modern.
Coalface	Underground area of a mine where the coal is exposed and extracted.
Cogs	See **Chocks**.
Corfe	(or Corve) A hazel basket in which coal was carried from the face to the surface. Later used to describe a small **Tub** or **Tram**.
Cupola	A ventilation furnace chimney.
Day Hole	A small **Drift** mine.
'Dosco'	Trade name for the large cutting machine used underground on **longwall** faces.
District	A defined or recognised area of a colliery for ventilation and daily supervision (by one or more officials such a **Deputy** or **Overman**.
Downcast Shaft	The shaft through which fresh air passes into the workings of the mine. Also see **Upcast Shaft**.
Dram	A term used in some areas, for example in Wales, for a wheeled **tub**.
Draw	A term used in Scotland and Lancashire for **tramming**. Also see **Putter**; and used in the context of the winding engine, for a descent/ascent of the **cage**.
Drift	A mine driven from the surface, accessed by an inclined tunnel rather than a shaft. Also see **Day-hole** and **Adit.**
Endless Rope Haulage	The use of two rail tracks, one for empty tubs and one for full tubs travelling **inbye** and **outbye** simultaneously on a flat or nearly flat gradient.
Firedamp	Inflammable gas whose chief constituent is methane, much feared by miners.
'Goaf'	See **Gob**.
'Gob'	Also known as 'Goaf': an area where waste material is lodged.

Headgear	or **Headframe** or **Headstocks**, the timber (or steel) structure erected over the mine shaft, with pulley wheels and ropes for raising and lowering the **cages**.
Heading	A drivage or **roadway** through rock and coal in advance of a **coalface**, in order to ascertain the conditions prior to working the coal. 'Hedin' in Wales.
Hoppit	Large iron bucket used by pit **sinkers**. A smaller version is known as a **Kibble**.
Inbye	Towards the coalface. Also see **outbye**.
Inrush	A sudden flow of water into a mine or underground workings.
Joy loader	A mechanical coal-cutter for continuous mining on a **longwall** face, named after its American inventor, in c.1920.
Kibble	See **Hoppit**.
Level	A main underground **roadway**.
Locker	See **Sprag**.
Longwall	A system of working coal originating in Shropshire where a number of men work along a **coalface**, with no supporting pillars needed. Widespread usage in modern-day mines.
Man-hole	Narrow recess in side of a haulage roadway so as to allow a miner to shelter during passage of hauled tubs.
Outbye	Away from the **coalface**. Also see **inbye**.
Pack	A wall of loose stones packed with debris, erected for support of a roof in **longwall** mining.
Paddy mail	Underground miners' train operated by a specialist driver.
Pan	A section of a chain conveyor.
Pillar and Bord	See **Pillar and Stall**.
Pillar and Stall	A system of mining a seam of coal via parallel stalls advancing onwards, leaving pillars of coal to support the roof. Also known as '**pillar and bord**' mining. Each stall was manned by two miners.
Pit	Another name for a coal mine or shaft.
Pit Bank	The colliery surface, especially around the shaft(s).
Pit Bottom	The area at the base of the shaft where the **cage** ascends and where men and materials are loaded under the supervision of the **Onsetter**. Usually a very cold workplace.
Pithead Baths	Purpose-built building where miners change and wash, established mainly through the Miners' Welfare Scheme.
Prop	Wood or steel roof support, set manually or hydraulically.
Roadway	Underground passageway driven through a mine, used for access or exploration.
Safety Lamp	Approved lamp used by miners, originally invented by Sir Humphrey Davy in 1815 but there were many other versions.
Screens	Place on the pit-top where coal is sorted (originally manually) according to size and dirt/debris removed. Part of the coal preparation process.

'Shearer'	Large coal-cutting/power-loading machine that makes a vertical cut in the coalface during modern **longwall** mining. Developed by James Anderton from c.1954 and generally known as the Anderton Shearer Loader.
Skip	A large rectangular (usually) steel container used to carry mined coal when which is then wound up the shaft.
Sprag	A temporary short roof support or prop, made of timber; also a term used for short piece of timber (sometimes called a 'locker') placed in the spokes of a **tram** or **tub** to stop it running away.
Stemming	Clay and/or other material used to ram into a shot hole after explosive has been inserted prior to firing.
Stopping	A barrier built across a roadway to prevent air flowing beyond it. Used to block dangerous gases, especially after an explosion or potential explosion.
Tippler	A mechanical appliance on the pit bank for emptying coal from a **tub** or **dram** above the screens of a colliery. Operated by '**pit brow lasses**' at some collieries.
Tram	See **Tub**.
Tub	A wheeled carriage or wagon used to transport coal and other materials on an underground railroad.
Upcast Shaft	A shaft carrying an ascending air current. Also see **Downcast Shaft**.
Windlass	A man-operated winding device at the top of a shaft.
Whim Gin	A horse-driven drum and rope winding device used at the top of shafts on early mines. Also see **Whimsey**.
Whimsey	Another term for a **Windlass** but later also used for a **Whim Gin**.

INTRODUCTION

I was born and brought up in several south Yorkshire mining villages. Just about everyone I knew – family, relatives, school friends, neighbours – had what might be called 'colliery connections'. The pit not only dominated the skyline at the bottom of our street, but also impacted on lives over several generations. Mining really was a way of life for most people; and it is one of those rare occupations where stories are passed down with remarkable clarity over many years. It was not until I spent some of my time away from home, as a college student in the late 1960s, that I began to develop an interest in local history and the history of coalmining in particular. I was able to visit and interview a good number of descendants of those involved in the 1866 Oaks Colliery disaster for my dissertation. After more than a hundred years their testimony proved invaluable, unobtainable elsewhere. Since then, research, writing and teaching, the latter in both school and adult education contexts, has been a major part of my professional and recreational life for well over forty years.

It was not until the early 1980s, in the pre-internet years, that I began to explore my own family history; and now thanks to much more accessible online sources I can trace several lines of my miner-ancestors back five or six generations. But the first thing that I did – and this is standard advice for anyone beginning research – was to visit relatives so as to collect information and memories. That was the only way I could 'get to know' my granddad Fred Elliott, as he died when I was only two years old. Much later, my research widened to include oral history and academic projects with a large number of mineworkers. Over the years I have tried to make the results of my work accessible to a wide range of people through articles, books and deposits in museums and libraries.

Much of the the contents of this book assumes that readers have at least a basic knowledge of the main sources for family history research. But please don't be put off if you haven't! From time to time I have tried to incorporate general advice into more specialist investigation routes and pathways, and I've referred to good family history advice that can easily be obtained, ranging from fact sheets to internet guides, the latter easily available online from some excellent libraries, archive offices and family history societies.

Of course there are many general books too. Be warned though: the bibliography of the coalmining industry is a massive one. Indeed, it can be

1

Fred Elliott (1887–1948), my paternal grandfather, at his pigeon loft in the village of Carlton, near Barnsley. Fred worked at Dodworth and Monckton collieries.

daunting for new and even experienced researchers. The standard work, *Bibliography of the British Coal Industry* (Oxford University Press, 1981), which is way out of date, lists 120 primary source collections, over 2,500 secondary studies and almost 3,500 parliamentary and departmental papers. Just think of the new books and papers – and internet sources – that have appeared since then. The standard academic source (but not yet digitised), is *The History of the British Coal Industry*, commissioned by the National Coal Board and British Coal. It is best consulted or obtained via a major library or library services as it will cost you a small fortune if you want to buy the five-volume set. Hopefully the reading/source lists that I have suggested at the end of each chapter of this book will direct you to some of the most useful sources available 'for family historians'.

A perhaps surprising number of miners themselves have published auto-biographical accounts of their life and times. Good examples of these can be extremely valuable for background information concerning one or more miner-ancestor. I have made use of several within the main chapters and certainly as part of source lists; and have made similar references to that most underrated source – oral history recordings. If I was to suggest one miner-author to read, with no hesitation I would say make use of the prolific writings of B.L. Coombes (Bertie Louis Coombes, b.1893). A miner in south Wales for forty years, his most famous book, *These Poor Hands: The Autobiography of a Miner Working in South Wales*, is a classic and easily obtainable. It is also well worth reading some of his less well-known writings, summarised and sampled by Bill Jones and Chris Williams (in *B.L .Coombes* and *With Dust in His Throat*) both published by University of Wales Press in 1999. Coombes' very humane writing really does capture the life and times of a miner from the First World War through to nationalisation and beyond. He deserves to be read by anyone with mining ancestry.

Unfortunately, coalminers are often portrayed in stereotypical extremis, banded together as militant agitators or habitual drunkards, even as a 'special breed'. In his 'urban rides' to Wigan and Barnsley, Orwell portrayed them in situations meant to shock 1930s society, echoing the work of the nineteenth-century commissioners. Other authors present the miners as archetypical proletariat workers. In reality – and this is where good family history research is so important – miners lived in communities where the pit, family, sport and leisure, politics and even religion combined and interacted in many positive ways; and especially manifested in deep friendships and an unspoken camaraderie engendered by the ever-present shared dangers of the job. If you get the chance do go and see Lee Hall's *Pitmen Painters* play, based on the painter-miners of Ashington, or, for life at a colliery, get hold of a copy of *The Price of Coal* (1979) by Barry Hines.

Although employment numbers were huge, coalmining family histories are not easy to research. Pits were usually short-lasting enterprises, relatively few surviving a hundred or more years in a single ownership. That's why miners were so mobile and not easy to track, even on the censuses. They might lodge somewhere for a short time and then move on. The coal owners and coal companies were not always the best of record-keepers anyway. Even when they were, their papers may not have survived or have been deposited in archives. What remains is well scattered among regional and national repositories. The Big Question that everyone asks relates to personnel records. If you are researching a direct and recent miner-ancestor then you may be able to find some or part of his employment records via application to the Iron Mountain repository, but otherwise finding personal information, if any, is difficult. However, there are still some very useful pre-1947 company and colliery records in regional and national archives. These can be used alongside general sources such as Ordnance Survey maps, local newspapers, estate and tithe maps and trade directories, and of course

This is the only photograph I have of my father, Fred Elliott (1917–2007: centre of image) in his mining clothes, pictured at Wharncliffe Woodmoor 1, 2 & 3 Colliery in the mid-1960s shortly before the pit closed. He had worked there since the age of 14 and later found a similar job, but on the pit top, at nearby Grimethorpe Colliery.

standard family history sources such as census, civil registration and parish registers.

There are remarkably few modern guides to researching coalmining ancestors: David Tonks' *My Ancestor was a Coalminer*, published by the Society of Genealogists, is a worthy exception. Also still useful is Alison Henesey's *Routes to Your Roots. Mapping Your Mining Past* (National Coal Mining Museum for England).

What I have tried to do in this book is run contextual information alongside research advice in the main chapters of Part One. I have also included several themes that have had relatively little coverage elsewhere from an ancestry viewpoint, for example 'miners at war', 'researching ancestry through objects and ephemera' and aspects of 'accidents and disease'. Part Two, the main reference section, relates to regional and national sources. When researching and writing this section it became clear that a good number of libraries, archives and museums were being revamped and/or rehoused. I have tried to be as up-to-date as possible but do check websites and social media sites for the latest news.

If you can place your miner-ancestor in a meaningful historical and social context it will have been a very worthwhile piece of research, not just for your family, but also for future generations – and for mining history as a whole. It really is worth all the effort: the subjects themselves deserve it. And finally, whilst the internet and commercial sites are wonderfully convenient tools for researchers, do make use of libraries, archives, museums and family history societies in person, where expert support and help is always available.

This c.1891 studio photograph shows my great-grandfather Jonas Elliott (1845–1892) with his wife Harriet and surviving members of the family (two children died young). They lived at Deepcar, near Sheffield, where Jonas worked in small coal and ganister mines. The constant inhalation of silica and coal dust in dreadfully cramped workings led to many premature deaths due to respiratory diseases in this area. Jonas looks far older than his 46 years and probably realized that he was dying when he took the family to a local photographer's studio. He passed away a few months later, and was buried in an unmarked grave in Bolsterstone churchyard. His eldest son George (standing) died aged 30 from the same 'complaint'. My grandfather, Fred Elliott, is the small boy sat on Jonas' knee: another boy miner in waiting.

Brodsworth Main Colliery in the Doncaster area was sunk to the famous Barnsley coal seam from 1905 to 1907 and the model village of Woodlands soon developed, providing comfortable houses for hundreds of miners and their families. During the 1920s the pit became one of the largest and most productive mines in Britain, employing well over 4,000 men and boys and even providing coal for the fires of Buckingham Palace.

Part 1

THE MINER IN CONTEXT

Sons often followed fathers in the coalmining industry. Here, are three generations of a Scottish mining family, the Grays, from Shieldhill near Falkirk, who worked at Gardrum pit.

Chapter 1

DISCOVERING THE WORKING LIFE OF YOUR MINER-ANCESTOR

Mining is one of the few occupations where working memories are passed down over several generations. Workplace camaraderie, close-knit families and living in distinctive communities have contributed to what might be called an inherited testimony; as has the very nature of the job. Even putting the very worst aspects of mining on one side: accidents, disasters and, the most underrated of all – industrial disease – your miner-ancestor worked in one of the dirtiest and most demanding of all British industries.

For most families in mining areas life revolved around the pit: it was the norm, it was what was required and there was little or no alternative. Dad went down the pit and so did his son or sons. Brothers and uncles did the same, as did most of neighbouring bread-winners. It would be rare if your miner did not have a family member or relative or friend or neighbour who also worked at the same or a nearby colliery. **That is why the neighbourhood and community should be an integral, rather than occasional or incidental, part of your research.**

Working in shifts underground for seven, eight or more hours a day, for five to six days a week, required considerable fitness as well as mental fortitude. But that was not the end of the story. The miner still had to get to work and go through a set preparatory routine before descending the shaft or drift; and may have had to travel underground, one, two or more miles to the place where the job actually started; and the point where he really got paid. Of course, the same routine was repeated in reverse order at the end of the shift – with the addition of getting washed at home (or in the pithead baths in later years); so in reality an average workday could easily be extended by at the very least a couple of hours. Not surprisingly, young and old miners (and a good number of middle-aged ones too) fell asleep in their pit muck, absolutely exhausted, well before starting their main home meal, or went straight to bed after returning from the night shift. And yet some men worked, albeit often on so-called 'lighter' jobs, well into old age; others, like

Almost naked and covered from head to boots in muck and grime, two haulage hands pause by their tub of coal, c.1915. Another black-faced lad, still with his shirt on, can be seen in the background. Once 'clipped on', an engine-powered 'endless haulage rope' dragged the tubs to a much cooler area: the pit bottom.

9

my paternal grandfather, a former 'trammer' and proud collier, suffering from illness and disability, worked in the pit top winding engine room, on maintenance work, keeping the place clean and tidy. He had no retirement though, passing away at the age of 60.

Much of this chapter is based on interviews conducted with former miners born well before the nationalisation of the mines in 1947. Although mainly from Yorkshire, their experiences are fairly typical of other regions. The older men, speaking in their 80s and 90s (and a few at the great age of 100 or more) refer to jobs and conditions that existed generations earlier. This oral testimony may therefore help us appreciate what work was like for a miner and his family during the nineteenth as well as the twentieth century.

Boy miners

The 1842 Mines Act prohibited the employment of boys under the age of 10 years working underground, as from 1 March 1943. However, the Act did not have full compliance in its first few years of operation, so don't be surprised if you find that your 8 or 9-year-old ancestor is listed as a miner in the 1851 census return. It was not until 1887 that the legal limit for working underground was raised to 12 years.

Boys were not allowed (or supposed) to work underground until they had reached the age of 13, as from 30 July 1900. The 1911 Coal Mines Act (effective from 1 July 1912) prohibited any boy under the age of 14 working underground, though of course they could be employed on the pit top, and very many were. After the First World War and the Fisher Act of 1918 the age of compulsory education was in any case extended to the age of 14. However, some youngsters were still allowed to leave when 13, something that one of my ancestors achieved – by 'getting his papers signed' (obtaining a certified basic standard of education). Thus some some 13-year-old boys (and very briefly [from January–August 1900] some aged only 12 years) did work at collieries before and just after the First World War, but not, again supposedly, underground.

The 1911 Act also restricted the employment hours of boys to 54 hours a week, and they were not allowed underground after the hours of nine at night and five the following morning. Sundays and Saturday afternoons were excluded for 'boy labour'.

The Butler Education Act of 1944 raised the school leaving age to 15, a figure that remained in force until 1972, when it was extended to 16 years.

Old miners

It was not unusual, before the introduction of the state pension, compulsory retirement age and nationalisation of the coal industry in 1947, for miners to continue to work well into their late 60s. Occasionally, even with disabilities, some veterans continued to work in their 70s, even 80s. There are many examples in nineteenth-century census returns of old miners. This was because, apart from minimal Poor Law relief, trade union and family support, there was little alternative other than to work. It was not until 1908, thanks to Lloyd George, that the first state pension – 5s (25p) a week for men who were aged 70 – was introduced; but it was means tested. In 1925, the pension, now for 65-year-olds, was based on contributions from the employer and employee. Established in 1952, the Miners' Pension Scheme (MPS) continues to provides small pensions to former mineworkers. Originally contributions were voluntary, but became compulsory from 1961. The MPS closed for contributions after the privatisation of the coal industry in 1994.

Tip

Talk to old miners and don't miss an opportunity if you have one to record the memories of any surviving mining relatives. Most of them will love to recall their experiences, good and bad. Keep the session fairly brief and visit them again after you have listened and transcribed the information. Don't barrage interviewees with loads of written questions; it's far better to stick to broad themes and events and keep the interchange informal. Even where some facts are wrong and/ or exaggerated, listening to mining terms and recording the person's voice is well worth the effort. Failing that, do make use of the many thousands of oral history recordings available online or at national and local museums, archive offices and libraries (see the regional and national reference sections of this book). Although the recordings are from non-related individuals they will help place your ancestor in far better context than otherwise.

Getting set on

For many years, leaving school and getting a job at a pit was an informal and fast process. After a few 'weighing up' questions it was just a case of the manager or his representative setting a starting day and time. Having a father or relative already working at the pit was a great advantage. Even religion might play a part. Many youngsters left school on the Friday afternoon and were working at the pit early on the Monday morning, some dispatched underground. Later, from the 1930s onwards and certainly after nationalisation (post-1947), matters were more formal, with youngsters being seen by 'training officers' at the colliery, and of course there were close career links with local schools and youth employment services.

New Starters

Tom Emms (b.1911): The pit was the only job to go to. I was 14 on the Thursday and on the Saturday morning my father took me to the colliery [Edlington Main] to see the clerks and the under-manager and I signed on. On the following Monday I was at the pit at 5.30 in the morning.

Johnny Williamson (b.1912): As soon as I was 14 I was told 'You had better get down the pit lad, they are setting men on'. I went there on my own and knocked on the manager's door. I was asked my particulars and who my father was. As soon as I told them that my father and grandfather were miners I was accepted and I was signed on as a 'nipper' [pit boy].

Roy Kilner (b.1923): The last week in December me and a friend went to Barnburgh pit to get a job. We went into the under-manager's office and enquired, 'Any vacancies, Sir?' He asked me if any of my family worked there. I said, 'Yes, my Uncle Ted.' 'Oh,' he replied, 'he's a good worker. You can start on Monday.'

Arthur Nixon (b.1931): I went on my bike to North Gawber pit one foggy day and was directed the manager's office, reached by some steps alongside some other offices. I knocked on the door and a voice called out 'Come in'. There were six chaps inside, in their pit muck, sat around a roaring fire. 'Now then lad, what can I do for you?' the manager said. I told him I was looking for a job. 'What sort of job?' he replied. I asked if there was a job in the electric shop. He looked at me and asked, 'Are you religious?' I said, 'Well, I went to Sunday school but that's all.' He told me that there were lots of 'bible-punchers' there but gave me a note and sent me to speak to Fred Moxon, the engineer. He asked me a few questions and asked me when I could start. I started the next day.

Homes and transport

Most mines worked a 24-hour day, so having labour close at hand was an essential requirement of estate owners and companies before major transport systems were fully developed. Rows of artisan cottages were built during the eighteenth century by great landowners such as Earl Fitzwilliam, at Elsecar, not far from his great house at Wentworth, near Rotherham, close to his colliery.

Throughout much of the nineteenth century many hundreds of small rural communities in mining areas were transformed into 'pit villages'. Carlton, the south Yorkshire village near Barnsley where I was brought up, was largely changed due to opportunistic private landlords, but a new coal company community consisting almost entirely of miners' families were housed in Carlton Terrace (or 'Long Row' as it was commonly called), right next to the mine. The top end had a working men's club but the bottom, right by the canal and pit, had an adjacent shorter row of superior quality houses where the officials and policeman lived. The manager lived in a small but imposing mansion in the old village.

Getting to the pit

John Williamson (b.1912): Gran would wake me up with a shout, usually several shouts, each getting louder, at 4am. My snap would be waiting for me, wrapped in the *Daily Herald*, which was the working man's paper. I would meet my mates at the end of the street and we would walk a mile and a half to the pit.

Bernard Goddard (b. 1917): I pedalled there on a second-hand bike, which cost me me £5 at 2s 6d a week.

George Kemp (b.1920): It was 4am when I got up. I had to walk from Winn Street into Barnsley and then caught a bus to Carlton, but sometimes would walk it to save money.

Roy Kilner (b.1923): Me and my brother walked to the pit. I was still dressed like a school kid, in short trousers. I walked two and a half miles. As we were going home I made up this little song:

> *With my snap tin on my belt*
> *And my Dudley on my bike,*
> *I'll be off to Barnburgh Main in the morning!*
> *With my hard hat on my head*
> *And my pit boots on my feet,*
> *We'll be off to Barnburgh Main in the morning!*

New off-shoots to old villages emerged, a mix of private and planned initiatives. Close to where I now live, in the Doncaster area, the pit village of New Edlington developed rapidly following the sinking of Edlington Colliery (later known as Yorkshire Main) in 1909/10, very different to the original Norman settlement, which became known as Old Edlington. In the space of twenty years the population of the new village exploded from about 580 in 1911 to over 5,000 in 1921.

Architect-designed model housing estates were created by the more enlightened companies nearby. Percy Bond Houfton, for example, designed 'Woodlands' for the Derbyshire-based Staveley Coal and Iron Company, serving what became the biggest pit in the country, Brodsworth Main, just before the First World War. Woodlands was laid out on garden-city lines and houses were 'individualised' via the fashionable Arts and Crafts style. The model village tradition continued well into the twentieth century when technology enabled large new deep collieries to be sunk through previously inaccessible land. After nationalisation, the NCB inherited and further developed its own huge housing stock, becoming one of the largest land-lords in the UK.

Despite the close proximity of pit houses, many miners walked to their pit from surrounding villages and towns, such was the great demand for labour and the pull of work. Perhaps exceptionally, one miner that I interviewed, Stanley Potter, worked at fourteen different pits in search of better pay and conditions prior to leaving home to get married, then settling down to work at a colliery where he remained until retirement. Every day Stan walked about six miles to a remote drift mine, attracted by slightly better pay than at his local pits. For most, however, getting to work was a communal rather than solitary journey, the miner meeting an increasing number of mates on the way. Towards the end of the century many miners used cycles to get to work and the rail and new tram networks greatly enhanced mobility. During the first few decades of the twentieth century a profusion of private omnibus companies provided special 'pit bus' services to collieries, further increasing access.

First days: working at the pit top

Many former miners will remember their first day at work, some recalling the occasion as a mix of fear and trepidation, others in a more relaxed and matter-of-fact way. The first few weeks and months might be spent on the pit top, say helping out in the timber yard, or doing a job such as working on the screens (where coal was sorted), alongside other boys and a few old miners who through age or disability were unfit to work underground. Ironically a good deal of the work was as dirty and noisy as working underground.

Boys sorting dirt from the coal on the picking belts/screens at a colliery near Bargoed, south Wales, in 1910. Note the elevated position of the man in charge, and the chalked tally list. (NUM)

Screen boys

John Bailey (b.1900): It was a rotten job. A chap from Darfield was the 'bummer'. He went to chapel but he was a lousy boss. We could never do anything right for him. He shouted at us but did not swear, forcing us to do things, for instance, if some of the belts halted he would find something for us to do while it was being repaired.

Arthur Clayton (b. 1901): I then got into this place and it wanted John Milton to describe it because it was Miltonic! It was dim and dusty and noisy and there was a little man in charge of us. He had been a teacher but had lost his job, through drink. There was a big belt, really iron plates, which went round an hexagonal thing ... there were some big mechanical riddles ... bump, bump, bump ... you could not see for dust. As it [coal and debris] came on the belt a boy stood at the bottom of a big riddle. He had a big rake and would spread it along the belt and there were boys on either side, picking out dirt and throwing it over their shoulders to a place at the back which had a trap door leading to the wagons ... A little Irishman was in charge. When you

15

were day-dreaming and not picking dirt out he would shout 'I will cut your liver out and put it back and swear I never touched you.' Later we used to laugh about it when some of us had retired.

George Rawson (b.1913): My job was to pick dirt out of the coal on the screens. I wore shorts and old clothes. The screens were large iron conveyors on which coal came out of the pit. It was tipped down chutes by tipplers. As the coal passed us boys we had to pick the dirt or muck out on to this big conveyor belt. At that time the cleaner the coal was then the more money the owners got.

First days: working underground

Many other young miners worked underground on their first day. Travelling down in the cage at great speed was an unforgettable early experience. Jobs below often involved basic haulage work (loading/unloading tubs in the pit bottom) or general duties. For some, their work was not that far removed from early Victorian child mining: as 'trappers', opening and closing air doors; and later as 'trammers' (also known as putters, hurriers and drawers), pulling and pushing tubs along rails.

A flat cap, old flannel shirt, waistcoat and moleskin trousers (or 'bannikers' – knee-length britches) and boots or clogs were the usual clothes worn by miners right up to the 1940s; and a good deal of the clothing might be reduced to shorts or pants in hot working conditions. Some miners would tie string to their trousers just below the knee, in order to keep the bottoms from getting wet and combat invasions of vermin. Infestations of insects, mice and rats were not unusual, accidentally introduced into the mine with bales of straw and horse feed. There were no toilets or washing facilities underground, and lunch or snap time was usually limited to a ten or twenty-minute break taken wherever work took place. Not surprisingly, in view of the working conditions, plus accidents and disasters, life expectancy for miners remained well below the national average throughout much of the nineteenth and twentieth centuries.

Pit bottom boys, lamp carriers, door trappers and trammers

Jack Steer (b.1898): When I got to the pit bottom my brother told me to sit there for a while while he reported to the deputy who took me to a corporal, the man that dished the jobs out, and he set me clip-carrying. These clips were put on the ropes and pulled the tubs to the districts and back again. I was dragging clips and chains from one end of the shaft to the other. It was very cold by No. 1 shaft but No. 2 shaft it was nice and warm, warm air coming from the districts.

John Clamp (b.1900): I wore shorts and had clogs on my feet. I was on nights on my first day working as a 'deputy's boy' and had to walk with him, but he sat me down and left me in the dark! I went to sleep until he came back.

Arthur Clayton (b.1901): My first job underground was lamp-carrying, getting four safety lamps from the lamp room and taking them down the pit, walking a long way with a lot of other boys and men. During the shift, if some colliers 'lost' their lamp I had to swap them. They frequently went out, just a jerk would do it. Then I had to walk back to the pit bottom.

Johnny Williamson (b.1912): I was given a CEAG electric hand lamp, which had recently been developed but it weighed 7lbs. I was only 4 foot 6 inches so the lamp dangled from my leather belt, knocking my knees. I soon got used to it. I wore clogs on my feet. When we went to work they would say 'Clogs are going!' Going down the shaft was a bit strange at first. I was told to stand in the middle, there were fourteen of us on one level of a 3-decked cage. We used to go down in 45 seconds, slowly to start off, then there was a 'whoosh' and we were down. From the pit bottom I walked about a quarter of a mile and tripped over just about everything I came across.

Ernest Kaye (b.1917): I was absolutely terrified that first morning, going down in the chair. My old lamp was on my belt and I held on to the safety bar, got off at the bottom, feeling frightened to death. I was told to stay with this man on an 8-hour shift. When I got home Mother asked me how I had got on and I said 'Shocking!' I was a door trapper. There were big wooden doors, two together, since when you opened one to go through you had to shut that one and open the other so the air was not stopped. I was shown what to do, allowing people to pass through, opening and shutting. The air pressure meant pulling the doors hard, using the bar on them, and going through with whoever was passing. I sat on a bit of wood or stood, waiting.

Stan Potter (b.1922): I soon found out what tramming was really like. First he (the collier) told me to get some clay out of the bankside near the pit (a drift mine) entrance and to keep it working with my hands, like plasticine, spitting on it and getting it going. Then he said, 'Here's your candle, lad.' The colliers had to buy their own candles. We went down and into the pass-by and he uncoupled a tub and started tramming it, to show me what to do. The candle was stuck in the clay

One of the loneliest jobs in the mine: a boy door trapper had to open and close a ventilation door – on demand – to allow tubs to pass through.

and placed on the tub. On the main level, about 5ft high, it was okay, but when it came to going along the low gate it was only a yard high and fairly steep. He pushed it up okay and and told me how to drop it off at the end of the rails, leaving a little gap to throw coal into the tub. When the tub was filled he just put a locker in the back wheel, lifted it on the rail and pushed and it slid along. It looked easy. Well it did not work for me. I could not push the tub like he did. I tried using my head against it as I had not enough strength in my arms and had not got his balance or his technique; and had not got his knack of going over the sleepers. My clogs hit them and my back kept hitting the roof. When I got to the end of the gate my back was streaming with blood, all along the vertebrae. I wore a pair of clogs, a pair of tramming drawers [long pants] and was stripped to the waist; and a cloth cap. Later I was in the kitchen getting washed and my mother came to wash my back and noticed all the torn flesh. She said, 'Oh Stanley, what a mess. You can't go there again'. I did. I got used to it and kept my back lower, tramming like my dad did.

James Reeve (b.1928): Dad took me to the box hole [hut-like underground office] and left me with the pit bottom deputy who gave me a sweeping brush! I had to sweep the box hole out and then nearby roadways. It was done to get me used to the pit bottom and get my underground eyesight. The first day seemed an eternity.

18

'Tramming' – pushing tubs of coal on rails – was an arduous job, especially along low roadways with only a candle for light.

Pony drivers

Young miners, from about the age of 12, were often described as 'pony drivers' in census returns and other documentation. Training was minimal and some miners will tell you that the ponies and horses were looked after far better than themselves. From the late 1870s there were strict rules and regulations so as to ensure that the animals were worked properly and not abused, reinforced further via the 1911 Coal Mines Act and subsequent amendments.

Responsible to the ostler or stableman, drivers were in charge of the working animal, when hauling tubs (or trams/hutches as they were also known) to and from the coal faces. It might be a single tub or two, or a train of linked tubs. The horses, despite the complicated logistics of getting them up and down the shafts, were given an annual break during the miners' paid feast or holiday week, after 1938. Occasionally, during the longer strikes they were also given a respite, even taking part in events such as agricultural shows and even races.

'Pit ponies', really horses of various breeds, were an essential though often controversial part of underground mining from as early as the mid-eighteenth century in the North East to well within living memory. In 1878 there were over 200,000 horses at work in British mines, according to the RSPCA. Numbers decreased to around 70,000 by 1912. Founded in 1927, the Pit Pony Protection Society was totally against the use of the animals for mine haulage work. Nevertheless, and despite mechanisation, horses remained useful in some mining situations, over 21,000 still at work in 1945. Numbers rapidly dwindled to 632 by 1971, mostly concentrated in Northumberland and Durham.

A young pony driver, water bottle in his pocket, collecting his horse from the stables. The animal also has some protection: a leather cap, with dual projections that served as blinkers, c.1940s.

Colliery horses featured in a 1976 Walt Disney film, *Escape from the Dark* (or *The Little Horse Thieves* [USA title]), about an attempted rescue of 'condemned to be killed' horses following the introduction of machinery at a Yorkshire mine. Robbie and Gremlin were probably the last colliery horses in Britain, retired from a small south Wales drift mine in 1999. Robbie continued demonstrating his skills, albeit to surface visitors, when pulling small tubs around the site of the National Mining Museum for England (NCM), for a few years afterwards. Patch, another veteran Welsh horse, was the last of the NCM's working horses, passing away in 2011.

Tip

For background reading about horses and ponies in mines see Ceri Thompson, *Harnessed. Colliery horses in Wales* (National Museum of Wales, 2008); Derek Hollows, *Voices in the Dark. Pit pony talk and mining tales* (lulu.com, 2011); also useful are John Bright, *Pit Ponies* (Batsford, 1986) and Eric Squires, *Pit Pony Heroes* (David and Charles, 1974).

Pony drivers remember

Arthur Clayton (b.1901): All the new lads had Dan because he ruled himself. He was a small pony and would do anything. There were some bad ones. One was called Snap! It used to stand and kick, breaking all the gears. On rare occasions two or three boys were killed when the pin jerked out and they fell and the truck ran over them. You used to sit behind the pony, like a drayman . . . taking three empties at a time and bringing three full trucks back.

The head stableman for the whole pit used to come and kill badly injured ponies with a 'peggy'. While it was on the floor they would hold two or three safety lamps before its eyes and then would suddenly remove them and let bang.

Tommy Hart (b.1905): There were about thirty-six ponies. Some were named after First World War battles such as Verdun. Ponies were well looked after. They would walk on their own to the stables and go in their own stalls. It was unbelievable, you did not have to guide them. Sometimes they could be awkward but I never got kicked. I remember that we rode them (against regulation). I got on top of the pony and laid down so my head was below the pony's head but we did not do it a lot. The stablemen were very strict and would inspect every horse and pony and you got a clip around the ear if there was something wrong.

George Rawson (b.1913): Father came home from the pit one day and told me he had got me a job working with him as a pony driver. I was 14 and 3 months. I had to report to the box hole ['office'] in the pit bottom and the deputy would tell me where to go. I walked to the stables where Mr Silcock was in charge. He was very keen and really did look after the horses. When you got back at the end of the shift he would examine them to make sure that there were no cuts, bumps or bruises. We put the collar on and the harness or gears, which were hung in the pass-by. The chain, which was about 5ft or 6ft long, was hooked on to the tubs. The miners would fill the tubs by hand and take them to the pass-by. My pony was called Midget, the smallest in the pit, but I was only small myself, 5ft 2 in. It was well behaved and intelligent but it would not stand still while I put his gears on at the start of the shift. Sometimes the ponies would catch their backs on the roof so the deputy would send the repair men to dint [lower] the roadway. Later I had a pony called George, the same name as me! If we rode the ponies we got into trouble. Every so far down the roadways there were man-holes where you could go for safety. The stableman might hide in there, with a brush and bucket of whitewash, so that when the drivers rode past they they were splashed, so there was no excuse when you got to the pit bottom. We then got a telling off but if you did it too often you got some money stopped from your wage – and that meant trouble at home as well!

Norman Rennison (b. 1922): At South Kirkby they were more like cart horses compared to ours, which were more like New Forest ponies. I drove one which was called Gypsy. It had its tail trimmed, a lovely little pony but it got killed, though not through me. The bloke was taking him out, through the doors, but he should have made sure that nothing was coming and it was hit by some tubs and put down. They used a spiked cap for this, the shape of the horse's head, with a hole in the middle and a spike went into the hole and was banged with a hammer. We used to have to fetch dead ponies off the units on trams which were like tubs with no sides.

You must not hang your coat up with an apple in your pocket anywhere near a horse or he would eat it.

At holiday times we took the ponies out of the pit and into the fields. A box with wooden sides was used to contain them on the chair and it was wound up slowly but they sometimes slipped on metal plates. The ponies got to know you. Some were Welsh mountain ponies and a few were Shetlands. One was called Dot, a great little worker. Another was called Pride, a grey, who used to bang his collar at the back of the tubs and would shove them with his collar, nearly a hundred tubs at a time but they were small, not like the big modern tubs. There were mice in the stables but we had a couple of cats and they got bottles of milk everyday.

Job variety and progression

Some miners were quite happy to work on a variety of jobs during their pit life. Day-labourers – 'datallers' as they were sometimes known – were paid a daily rate for miscellaneous tasks. Many others preferred to progress to 'learning a trade' or specialising and there were plenty of opportunities to do so: as electricians, surveyors, fitters (repair and maintenance workers), engine drivers, plumbers, joiners, blacksmiths, bricklayers, and so on. A National Schedule of occupations and and job descriptions drawn up by the NCB identified 194 underground jobs, 221 surface jobs and 120 jobs in central workshops; and there were many locally-named variations of each one.

Colliers

For many young miners, progressing to work at the coalface – often alongside a father, uncle, even grandfather – was the ultimate ambition. Colliers were an elite workforce. Status and hard work apart, it also meant top pay, especially when working with a good team of men on a productive face. After nationalisation of the industry in 1947 the job of a collier was defined as:

> Getting and filling coal on to a conveyor or into trams [tubs]; getting and filling coal, setting necessary supports, on either machine-cut or hand-got faces; hewing coal by hand-got methods; engaged on stall work and responsible for taking forward rippings, etc., carrying out any operation in connection with a mechanized heading or longwall face; hewing coal with pneumatic picks; developing headings in coal preparatory to opening out stalls.

Coalface-related jobs included that of a 'ripper', who would make and brush roadways to obtain a suitable height, erect supports, bore shot holes, load materials and assist getting coal by hand. Other key jobs included that of the 'packer' (who built pillars or blocks, using stone and dirt to support the roof in the waste area or roadway), 'timberman' (who set wooden props as supports), 'cutterman' (working the coal-cutting machine), 'gummerman' (dealing with waste material after cutting), 'borer' (drilling shot holes), 'conveyor loaderman' (loading coal from conveyors on to tubs), 'fanman' (operating ventilating fan at the face), and so on.

Getting the coal varied tremendously due to geological conditions. The type of coal, angle of dip, faulting, thickness of seams and working conditions, including high temperatures and wetness, were all crucial factors affecting extraction. Many colliers adapted remarkably well when working in low and awkward seams. Some were 'complete colliers' in the sense that they worked alone with little light, many yards from any help or companionship, setting timber props as they progressed each shift.

A Yorkshire NCB photographer, Jeff Poar, captured traditional hand-got coal getting (or 'hand-filling') at Emley Moor colliery in 1983. The Beeston seam here narrowed to only 16 inches (40cm) high and could not be worked by machine. The collier, 59-year-old Reuben Kenworthy, worked most of his shift laid on his side and belly, a pad of cloth the only protection against the floor, using a pick and shovel to get the coal. He was replicating the kind of work that your collier ancestor would have done many generations earlier. Coal extraction was achieved via the power from the muscles in his arms, chest and stomach, combined with years of skill; and from time to time his back would snag against the roof. Reuben worked continuously for three hours until 'snap-time', then took a 20-minute break, then it was back to work in a ridiculously confined space for a further four hours. In this way he extracted twenty-two tonnes of coal on average per day (approx 2,500 shovelfuls!), an extraordinary achievement. The seam record, however, by a Polish miner, Marion Rokicki (or 'Rocky'!) was almost forty tonnes a day. The legendary Rocky never missed a day's work, travelling seventeen miles on a bus to get there every day, even walking it in bad weather, producing over a quarter of a million tonnes of coal single-handedly as a traditional collier.

Reuben Kenworthy, when offered a more comfortable job on a higher face, refused, saying that he was used to working in the old way. To get to his place of work, after a 120-yard shaft descent, he had to take a 600-yard 'man-rider' journey, precariously laid on a conveyor belt, which was also used to carry materials. Then there was a 20-minute walk and crawl to the face. Preparation work, that is undercutting the dirt below the coal, had been done by a machine, as had some blasting by the shot-firers to loosen the valuable coal.

The use of electronic coal-cutting machines, hydraulic roof supports, and great machines known as shearers, greatly increased production at coal faces, though the noise, dust and dirt generated had to be dealt with as part of the health and safety process.

Reuben Kenworthy at work on the Beeston seam in 1983. (Jeff Poar)

Colliers remember

The recollections of old miners provide us with wonderful insights into the organisation, type and conditions of work in the pre-mechanisation era.

Jack Steer (b.1890): It was hard work. I wore a pair of pit pants, nothing else apart from shoes as it was so hot. The sweat ran down my chest. I've seen colliers take their pants off to wring them out. Every collier had his own way of getting the coal. It wasn't just strength as you used your brains. An experienced collier would cut out one side, cut underneath and over the top, but a strong man might just use brute force, but would achieve less. You would work on your stomach, 'spragging' (supporting with timber) the coal to hold it up and then knock the sprags out and the coal would fall. When cutting you had to lay on your side with room just to swing your pick. You kept putting sprags under, until about 5 foot, then knocked them out and it was then easy coal to chuck on. This was the old method of 'holing' as they called it.

Tommy Henwood (b.1911): I worked in the New North East face, a Barnsley seam, which was 5ft 6 in. You had to fill a stint [in a shift, say 3 cubic yards] of coal. I used a pick and shovel, hammer and wedge and a ringer [long bar]. At the bottom by the floor we put wooden blocks under the coal and knocked them out and put wooden props up so we could get cover and knock the props out and the face would come down. If the props didn't hold then you got out of the way fast. I have been buried up to my neck but when mechanisation came steel props came in. We preferred timber as they would split and crack to warn us.

George Rawson (b.1913): Four men worked a pillar of coal or stall, two on day shift and two on afternoon shift. They had to hew under the coal with picks. There was no shot firing. After holing under the coal, by lying on your side, iron wedges were driven into the top pillar of coal to make it leave the roof, then the coal was broken up with a sledge hammer. One of the hammers was bigger than the other and was called a 'Monday' as no one liked using it after having a weekend off! The coal was then filled into tubs and the tubs taken by the pony driver to the pass-by where they were sent to the pit bottom by the rope haulage. Hand filling and hewing was very hard work.

George Kemp (b.1920): I would sneak on to the face to the colliers and help them, learning how to go on. I progressed to become a collier when I was 19. The Silkstone was about 2ft 8inches in height. Faces were 200 yards long and ten men worked up at the top side and ten at the low side. You worked on your knees. Getting to your place, you each had 10 yards of coal, about 14 tonnes, to shift. This was a stint. You carried an oil lamp, an electric lantern, a pick, shovel and hammer. You got rid of the gummings [waste] so that it would be higher to work in. The face was prepared for us by the previous shift by the shot-firers. By 10 you felt buggered but three or four slices of bread and fat would revive you. We did not leave the face but occasionally went to the tailgate to have a stretch. Going to the toilet, well you just had to manage where you were working, shovel it into the gob [waste area] and cover it. You could not do anything else. Some might do it on a shovel and put it on a belt but this was not fair on the lads working on the screens!

Bathing and women's work in the home

The pit-head bath was full of naked and chattering males of various ages. Almost every bare body there was slim and well shaped. Very few pitmen are ever podgy; their work and bending see to that. New energy and cheerfulness stir our bodies as the hot shower sluices the coal dust downwards in black streams.

B.L. Coombes, *Home on the Hill. An autobiography*
(1959: unpublished)

As a small boy growing up in a Yorkshire pit village I can still remember a few black-faced miners coming home from work in their 'pit muck', despite the provision of colliery pithead baths. For generations miners had little option but to strip to the waist and bend over an oval zinc bath or bathe in a tub in front of the fire or in the backyard after each shift. What a job it must have been to wash away so much muck and grime. The role of women in this process should not be underestimated! Meal-making apart, mothers, wives and sisters would spend many hours in preparation in a household that might include anything from three to ten or more male miners coming home at three crucial shift times: days (about 2pm); afters (about 10pm) and nights (about 5am). Goodness knows how they coped when several men and boys arrived home at the same time. As each shift ended water had to be heated in the 'copper' (an integral boiler) or in receptacles placed on the fire in readiness to fill and replenish the bath. What's more, the water had to be carried in enamel bowls or jugs to the bather, a back-breaking daily chore; and women were expected to scrub the man's back (though the superstition of avoiding this as it 'weakened the spine' may have persisted for some old miners). Many women developed arthritic and other problems in later life, and even suffered miscarriages. Scalding was also common, occasionally with fatal consequences. Allied to this work was the endless task of the drying of damp pit clothes and associated wash days, which for large families must have taken many hours. In a very real sense women were the unpaid home workers of the coal industry.

The provision of pithead baths – often viewed suspiciously by miners at first – was undoubtedly one of the most important social and practical

Filling the old 'tin bath' with hot water was a back-breaking and potentially dangerous task for women.

In the showers at Woolley Colliery, near Barnsley. The pithead baths here opened in 1939.

innovations of the industry. And linked with this development was the provision of canteens and medical rooms, staffed by a 'pit nurse' and/or 'ambulance' man.

Further reading: Ceri Thompson, *The Pithead Baths Story* (National Museum Wales Books, 2010); Brian Elliott, 'Muck and grime. Home and pithead baths' in *Memories of Barnsley* [magazine], Issue 25, Spring, 2013.

Pithead baths

- The 1911 Coal Mines Act stated that if two-thirds of mineworkers submitted a request for pithead baths (and were willing to pay half the cost of maintenance), the owners would build them, provided the upkeep was no more than 3d per miner.
- The Sankey Commission (1919) recommended that pithead baths should be provided at collieries.
- The Mining Industry Act (1920) inaugurated the Miners' Welfare Fund, which enabled money to be allocated for the erection of pithead baths.
- By 1936 pithead baths were built or planned for 244 collieries, making provision for 304,000 men and 592 women (female baths were needed in some coalfield regions for 'pit-brow lasses').
- The term 'baths' was a misnomer as the washing facilities were in fact showers.
- A key feature of the interior design was the separation of clean and dirty locker areas.
- Miners were issued with 'how to use the baths' handbooks by each pit after the official opening.
- For cash, miners could purchase bathing items such as soap, towels and sandals.
- The new baths were usually contained in architect-designed modernistic buildings.

Officials: deputies and overmen

Some experienced miners (usually with at least five years' underground experience, including two years' facework) either aspired or were encouraged to take on a more senior role at their collieries, as an 'official' or deputy. Becoming a 'shotfirer' was regarded as a step to becoming a deputy. Occasionally known as a 'fireman', a deputy was responsible for the safety of the men in a specified area or district of a mine. It meant obtaining suitable qualifications, through attendance and examination at a mining college or mining department in a technical college. A deputy also had a supervisory role and his yardstick was a symbolic as well as practical badge of office. An overman was a senior official responsible for a larger underground area of a colliery, say two or more districts, an intermediary in status between a deputy and under-manager. From 1910, deputies and overmen had their own national union, the National Association of Colliery Overmen, Deputies and Shotfirers (NACODS).

Officials' stories

Tommy Emms (b.1911): At age 22 I had a lot of mining experience and one of the managers came round and told me he was looking for officials. I was asked if I would consider becoming a deputy. I had not done very well at school but was told I would be taught how to go on. I was asked to go to Edlington night school and Doncaster Tech for the examination which I passed aged 27. First of all I was a 'pit bobby' going around the face and checking for any hidden props, which were valuable items. I had to find them and tell the men to dig them out. I carried a bullseye lamp with a bright light that shone a long way. I did this for six months and then trained on the face and became a deputy. I had a lot of respect when I was a deputy. I always asked the men questions and they gave me questions. That's the way we got on. Learning their way and they learning my way. I had forty-five men to look after on a shift. I set the men off, with my book, six front rippers, six tailgate rippers, fourteen to sixteen putting packs in, men boring holes, cutter men and so on.

Sydney Cutts (b.1919): I witnessed many accidents because when someone got hurt I was called for … there were some really bad ones. One young chap was killed on the face … he'd been sat down and had not noticed the roof coming down and was buried with his head on his knees. You almost got hardened to it. Deputying was a lot of responsibility. I was as soft as a boat with the men at first. Some deputies could be bullies but I let the men know I was one of them, not one of the upper crust. I would help if someone was behind, give them a hand, especially the old 'uns. Later I became an overman. I was well liked by the men as I did not believe in pushing them too much. If I saw someone getting a bit extra or a bit less then I would sort it out. We looked after about three districts and helped each other (overmen). We had to see the manager after each shift. I would sooner have worked with the men. We had a rough time going to the pit to examine things during strikes but we had to check on safety. We refused to do anything else. Most of the men were great, just like brothers.

29

> **Eric Crabtree** (b. 1932): A good official has to be able to organise the work well and have good eyes to know what needs doing. You also needed to be able to handle men. I gave the men an hour's overtime for a big job and got them together in the conference room to discuss the job, and also asked for suggestions. This was much better than ordering people about. I treated men as my equal and got a lot of respect as a result.

Under-managers and managers

Colliery under-managers and managers in the modern era not only had wide experience of the mining industry, but also had to have a variety of qualifications under various mines Acts. Many were also members of professional bodies. They were responsible for safety and production in part of or for the entire mine.

> ## Tip
>
> A managers' database at the North of England Institute of Mining and Mechanical Engineers (NEIMME) in Newcastle is currently under development and members' lists can be seen in the back of the proceedings of the National Association of Colliery Managers held at the NEIMME (www.mininginstitute.org.uk).

> ## Screen lad to Manager, Inspector, Mining Engineer and Director
>
> Bernard Goddard (b.1917) started work on the pit-top screens at Grange colliery, near Rotherham, at the age of 14. Whilst still in his twenties, through study and examination, he had obtained deputy's, under-manager's and manager's certificates, attending day and evening classes. Aged only 31, he was appointed His Majesty's Inspector of Mines for the Northumberland, Durham and Cumberland area, the youngest mines inspector in Britain. After five years Bernard returned to colliery management in Yorkshire, eventually becoming Chief Mining Engineer and and Head of Production for the NCB South Yorkshire and Doncaster areas. His career then extended to that

of Director (and spokesperson) of Mining Environment, with offices in Doncaster and London. Bernard's senior role with the NCB involved visiting many European countries, as well as North and South America and the USSR, and working with leading figures in the industry, including the NCB chairman, Derek Ezra and miners' leader Joe Gormley. After official retirement Bernard worked as a mining consultant, his total mining experience extending to almost sixty years.

Bernard Goddard.

Mining engineers

Mining engineers were of vital importance for the operation and development of mines, as well as for safety and emergencies. Professionally qualified, via regional institutions, they usually worked within or had their own independent practices, and were used on a consultative basis by the colliery companies, swiftly so during times of crisis. Mining engineers were referred to as 'viewers' in the nineteenth century.

Tip

A biographical database based on information held in the Transactions of the Institution of Mining Engineers is available for consultation in the library at the National Mining Museum for England at their Caphouse colliery site near Wakefield (www.ncm.org.uk/collections/library or email: curatorial.librarian@ncm.org.uk). The database, which covers the period 1889–1983, concerns the more prominent members and includes reference to obituaries, photographs etc. Transactions and printed material relating to some mining engineers are held at the Institution of Mechanical Engineers in London (www.imech.org), as well as other places referred to in the reference section of this book. For high-profile managers and mining engineers do also check the DNB (Dictionary of National Biography) as there may well be an entry.

Parkin Jeffcock, civil and mining engineer (1829–1866)

On 12 December 1866 a telegram from Barnsley reached the office of Thomas Woodhouse, mining engineers, in Derby. It read: 'The Oaks pit is on fire. Come directly'. Woodhouse was unavailable, so Parkin Jeffcock, the younger partner, set off by train to Barnsley. Assisting with the rescue operations in terrible conditions, Jeffcock was one of twenty-seven brave volunteers who lost their lives after a second underground explosion the following morning. This pushed the total fatalities to 361, making it Britain's worst-ever mining disaster. Jeffcock's body was not recovered until 5 October 1867, identified by his name on his shirt tag, and he was then buried in Ecclesfield churchyard. Jeffcock attended the College of Civil Engineers at Putney and trained under an experienced Durham viewer and engineer, George Hunter, becoming a partner in the Woodhouse practice in 1857. St Saviour's church at Mortomley, near Sheffield, was built in Jeffcock's memory. A spectacular memorial to Jeffcock and other Oaks volunteers can be seen overlooking Doncaster Road at Kendray, near Barnsley, erected there in 1913.

Pit sinkers

As we have already seen, from the nineteenth century onwards there was a great diversity of jobs at coal mines. Undoubtedly one of the most specialist and most dangerous at the start-up stage was that of the pit sinker. Once a mine location had been carefully chosen (after test bores) and the site marked, by a ceremonial 'cutting of the sod', a small, very distinctive team of workers – usually employed by a specialist contractor – arrived to begin the long and dangerous process of sinking. Led by a master sinker, these men might spend a year or two (even longer sometimes), maybe living in lodgings until the task was complete and then move to the next job. Like pioneer gold miners, they sometimes lived in flimsy huts during the sinking process, prior to the great influx of miners into the area. At Dinnington, in south Yorkshire, for example, the sinkers lived in impromptu properties made of corrugated steel sections, located near the pit, an area that became known as 'Tin Town'. However, it was not unusual for some sinkers to live in purpose-built cottages near their place of work, occasionally identified on large-scale maps as 'sinkers' row'.

Early shafts could be little more than a few feet in diameter and quite close to each other, but from about 1850 usually extended to several yards, enabling a pair of substantial cages to be accommodated. However, shafts were not just for winding men, materials and coal, but also had to be suitable for ventilation, pumping, power and communication (signalling).

Starting off was relatively easy, even in the pre-mechanised era, manually digging through the top and sub-soil until the rock strata was reached. A large iron sinking bucket was used to contain the waste material, and for inspections. On occasions, due to the confined space in the bucket, several sinkers had to dangle one of their legs over the side during precarious descents and ascents. The bucket was suspended, lowered and raised via either a crane and jib at the surface or a basic pulley-frame system. Temporary timber lining was often used to support the shaft sides, and then replaced by brickwork (and in later years by cast iron or concrete blocks). There was immense danger during the whole process, especially from falling rocks and inrushes of water. Accidental explosions and gas emissions were further hazards to contend with, blasting being used to loosen rock as sinking progressed; and of course as work proceeded there was always the real prospect of falling down the shaft to a certain death. Safety was always undermined in that the sinkers were usually paid 'per yard' of progress.

Early photographs showing pit sinkers in dangerous situations, standing on platforms and clinging to buckets, with little protection other than oil-skins, are perhaps the most compelling images of mining.

A team of pit sinkers at the Victoria Colliery, Barnsley, c.1905. (Chris Sharp)

Initially ignoring planning regulations, the legendary Lancashire steeple-jack and television personality Fred Dibnah (1938–2004) sank a 30m brick-lined mine shaft in his back garden in Bolton during his last series, in 2003, using many of the old skills of the pit sinkers.

Tip

Peter Ford Mason's *The Pit Sinkers of Northumberland and Durham* (The History Press, 2012) is essential reading if your ancestor was a pit sinker.

Thorne Colliery: a sinking nightmare

Set in the flat land east of Doncaster, barely above sea-level, the sinking of Thorne Colliery must rank as one of the most difficult, most prolonged, most expensive (£1.5 million: about £45 million today) and most tragic engineering tasks in the history of modern British mining. Progress on the two shafts was beset with flooding and technical challenges that spanned the First World War and was not completed until 1926, after seventeen years of stop-start work. During the early phases of sinking one man was killed when he fell from the hoppit (sinking bucket); another worker died from carbon monoxide poisoning; and on 13 December 1910 a sinker was killed and seven others injured when a pump fell down the shaft, crashing through a work platform. But mishaps climaxed in the early afternoon of 15 March 1926, during the final stages of sinking. Six men were hurled to their deaths when the scaffold on which they were standing collapsed following the failure of a supporting engine on the surface.

Engine winders

An extremely important occupation at the pit-head was that of the engine winder, who was responsible for operating the steam-powered (and later electric-powered) engine that hauled the single or multi-decked cages of men, coal and materials up and down the shafts. Before the 1842 Mines Act a boy as young as 12 years old could work as a 'winder' and accidents were not unusual. The minimum age was raised to just 15 after 1842. Subsequent safety measures, regulation and inspection were of massive importance, the operators subject to severe interrogation after accidents and mishaps, at inquests, inquiries and in courts, where criminal prosecution might be faced. It was not unusual for winders to be in the job for many years, keeping the role in the same family over several generations. Winding engine houses were usually kept in immaculate condition via the engine-man and his assistants. This small but vital group of workers had their own local unions or associations and, from 1878, national representation through membership of the National Union of Winding and General Enginemen.

Pay

Prior to national agreements, the calculation of miners' pay was complicated, though the actual process was fairly straightforward, at least for much of the twentieth century, and for a good number of years earlier too.

Pay-day was usually on a Saturday after the last weekly shift, and then on Fridays when five-day weeks were established. The usual procedure was for the miner to go to the pay cabin/office and exchange a numbered pay check for cash earned during a set period, say a fortnight. At some pits the money was handed over via small numbered tins. A pay summary sheet or strip usually accompanied the cash, showing what had been earned, along with stoppages, which might include deductions for contributions to hospital and relief funds, insurance and so on, and even materials, such as explosives.

However, in some regions many miners worked under a sub-contracting or 'butty' system, where an experienced man such as a collier had an agreement with the management/coal owner/coal company, to pay out a group of men. Pay-outs might take place in the pit yard or a convenient location nearby. My grandfather, Fred Elliott, got paid – rather temptingly – in the yard of a pub about half a mile from his colliery. On occasions my father would be dispatched to the location to make sure that he did not go into the pub and spend some of his wages, every penny being required for a family of eight. Weekend 'binges' did take place, of course, and the first Monday morning back at work after a fortnight's pay-day was never the best-attended shift.

Before about 1850 miners were often subjected to a signed and witnessed hiring agreement, known as the yearly or monthly bond, in exchange for a nominal wage. Akin to a master and servant arrangement, the bondage system was rightly regarded as slavery, and was particularly vicious and prevalent in Scotland and the northern coalfields during the eighteenth century. Miners breaking their agreement could be blacklisted, or even transported. The truck or 'Tommy' system was widespread in some areas, with mining families having to purchase basic food and commodities from the colliery companies/owners via the issue of pay in the form of tokens.

Miners were usually paid through piecework, performance-based work agreed between the miner and/or union and the mine manager/company. Typical examples would be based on the amount of coal extracted (per ton or cubic yard removed) or the yardage of advance during the making of a heading. Labourers, however, were paid a daily wage.

After 1911, performances for piecework depended on locally agreed (between management and miners associations/unions) documents known as *Price Lists*, small booklets containing the rates of pay for working in different seams of coal in a named colliery or area. The lists included rates for 'boys' working underground, aged 14 to 23 (later amended to 21). The various miners' associations and employers also published joint booklets relating to minimum wage rates for men and boys, following the Coal Mines (Minimum Wage) Act of 1912.

An elected and union/workers'-paid pit-top worker known as a check-weighman was a key pit-top figure when miners were paid by weight of coal, monitoring the calculations of the mine owner's weighman at the weigh house.

From time to time the Miners' Federation of Great Britain published average wage lists, according to various classes of workers. The largest and best-paid category (with 350,000 members) were 'piecework getters', colliers in the main, who got almost 9 shillings in 1914, rising sharply to 21 shillings in 1920 after the substantial Sankey Commission award. 'Underground labourers' (163,800) were ranked sixth in the wage table (after day-work getters, fillers, timbermen and deputies), receiving just over 15 shillings after Sankey. Youths and boys working on the surface (42,120) were joint bottom of the listing, with a post-Sankey wage of 7s 6d, the same average earnings received by the smallest category: 3,030 mainly 'pit-brow' women and girls.

Pay days recalled

Jack Steer (b.1890), a collier: I was employed by a contractor who was in charge of the haulage system. He paid me from a kitchen window in Ranskill Road [Sheffield]. The collier paid you if you worked for him. You got 6 shillings a day for filling and he would keep what was left over. If I earned £1 he would get 14 shillings and I would get 6 shillings. If there was a filler short the deputy would send you elsewhere. Once I had to work on five different stalls so had to go to five different pubs to get my wages. In 1932 a filler still only got 8 shillings a day. The pit was on a four-day week, which meant a 32-shilling wage.

Gerald Booth (b.1909), pit-top haulage worker: It was a day wage, 13s 7d a week at 14 and a shilling rise each birthday. Saturday was pay day. We went to the pay office and received our money in little tins after handing in a pay check.

Stan Potter (b. 1922), trammer and collier: The best thing about mining life was pay day!

Frank Johnson (b. 1922), collier: The best thing about nationalisation was that everyone got the same rate of pay.

Frank Beverley (b.1923), screen lad and underground haulage boy: We had 'tipple tin day'. On a Friday you went to this window where there was a bob hole, and you put your hand in. On the inside there were little tins with money in and the bloke might say, 'Tally number 1322' and put number 1322 tin in your hand. It was 10s a week, which I gave my mum. Then it rose to 12s 6d and Mum gave me 2s 6d back.

Further reading

Bess and Ralph Anstis, *The Diary of a Working Man. Bill Williams in the Forest of Dean* (Alan Sutton, 1994)

Harold Brown, *Most Splendid of Men. Life in a* [North Staffordshire] *Mining Community 1917–25* (Blandford Press, 1981)

Jim Bullock, *Bowers Row. Recollections of a Mining Village* (EP, 1976)

B.L. Coombes, *I Am a Miner* (Fact, 1939)

B.L. Coombes, *Miners Day* (Penguin, 1945)

B.L. Coombes, *These Poor Hands – The Autobiography of a Miner Working in South Wales* (Victor Gollancz, 1939)

David Douglass and Joel Krieger, *A Miner's Life* (Routledge & Kegan Paul, 1983)

Brian Elliott, *South Yorkshire Mining Veterans* (Wharncliffe, 2005)

Fred Flower, *Somerset Coalmining Life* (Millstream, 1990)

John Graham, *A Miner's Life* (Tyne Bridge Publishing, 2009)

Michael Pollard, *The Hardest Work Under Heaven* (Hutchinson, 1984)

Ian Terris, *Twenty Years Down the Mines* (Stenlake, 2001)

Mary Wade, *To the Miner Born* [Bedlington] (Oriel Press, 1984)

Maurice Woodward, *A Coalville Miner's Story* (Alan Sutton, 1993)

Chapter 2

ACCIDENTS, DISASTERS
AND DISEASE

I t is useful to be aware of the context and history of everyday accidents, disasters and disease rather than just concentrating on what happened to your particular mining ancestor. This chapter therefore aims to provide background information as well as practical suggestions for your research and concludes with information and guidelines about the important subjects of mines rescue and gallantry awards.

Everyday accidents and dreadful disasters

Working in a coal mine has always been regarded as a dangerous occupation. Ian Winstanley's database of mining deaths (see below) has more than 100,000 searchable entries, but his complete listing extends to over a quarter of a million names, from pre-1840 to 1949. According to statistics extracted from HM Mines Inspectors' Reports, annual deaths from accidents underground and on the pit top averaged 1,129 between 1873–1882. This level increased to 1,275 for the years 1903–1912 and climaxed at 1,753 in 1913.

It is highly likely that your coalmining ancestor will have had personal experience of one or more accidents, either to himself or to a workmate.

When a major disaster occurred, just about everyone in nearby communities was directly or indirectly affected by the event. Almost entire age groups of young and adult males were removed from streets, neighbourhoods and pit villages, leaving scores of widows and hundreds of dependant children. There are many cases where fathers died alongside sons. Five brothers, aged 17–32, were killed in the Oaks disaster of 1866, where twenty-seven rescue workers also died. Only a generation earlier, in 1838, at the Huskar pit near Barnsley, the nation was shocked to hear about the deaths of twenty-six children, trapped and drowned underground following a freak storm. The youngest, James Birkinshaw, was aged 7 and Sarah Newton was 8. The average age of the fifteen males and eleven females was only 10.8 years.

However, throughout the nineteenth century, and well into the twentieth, it was the day-to-day loss of life that was the main feature of the industry. So-called 'safe pits' usually meant collieries that did not experience major

A mine disaster widow: Mrs Sarah Hyde, whose husband, Thomas Hyde, lost his life in the Oaks Colliery disaster on 11 December 1866. Thomas's body was not recovered until eighteen months later, his remains identified by a patch that Mrs Hyde had sewn on his trousers. Sarah is sitting in her small front garden, attired in mourning clothes and holding a small bible or prayer book. This striking image was taken in c.1900, about forty years later. The couple were both aged 25 and had two small children when disaster struck. They appear to have migrated to Barnsley from Swadlincote, Derbyshire. Thomas is described as 'coal miner' in the 1861 census for Swadlincote and was a collier at the Oaks at the time of his sudden death. Almost the entire male colliery-working population of Hoyle Mill, a small but thriving mining and glassmaking community where the Hydes lived, was lost in what remains England's worst mine disaster.

(i.e. multiple-death) accidents or disasters. Jim MacFarlane's research concerning a typical Doncaster area colliery revealed that in the one hundred years of coal production at Denaby Main there were 203 fatal accidents, therefore an average of over two per annum. The worst year was in 1896 when there were seven deaths. Six Denaby miners lost their lives in 1904 and also in 1907; and there were five deaths in 1872, 1906, 1930 and 1932. In the twenty-two years after nationalisation (1947–1968) there were still only six years free of any fatalities, though the average annual death-rate had fallen to one per year. Accidents were ever-present in the minds of mining families. For the widow or children the loss of a loved one remained long after the wider public memory had faded.

Relatively minor injuries, keeping a miner off work for a few days or several weeks, were also common, even in relatively recent times. Growing up in a 1950s mining community, the sight of the NCB ambulance, though not unusual, sent shivers through our household. Would it be bringing Dad home again following a 'pit accident'? 'Ambulance men' and 'pit nurses' were important pit-top staff, kept especially busy at the big pits. Dad was often grateful for their help. Keen to help colleagues in emergencies, some miners were involved in first-aid training, taking great pride in their skills when entering competitions.

Those miners who 'won the coal' at the coalface – the 'hewers' or 'getters' – were in most danger, injured or killed through falls of roof or side collapses. Accidents involving underground haulage – the movement of coal – was also a major cause of death, and one that usually involved young miners. Violent death through explosions was a far less common occurrence. Some pits and some regions, however, noted for their 'fiery' seams, stand out as 'explosion black spots' at various periods, none more so than at Whitehaven in Cumberland, parts of County Durham, Lancashire and Yorkshire, Somerset and Staffordshire and especially in the anthracite mines of south Wales.

Though employment on the pit top was regarded as an 'easier' and 'safer' job, in practice it was a noisy, dirty and dusty place to work, certainly not free from fatal accidents – for men and boys as well as women in some regions (see Chapter 4). Working on the screens (sifting 'muck' from the coal), and moving and emptying tubs accounted for one in ten of all fatalities at Denaby Main, which was quite typical of other mines.

The accident record at Denaby's close neighbour Cadeby Main would have been 'normal' but for one single event: the explosion that killed thirty-five men towards the end of their night shift, early in the morning of 9 July 1912. A second explosion not long afterwards then took the lives of fifty-three men involved in rescue operations, including three HM Inspectors of Mines and the managers of both collieries. The death toll would have been far greater, but for the fact that many Cadeby miners had taken the day off

'Waiting for news' is the caption for this postcard, one of several produced to commemorate the Cadeby Colliery disaster of 1912.

on account of a royal visit to Conisbrough Castle by George V and Queen Mary. Whereas the day-to-day accidents at Denaby and Cadeby attracted only small amounts of local press, the 1912 disaster attracted massive media coverage, regionally and nationally, even internationally. A local reporter estimated that a crowd of 80,000 had flocked to the pit. Disasters had long been 'tourist attractions', with special railway excursions laid on to cater for a voyeuristic public.

Under the 1911 Coal Mines Act those regarded as 'killed' in a mining accident were supposed to include those who died within a period of a year and a day of the date of its occurrence. In reality it is doubtful if this requirement was totally adhered to. And in earlier times there must have been many unrecorded deaths of miners who only survived for a few months after an accident or for those who died from 'complications'. That is why it is important for researchers not to rely wholly on death certificate evidence.

Statistics will never demonstrate human stories, which is why our family histories are so important to social and industrial history as a whole. In 1936, when my father Fred Elliott was a teenage miner, part of the mine where he worked – Wharncliffe Woodmoor 1, 2 & 3 Colliery, near Barnsley – exploded and fifty-eight men and young lads, some not much older than

42

himself, were killed. Dad was not working on that fateful nightshift, but of course knew many of those who died. Not surprisingly, years later, there were always moments of unease for my mother after Dad had set off to work; and this apprehension increased if ever he was late home. This almost unrecorded situation was repeated in countless households wherever coal was mined.

After the nationalisation of the coal industry in 1947 improved health and safety measures resulted in a marked reduction in mining deaths through-out British coalfields, though this also coincided with a great decrease in employment due to pit closures. But as late as 1968 there were 115 fatalities in British mines. In 1971, my cousin George Eastwood, aged 37, lost his life in an underground machinery accident, one of the last recorded deaths at Grimethorpe Colliery. My uncle, Frank Elliott, was a miner at Houghton Main Colliery in 1975 when an explosion killed five of his colleagues. Barry Hines' two television plays and book *The Price of Coal* (Michael Joseph, 1979 and Pomona, 2005) were inspired by the Houghton Main – and the earlier, 1973, Lofthouse disaster. Although few working mines remain, occasional pit deaths continue to remind us of the dangers that our mining ancestors endured. This was no more apparent than in 2011 when four men perished in a flooding at Gleision Colliery, a small drift mine in south Wales. Single fatalities have also occurred in three UK Coal pits: Kellingley, Daw Mill and Welbeck; and at the Hargreaves Services' Maltby colliery.

Occupational diseases and ailments

Although I have interviewed many sprightly former miners in their eighties and nineties (and several centenarians), occupational health problems often remained with them. For many unluckier younger men, years of breathing in large amounts of coal and stone dust led to debilitating and sometimes deadly respiratory problems, generally referred to as 'miners' lung'. Even so, sufferers may not always have pneumoconiosis, silicosis and emphysema – or chronic bronchitis – recorded on their death certificates. My father was an underground fitter for much of his working life. He installed, maintained and repaired machines and equipment such as coal-cutters, pumps and hydraulic props. I remember him being off work due to injuries to his legs, arms and back in particular. By necessity he had to work in places that were very cramped and hot as well as cold and damp. For 'compensation' when working in wet conditions he received 'water money', a pittance really. Dad, a great sportsman in his younger days, had to finish his employment before full retirement age, pretty well damaged by his work. When he was in his eighties and quite frail I helped him get a small amount of compensation following medical tests that confirmed respiratory disease.

By 2003, the Labour government via the Department of Trade and Industry ran two compensation schemes, one for respiratory disease and the other for Vibration White Finger (VWF). The number of registered claims from former miners and their dependants reached almost 400,000, some relating to men born as long ago as the 1880s.

Many miners also suffered from arthritis and rheumatism in later life. Conditions such as dermatitis and nystagmus (an eye impairment) were also officially recognised as occupational diseases in mines inspectors' reports. Relatively minor but painful conditions such as 'beat knee' (or beat hand, wrist or elbow) were also prevalent, though less easy to claim damages for. One veteran miner told me about his difficulty in getting compensation for his 'bad knees'. On his application form he estimated that he usually crawled about 300 yards in order to reach low workings – three times a shift – and had done this for fifty-one years, covering several thousand miles. Miners were easily recognised by the wider public in swimming baths and when shirtless at the seaside. The small blue marks embedded in the skin were evidence of old cuts containing coal dust that later healed. For young haulage lads (and lasses) who pushed trams or tubs of coal through low roadways, their 'badge of office' was a line of small scars along their vertebrae, occasionally known as 'trammer's scab'.

I never knew my paternal grandfather, also called Fred Elliott, as he died aged 60 in 1948 when I was 2 years old, ostensibly of cancer, but he was pretty well worn out by a life of mining. Fred worked at Dodworth and Monckton collieries in Yorkshire and had a hard life by all accounts, finding solace, as many miners did, through his working men's club, pigeon racing and allotment. Earlier, before the introduction of the compulsory retirement age of 65 for men, it was not unusual to find some miners working in their late sixties, seventies, or occasionally even older, employed on 'lighter' jobs. Fred, due to his health situation, worked as an 'engineman's attendant' on the pit top. Older and disabled miners were often employed on the screens.

During much of the the nineteenth century the life expectancy of miners was about ten years below the national figure of about 49 for a male worker. It was only after an Act of 1918 that compensation for those miners who could prove disability or partial disability by silicosis was possible.

Tip

If your recent relative was involved in a miners' compensation claim his employment details will have been obtained by a solicitor, so try contacting the relevant law firm in order to access information that otherwise would be difficult, costly or impossible to obtain.

RESEARCH GUIDE

Parish and chapel burial registers, and from 1837 death certificates, are the basic sources for fatalities and deaths of coalminers, though the information provided is usually minimal – and occasionally incomplete or missing.

Burial registers

If your ancestor was killed in a coalmining accident after 1812 the 'cause of death', albeit brief, should be recorded in the standard burial register for Church of England parishes, on printed forms, easily accessible via your local studies library/record office, family history society/Church of Latter Day Saints' (Mormon) research centre; and via online sources. Although nonconformity, especially Methodism, was a major influence in mining communities, details were usually recorded in parish registers even after civil registration commenced. Do take stock of other mine fatalities around the time that your miner died, so as to give some context to your ancestor's demise. Before 1812 any reference to the cause of death of a single miner in registers is extremely rare and likely to be limited to a few words such as 'killed in a coal pit'. For multiple fatalities there may be a little more information. Peculiar to Yorkshire, the Archbishop instructed clergy to record the occupations, ages and cause of death of parishioners in 1777, though not every incumbent obliged, even diligent ones stopping by 1779. However, the practice was resumed between 1796–1812. If you have a Yorkshire mining ancestor for these periods the registers are worth a check.

Civil registration

Death certificates are available for England and Wales from 1837 and from 1855 for Scotland. But, once again, only brief details of the cause of death will be recorded. Do bear in mind that your mining ancestor may have lost his life at or in a colliery located in a different registration area to that of his place of residence.

By far the most useful sources of information on coalmining injuries and fatalities are:

- mines inspectors' reports
- newspapers and periodicals
- internet websites

HM Mines Inspectors' Reports
1850–1855

In the wake of growing public concern over the number of deaths in coalmining accidents, a Bill 'for the inspection of coal mines' was passed by Parliament in 1850. The Home Secretary, Sir George Grey, on behalf of the Crown, created four inspection areas, each controlled by a qualified engineer:

- Durham, Northumberland, Cumberland and Scotland (Mathias Dunn)
- Yorkshire, Nottinghamshire, Derbyshire, Warwickshire and Leicestershire (Charles Morton)
- Lancashire, Cheshire, Staffordshire, Shropshire, Worcestershire and North Wales (Joseph Dickinson)
- South Wales, Monmouthshire, Gloucestershire and Somerset (John Kenyon Blackwell, replaced by Herbert Mackworth).

It was soon realized that the areas were too large and the number of inspectors insufficient for the job. Three new appointments were made during 1852/53: Thomas Wynne (for Staffordshire, Shropshire and Worcestershire) and Robert Williams and William Lancaster (for Scotland). The 1850 Act, which was only meant to last five years, was extended in 1855 for a further term and inspectors' powers were increased. By 1856 the inspection districts were increased to twelve. These and their respective inspectors, soon to be known as 'Blackcoats' (you can imagine the smartly-dressed visits to a pit), were:

- North Durham, Northumberland and Cumberland (Matthias Dunn)
- South Durham (John Atkinson)
- West Scotland (William Alexander)
- East Scotland (Robert Williams)
- Yorkshire (Charles Morton)
- Nottinghamshire, Derbyshire, Warwickshire and Leicestershire (John Hedley)
- North and East Lancashire (Joseph Dickinson)
- West Lancashire and North Wales (Peter Higson)
- North Staffordshire, Shropshire and Cheshire (Thomas Wynne)
- South Staffordshire and Worcestershire (Lionel Brough)
- Monmouth, Gloucestershire and Somerset (Herbert Mackworth)
- South Wales (Thomas Evans).

It is useful to be aware of these and later districts and inspectors when accessing the reports.

Under the new Act any fatality had to be reported to the inspectors who had the right to enter every mine. It was an almost impossible task as the pioneer inspectors were grossly overworked, underpaid and had no clerical assistance. Thomas Wynne, working in a geographically compact district, travelled 10,000 miles in a year. Just think of the time and logistics of this in the mid-1850s. In 1877, Frank Wardell, responsible for 543 mainly Yorkshire mines, travelled 16,000 miles to visit seventy-one collieries, investigate nineteen complaints and attend seventy-one inquests. Wardell also had to write

46

4,000 letters, probably late in the evening and when nearly exhausted. Not surprisingly many collieries operated for years without inspection: the black-coats just could not get round to them all. Very few miners knew the name of their district inspector. But there is no question that the inspectors were very able and conscientious men and this is reflected in the great care that was expended in producing their annual reports.

The *Reports of HM Inspectors of Mines* (January 1851–December 1855) were published as irregular reports until mid-1852 and then as half-yearly reports, though due to an oversight the following were overlooked for publication: Durham, Northumberland, Cumberland and Scotland (June–December 1851 and December–June 1852); Scotland (January–June 1852); Lancashire, Cheshire, Staffordshire, Shropshire, Worcestershire and North Wales (June–December 1851, January–April 1852 and May–June 1852); Thomas Wynne: Lancashire, Cheshire and North Wales (January–April 1852); Staffordshire, Worcestershire and Shropshire (May–June 1852); and South Western: South Wales, Gloucestershire and Somerset (December 1851–July 1852). The originals can be found in The National Archives: HO 87/53.

A one-off volume appeared in 1853: *Coal Mines: Return of the number of accidents in coal mines during the years 1850, 1851, and 1852, specifying each particular accident ...*

Although all notified fatal accidents were listed there are small dis-crepancies when entries are compared with the half-yearly reports.

A tabular list of fatal accidents for each district included columns for the date of the accident, colliery details (name, location and owners), persons killed, cause of death and the basic type of accident (statistically entered under falls of roof, explosion, shaft and miscellaneous). The cause of death entry is usually quite brief, as can be seen in the 1853 report page illustrated (p. 48), taken from Joseph Dickinson's report for Lancashire, Cheshire and North Wales. Interestingly, this includes a reference to the death of a female 'pit-brow lassie', Elizabeth Jolly, who was 'killed on the surface by a chain breaking' at the Ince Hall pit in Wigan.

Tip

For all of the reports do read the whole text for the district in which your ancestor was killed as inspectors often commented and made recommendations about a particular accident or type of accident. Do this and you will be better placed to appreciate the context and social conditions of the death. And cross-reference the death using other sources such as death certificate, parish register entry and inquest/newspaper report.

List of Fatal Colliery Accidents—continued.

Date.	No. of Accidents.	Name of Colliery.	Where situate.	Owners and Agents Names.	Persons killed.	Cause of Death.
1853: Oct. 24	7	Ince Hall Coal and Cannel Works.	Wigan, Lancashire	Ince Hall Coal and Cannel Company.	Elizabeth Jolley	Killed on surface by a chain breaking
26	8	Clifton	Clifton, Lancashire	Trustees of the late Ellis Fletcher.	J. Cranksbrow (boy)	Fall of roof
27	9	Bayley Field	Hyde, Cheshire	T. J. and J. Ashton	William Schooler	Ditto
Nov. 2	1	Tryddyn	Mold, Flintshire	Haworth and Thompson	John Jones	Run over by a tub of coals
4	2	Bispham	Wigan, Lancashire	Wm. Hill Brancker, and Co.	William Wiswell	Fall of roof
15	3	Breightmet	Bolton, Lancashire	James Hardcastle	Jos. Rostron (21)	Crushed by a tub of coals
18	4	Glade Hill	St. Helen's, Lancashire	John and Thomas Johnson	J. Manchester (41)	Fall of coal
24	5	Ince Hall Coal and Cannel Works.	Wigan, Lancashire	Ince Hall Coal and Cannel Company.	Geo. Dinsdale	Fall of coal in Pemberton pit
28	6	Raikes	Bolton, Lancashire	Earl of Bradford	Wm. Haslam (18)	Piece of coal falling upon him from the top of the pit whilst he was standing at the bottom.
"	7	Hulton	Hulton, Lancashire	William Hulton	Jos. Aspinall	Falling from cage in ascending the Park pit.
" 29	8	Mostyn	Mostyn, Flintshire	James Thomas Cookney	T. Wynne	Fall of roof
29	9	Worsley	Worsley, Lancashire	Bridgewater Trust	Ellis Morris (12)	Run over by his waggons
Dec. 1	1	Agecroft	Pendlebury, Lancashire	Andrew Knowles and Sons	Hilton and Beckett	Fall of roof
3	2	Vron	Wrexham, Denbighshire	Maurice and Low	— Lloyd	Explosion of gunpowder

Extract (p.70) from HM Inspector Joseph Dickinson's Report for Lancashire, Cheshire and North Wales for the half-year ending 31 December 1853.

48

No. of Accts.	Date	Name of Colliery	Where situate.	Owners' Name.	Persons killed.	Occupation.	Cause of Death, and Remarks.
16	1860. Apr. 27	Cowden -	Near Dalkeith -	Duke of Buccleuch -	Abram Reid -	Collier -	By stone falling from roof at face of working.
17	May 2	Morningside -	,, Wishaw -	Shotts Iron Company -	William Johnston -	Collier -	,, fall of stone from roof at face of working.
18	,, 11	Airdriehill -	,, Airdrie -	Tod and Colquhoun -	William Wright -	Sinker -	,, falling off a scaffold whilst repairing pit pump.
19	,, 24	Reading -	,, Falkirk -	James Russell and Co. -	Richard Thomson -	Drawer -	,, fall of coal at face of working -
20	,, 29	Carfin -	,, Hollyton -	William Dixon -	Stiven Laughland -	Collier -	,, fall of stone from roof of draw road.
21	,, 29	Carnbroe Iron Works.	,, Airdrie -	Merry and Cunningham -	Andrew Hutchison	Horse driver	,, falling into a small well, whilst lifting a pail of water.
22	June 20	Arniston -	,, Dalkeith -	John Christie -	Thomas Cornwell -	Drawer -	,, fall of stone from roof at face of working.
23	,, 25	Townhill -	,, Dumfermline -	Andrew Christie -	Margaret Paterson -	Pitheadwoman.	,, falling off a scaffold at pithead -
24	,, 28	Armidale -	,, Bathgate -	Shotts Iron Company -	Richard Wardrope -	Pitheadman -	,, struck by a rope getting detached from winding drum.
25	July 5	Balyonie -	,, Kirkcaldy -	Charles Balfour -	Robert Hutchison-	Collier -	,, fall of stone from ,, at face of working.
26	,, 7	Carfin -	,, Hollyton -	William Dixon -	Hugh Dolloughan-	Collier -	,, fall of stone from ing a prop.
27	,, 11	Wallyford -	,, Dalkeith -	A. and C. Christie -	William Watters -	Collier -	,, fall of coal at fa
28	,, 20	Airdriehill -	,, Airdrie -	Tod and Colquhone -	W. B. Colquhoune-	Engineman -	,, coming in conta ing crank.
29	,, 21	Muirhouse -	,, Wishaw -	John Davidson -	Patrick Bucke -	Sinker -	,, falling down p ing from a shot

An interesting statistical page from HM Inspector Thomas Williams' Report for the Eastern District of Scotland, for Apr

Unfortunately for family history research, not all accident victims are named. Vague entries such as 'a boy', 'a person' and '2 men' might appear – or even a dash signifying the person's name was unknown when reported. Ages are not always given. Also bear in mind that occasional fatalities, especially where the person died a few hours or days after the accident, may not be recorded, and that despite the legal requirement, some fatalities were probably not reported during these early inspection years.

1856–1915

From 1856, *Reports of H.M. Inspectors of Mines* were published annually. There remained some variances in the way each Inspector commented about safety issues, but the Annual Reports assumed a more common form from the 1860s.

Furthermore, the addition of 'remarks' to the cause of death listings meant more 'death details', especially after the 1890s. A table was also added for occupations: names such as 'drawer', 'haulier', 'horse-driver', 'door boy', 'sinker', 'engineman' were used, as well as more the more generic 'collier' (or 'collier boy') – and 'pitman'.

Robert Williams' Eastern Scotland report, for 1860, includes an entry for the death of Margaret Patterson, a 'pitheadwoman' killed 'by falling off a scaffold at pithead' at Townhill colliery, near Dunfermline, on 25 June. Some inspectors, such as those representing Scotland and Yorkshire, continued to omit the age at death but others, for example in the south Wales and Midland districts, were more diligent.

Case study 1

John Cardwell ('a boy') was 'crushed by corves' in Earl Fitzwilliam's Low Elsecar pit in Yorkshire on 10 May 1860, according to Inspector Charles Morton's report. The *Barnsley Record* of 19 May 1860 described the inquest, though Cardwell's first name is now given, more correctly, as 'George', and we now learn that he was only 10 years old, the minimum age for working underground since the 1842 Mines Act:

FATAL COLLIERY ACCIDENT
On Saturday, an inquest was held before Mr Badger, at the Ship Inn, Elsecar, on view of the body of George Cardwell, miner, aged ten years, son of John Cardwell, miner, Elsecar, who was killed in the Lower Elsecar pit on Thursday. Deceased was a trapper, and it was his duty to sit behind a trap-door, which he opened by means of a string when corves passed to and fro. About noon, instead of

---

opening the door with the string as usual, he seems to have got up to do so, when the corves forced him against the door and crushed him so seriously about the head and body that he died almost instantaneously.

'Killed by being crushed against a Trap Door' is the cause of death on George Cardwell's death certificate and a little more information is provided about the name and location of the colliery: 'Elsecar Low Pit near Tingle Bridge'. Tingle Bridge was a canal-side hamlet situated just to the north of Elsecar village, at Hemingfield. Earl Fitzwilliam, the aristocratic mine owner, lived nearby in one of the largest country mansions in the country, Wentworth Woodhouse. His colliery, employing 150–200 men and boys, was managed by the Earl's 'servant' Joshua Biram. Inspector Charles Morton had visited the pit some eight years earlier, following the death of ten miners who were killed in an explosion. One of the injured, 22-year-old George Lindley, a trammer, was partly blamed for the disaster, as he had left a trap door open, an error that led to a build-up and deadly ignition of methane gas.

The Elsecar colliery manager and his 'fire-trier' were therefore well aware of the importance of closing trap doors. But picture this lonely boy trapper sat for hours and feeling sleepy in almost pitch dark with only an occasional light of a candle or dim lamp; and then, rather than using his string to tug open the door, jumping up to attend to the approaching tubs. This sort of children's work was described in Commissioners' evidence collected for the 1842 Report, eighteen years earlier, when girls worked underground:

I'm a trapper in Gawber pit [near Barnsley]. It does not tire me but I have to trap without a light, and I'm scared. Sometimes I sing when I have a light, but not in the dark ... I don't like being in the pit.

(Sarah Gooder, aged 8: 1842 Mines Report,
vol. XVI, pp. 252–3)

Lord Londonderry, one of the most wealthy and influential of the coal-owners, was a major opponent during the course of the 'Children in Coal Mines' bill passing through Parliament. He scoffed at the way in which evidence was collected from 'artful boys and ignorant young girls' and presented a petition which included the following:

The trapper's employment is neither cheerless, dull, nor stupefying; nor is he, or can be, kept in solitude and darkness all the time

51

in the pit ... The trapper is generally cheerful and contented, and ... occupied with some childish amusement – as cutting sticks, making models of windmills, waggons etc., and frequently in drawing figures with chalk on his door ...

(*Hansard*, House of Lords, 24 June 1842)

A more realistic portrayal of a trapper, in verse, appeared not long after Cardwell's death:

> *Beside the ventilating door*
> *The Little Trapper lay,*
> *And sleep had closed his weary eyes*
> *As night shuts out the day.*
> *He left his home before the sun*
> *Had filled the earth with joy.*
> *And to the pit did wend his way*
> *An English Trapper Boy*

(*The British Miner*, 1862)

To re-emphasise: do combine sources whenever possible as this will put the fatality in its historical context.

There were several changes in the names of inspectors over the next few years and in 1874 assistants or sub-inspectors were appointed for each district. From 1889 District Reports were issued. In 1908, a former 'mines apprentice' and Northumberland pit manager, Richard Redmayne, was appointed HM Chief Inspector of Mines, a new post, and an annual overview of the work of the inspectors began to be published. Aged 43, it was Redmayne who was the main author of the *Royal Commission on Accident in Mines' Report*, which appeared in 1908. The Report's recommendations formed the basis of the landmark 1911 Mines Act or 'The Miners' Charter' as it became generally known. Redmayne's period of office, to 1920, coincided with six major colliery disasters: Maypole (Wigan, 1908), Wellington (Cumberland, 1910), Pretoria (Bolton, 1910), Cadeby (Yorkshire, 1912), Senghenydd (south Wales, 1913) and Podmore (Staffordshire, 1918). His autobiography, *Men, Mines and Memories* (Eyre & Spottiswoode, 1942) is well worth reading as he was such an important figure in the coal industry, especially concerning accidents and safety.

As can be seen in the illustrated example (p. 53) for the year 1908, taken from Appendix I of Gray's District Report for South Wales, comments had become far more detailed. Even so, cross-checking with newspapers is still well worthwhile.

Date	Colliery	Details
January 4.	Ely, Glamorgan, Naval Colliery Co. (1897), Ltd.	Frank Grearson, 38, *Hitcher*. Deceased and other hitchers were clearing the pit sump, through an arched cross measure drift, served by a small crab engine. One hitcher drove the crab, two others filled the trams, and deceased acted as rider. When riding up on the rope in front of a full tram, he was squeezed between the top of the tram and either a low collar 4 feet 6 inches above the rail, or a low piece of arch where the height was 3 feet 6½ inches over one rail, and 4 feet 0½ inches over the other. Riding on such a road was most improper, and should have been definitely prohibited. He died in four days.
January 6.	Fforchwen, Glamorgan, Cwmaman Coal Co., Ltd.	Samuel Beard, 66, *Labourer*. Owing to the pointers not having been altered a journey of empty trams was run unexpectedly into a double parting, where deceased was cutting cog wood, and crushed him to death. The pointers had not been altered through a mistake of the two riders in charge of the journey.
January 9.	Ferndale, No. 8, Glamorgan, D. Davis & Sons, Ltd.	Edwin Emerson, 38, *Shackler*. The driver of a small hauling engine had pulled a journey of three full trams by means of the main rope to a point, opposite his engine house, where it was necessary to attach a tail rope owing to a change of gradient. Mistaking a shout from the rider to a lad who was standing on the road, for a signal to pull in the main rope, he did so, but before the rider had attached the tail rope to the rear of the journey. As soon as the trams were over the brow they started off towards the pit down a gradient of from three to six inches per yard, over-ran the main rope and broke it off at a return pulley, and crashed into some empty trams on a double parting 118 yards outbye. Deceased, who was between the empty trams, received injuries from which he died in six days. It appeared that although the haulage road was provided with proper electric signalling appliances, the rider and engineman always did their work by means of verbal signals when the tail was being attached. This was without the knowledge of the manager.
January 16.	Navigation, Glamorgan, Nixon's Navigation Co., Ltd.	David James, 53, *Labourer*. As deceased was walking along the Six-feet engine plane he was overtaken by an empty journey, and injured so badly that he died next day. There was considerable noise produced by the sheaves at the turn, and, as he was rather deaf, he most probably did not hear the approaching journey. There was ample room on the sides of the road, and manholes were plentiful.
February 5.	Maindy, Glamorgan, Ocean Coal Co., Ltd.	Wm. Aldridge, 29, *Haulier*. Deceased was attempting to replace on the rails a tram of rubbish which had left the road on a gradient of 10 inches per yard. Owing to the gradient the tram was controlled by a chain attached to the back end of the drawbar and passed twice round a post. In the operation of getting the tram on the rails, the man who was attending to the chain at the post got his fingers pinched by it and let go, with the result that the tram ran down the road for a few yards with deceased in front, and crushed him to death against a post.
February 17.	Ferndale, No. 7, D. Davis & Sons, Ltd.	Roderick Roderick, 26, *Assistant repairer*. Deceased was expecting some empty trams, and hearing the journey he went a short distance up the drift to secure them. The journey was stopped about 50 yards higher up the drift for the purpose of discharging a tram of timber, when by some means, probably by the pin of a shackle rising, two trams were liberated. These ran for 50 yards, jumped the rails, and crushed deceased against the side. He died on April 12.
February 18.	Maindy, Glamorgan, Ocean Coal Co., Ltd.	Richard Rowlands, 21, *Haulier*. Deceased was taking a tram of rubbish along the Six-feet level when by some means he fell, and was run over. He had just removed the sprags, and it was thought that after doing so he started his horse, and in jumping on the gun slipped and fell.
March 18.	Ferndale, No. 7, Glamorgan, D. Davis & Sons, Ltd.	Wm. Rowe, 23, *Repairer*; Wm. Hughes, 40, *Assistant repairer*. The deceased were filling rubbish into trams when a journey of eight trams of rubbish ran back down the dip and killed them. The rider had left them two empty trams, and was taking the full journey up towards the pit, when it ran against a piece of timber lying on the road. The sudden check caused a link of the chain attaching the rope to the journey to open at a bad weld, and liberate the journey. The rider had neglected to attach a barboot.
April 3.	Ferndale, No. 2, Glamorgan, D. Davis & Sons, Ltd.	John Devereaux, 26, *Rider*. Deceased had held a door open for his journey of nine trams to pass through, and was in the act of jumping on the last shackle, when he struck his head against the roof, and fell under the last tram. The drift was five feet high at this point, and the speed of the journey did not exceed four miles per hour. He was the regular rider on this road.

Page 44 of HMI Gray's Report for the South Wales District, 4 January to 3 April 1908, showing in more detail the circumstances of death, mostly relating to haulage accidents.

53

Case study 2

In Inspector Gray's District Report for South Wales, for 1908, an entry for 4 February 1908 records – under miscellaneous – the death of Mark Hudd, aged 42, 'a collier', who worked at 'Eastern [Pit], Glamorgan [owned by the] Ocean Coal Co., Ltd', in the Rhondda. Hudd's death is described as follows:

> Deceased, who was standing near the shaft top as a cage filled with men began to be lowered, jumped forward to get in, and was crushed to death against the collar boards. It was a mad act to attempt, and if he had succeeded in getting in the cage he would not have gained more than a minute's time.

Note the inspector's comment concerning Hudd's apparently foolhardy act. His death certificate, obtained from Pontypridd RO, confirms the date of death as 4 February but states that he was aged 48 years, six years more than that recorded by the Inspector. The cause is given, quite factually, as 'Accidental death from being crushed between a descending pit carriage and the framing at the pit head'.

By referring to the *Rhondda Leader* (15 February 1908), a more detailed account of the accident and the Hudd family circumstances becomes apparent, although his pit is named as Bwllfa Colliery:

> On Tuesday last, the coroner, Mr. R.J. Rhys, held an inquest at the Workmen's Hall, Ton, touching the death of Mark Hudd, collier, who met his death at the Bwllfa Colliery on Tuesday in attempting to enter a bond [cage] whilst in motion. Jenkin Thomas, assistant banksman, said deceased and three others were waiting to descend the mine in the last bond, and after the signal had been given to lower a full complement of men, Hudd made a dash for the cage and was struck by it, and killed instantly. A verdict of 'Accidental death' was returned. The body was removed from his residence, 143 Ystrad Road, to Ystrad Station en route for Bristol, where interment took place. Deceased was a widower and leaves 8 children to mourn his loss.

Thus Hudd's demise may well have been due to him not wanting to miss the last descent of the cage, therefore losing a day's pay and letting his mates down. A daft thing to do, yes, but this context needs bearing in mind. Perhaps the Inspector did not receive the full story. The reference to Bristol suggests that Mark Hudd was one of the thousands of men and their families who migrated from the West Country to work in the Valleys during the late nineteenth and early twentieth centuries. The Ton Pentre Workingmen's Hall and Institute (where the inquest was held) closed in 1989 and was derelict for two years until it reopened as 'the Phoenix Cinema' in 1991. It is a Grade II listed building. The 'Eastern Pit' was sunk near Ystrad in 1877 and was one of the mines in the ownership of David Davies and the Ocean Steam Coal Company. Eastern appears to have had mixed fortunes, employing over 800 persons in 1923, but less than 200 a decade later.

1 1908	Registration District Dosbarth Cofrestru		Pontypridd						
	Death in the Sub-district of Marwolaeth yn Is-ddosbarth		Ystradyfodwg			in the yn	County of Glamorgan		
Columns:- Colofnau:-	1	2	3	4	5	6	7	8	9
No. Rhif	When and where died Pryd a lle y bu farw	Name and surname Enw a chyfenw	Sex Rhyw	Age Oed	Occupation Gwaith	Cause of death Achos marwolaeth	Signature, description and residence of informant Llofnod, disgrifiad a chyfeiriad yr hysbysydd	When registered Pryd y cofrestrwyd	Signature of registrar Llofnod y cofrestrydd
93	4 Feb 1908 Eastern Pit Ocean Collieries Rhondda U.D	Mark HUDD	Male	48 years	Collier	Accidental death from being crushed between a descending pit carriage and the framing at pit head	Certificate received from R J Rhys Coroner for Glamorgan Inquest held 6th Feb 1908	Seventh February 1908	Geo Williams Registrar

Detail from the death certificate of Mark Hudd, collier, 1908.

The annual Reports of HM Inspectors of Mines continued to be published until 1914 after which they were suspended due to the First World War. A retrospective and summary 1915–20 report was published by the Chief Inspector but this has little value for family history research as it is mainly statistical. From 1920, now via the Board of Trade and the new Mines Department, the status of the mines inspectorate changed, and the annual reports were no longer issued as Command (i.e. parliamentary) Papers. Names of fatalities and details were not given in the reports, though they can still be useful to read because of the background information contained in them.

For family history research, the great advantage of the reports published up to and including 1914 is that most fatalities are actually named and the cause of death given.

Accessing annual mines inspectors' and disaster reports
The Annual Inspector of Mines reports (seventy-five volumes) are in HO 87/53 and POWE 7 and POWE 8 (search using keyword '11') and POWE 8 (keyword '7' and '12') at The National Archives. Other national and major libraries, museums and archives have complete (or near complete) runs of mines inspectors' reports. Part-runs and district reports are also held in the regions: see the national and regional reference sections in Part Two of this book.

Inquiries into major disasters were published as separate Special Reports (as Command Papers) by the mines inspectorate, and most recently by the Health and Safety Executive (HSE). Most major disaster reports, printed as Parliamentary Papers, can be accessed online free of charge at The National Archives. Parliament's website is www.parliament.uk/business/ publications/parliamentary-archives where a useful family history guide can be downloaded via their Learning Resources scheme. However, searching the catalogue is not straightforward. The papers are contained in HL/PO/ JO/10/9 (for 1850–1899) and HL/PO/10/10 (1900–1949). The Chadwyck Healey (CH) Index to House of Commons Parliamentary Papers offers alternative and has an excellent search feature, but is a subscription website (accessible via some libraries). If you visit the Parliamentary Archives in person you can use the CH site and download reports that can then be burnt to a CD/DVD for a small charge. However, many of the national and regional libraries and museums also hold disaster reports. Again, please refer to information listed in Part Two of this book.

Newspapers and periodicals

Local newspapers in coalfield regions often contain a wealth of information about accidents, disasters and inquests. Although roof falls were the most common causes of death, a variety of other mishaps become apparent, both above and below ground. Several pre-1850 single-fatality accident examples, pre-dating inspection reports, are shown below, perhaps the only detailed accounts available:

> On the 4th instant. William Knighton, a coal miner of Ilkeston, was unfortunately killed by the fall of a piece of timber in the shaft of a coal delph which is sinking at Hallsworth, in the neighbourhood.
>
> *Derby Mercury*, 12 May 1814

> W. Joiner, coroner. On the body of John Morton, a coal-miner, who fell to the bottom of a coal-pit (nearly 8 fathoms) at Siston-hill, from the untwisting of a rope, by which he was descending.
>
> *Bristol Mercury*, 15 November 1824

> On Thursday, a man of the name Emery, who was employed at the foot of the shaft at Hetton, to attach the corves [tubs] to the rope by which they are drawn to bank, was killed by a corfe slipping from the rope and falling upon him ... The deceased was a married man, and has left a wife, and a family of three children, to lament his premature end.
>
> *Durham Chronicle*, 22 April 1826

> On Friday last, a boy, about fifteen years of age, son of George Lowrey, of Easington Lane, whilst attempting to place himself on a rope to descend Elemore Pit, unfortunately missed his hold, and fell to the bottom, a depth of 135 fathoms. He was of course dashed to pieces ...
>
> *Durham County Advertiser*, 3 April 1830

Here are two later examples, taken from a short-lived Barnsley area newspaper:

> About half-past one o'clock on the afternoon of yesterday, a serious accident occurred at the Oaks Colliery, near Barnsley, to a married man

named William Gaunt, residing at Raywood Row, Barnsley. Gaunt was employed as the cupola tenter, and was going down the pit to commence his afternoon work. When he had got within fifteen yards of the bottom of the shaft he fell out of the cage into the pit bottom. He was removed to his home in a cart, where he was attended to by Mr Ibbeson, surgeon, who found that the unfortunate man was very severely injured in his back, and we understand has since died.

Barnsley Record, 31 December 1864

We regret to announce that a melancholy and fatal accident occurred on Thursday morning at the Oaks Colliery, to a young lad about fifteen years, named Hewitt, living at Barebones. He was engaged greasing some corves at the pit hill, and whilst doing so accidentally fell down the shaft and was killed instantly.

Barnsley Record, 25 November 1865

From early to mid-Victorian times the Oaks Colliery was one of the most dangerous workplaces in the north of England. Operational from 1841–2, an explosion killed three miners in 1845 and the whole pit fired at the end of the same year, flames issuing from the shaft 'as if from a volcano', though, luckily, only nine men were underground at the time, every one of them escaping serious injury. But then, on Friday 5 March 1847, seventy-three (of ninety) men and boys still underground in the late afternoon lost their lives in a massive explosion which blasted debris from the bottom of the 290-yard deep shaft some 50 yards above the surface headstocks. But that was far from the end of the story. On Thursday 12 and Friday 13 December 1866, two explosions killed 361 men and boys, including twenty-seven volunteer rescue workers. Statistically, this was Britain's worst mining disaster, until the Universal Colliery, at Senghenydd in south Wales, exploded in 1913, with a death-toll of 439.

The really big disasters decimated the nearby communities that served ill-fated pits. There were only about sixty houses at Hoyle Mill, near the Oaks Colliery, in 1866. From these alone 103 men and boys lost their lives in the disaster, leaving 167 widows and 366 children under the age of twelve. Every house in Ash Row – apart from the policeman's – was directly affected by one or more fatality. There were scarcely any adult males that survived. The funeral and mourning-wear businesses of Barnsley were kept busy for several years, and the bereavements were much prolonged as bodies were still being found up to four years afterwards.

Local newspapers often contain reports of smaller accidents from neighbouring, even distant areas, so it is always useful to widen your search and not rely on a single newspaper source. Here are two, sadly gruesome, examples:

Shocking Catastrophe – Robert Moore, a coal-miner at the Dry Clough Colliery, near Royton [near Oldham], being too late to descend with the coal tubs, which had just left the shaft on Friday morning, was enraged and took the desperate resolution of slipping the rope to the tub, when he was so unfortunate as to be precipitated head-long down the pit, nearly 130 yards. His head was severed from his body, and also was a mass of bruises.

The Examiner (London), 18 August 1833

On Wednesday, an inquest was held before Mr Busby, coroner, at Clay Cross [Derbyshire], on the body of two colliers named Augustus Cubit and George Holmes, who were killed in the No.4 pit, Clay Cross, on Monday last. The men were at work lengthening a siding in the pit, when a large piece of bind, weighing three tons, fell upon them and killed them instantly. The men had used timber to support the roof but the bind slipped between the props. A verdict of 'accidental death' was returned.

Barnsley Record, 16 June 1866

Even national newspapers such as *The Times* occasionally reported mine accidents involving a single or small number of fatalities, so it is well worth a search via digital or microfilm sources (see below pp. 63–4).

When a serious accident involving one or a small number of persons occurred (and certainly in a disaster) it was a natural tendency for a respectful 'downing of tools' to occur, albeit for a short period of a shift or a day. But there were also technical, repair or safety reasons why pits or parts of pits closed after an accident. The following are fairly typical examples from the south Wales and Durham coalfields:

Over 500 men were thrown out of work on Wednesday night at the No. 7 Pit [Tylorstown] through an accident by which two repairers, named W. Rowe, married with one child, 17 Donald Street, Tylorstown, and William John Hughes, single, 9, Frederick Street, Ferndale, lost their lives. It appears that the unfortunate men were doing special work, timbering, when a journey of trams became unhitched near the spot where they were engaged, the heavy vehicles running wild; and before they had an opportunity of gaining a place of safety, the poor fellows were buried alive, the staging being knocked away and tons of rubbish falling on them.

Rhondda Leader, 21 March 1908

On Wednesday morning, a lad named Henry Potter, engaged as a driver at Beamish Air Pit, was crushed by some tubs and fatally injured. Deceased, who was sixteen years of age, resided at Stoney Lane, near

Beamish. The pit, according to custom, was laid idle on account of the accident.

Consett Chronicle & West Durham Advertiser, 5 January 1912

Even during the NCB era it was not always possible for miners to be given 'official leave' to attend the funeral of a work colleague. Those that did usually lost a day's pay.

Serious injuries are also occasionally reported. The following two examples, taken from the *Barnsley Record*, are fairly typical of the mid-Victorian period, both persons apparently surviving, and certainly not mentioned in the mines inspector's reports:

COLLIERY ACCIDENT

On Friday last an accident occurred at the colliery belonging to Messers Day and Twibell, at Old Mill, to a young man named Thomas Woofinden, employed as a hurrier at the colliery. While at work a corfe ran over one of his legs, the flesh being torn from the leg, and the bone quite bared for three or four inches. Mr Ayre, surgeon, was sent for, and the lad is doing as well as can be expected.

Barnsley Record, 26 February 1859

SHOCKING COLLIERY ACCIDENT

Another fearful colliery accident happened on Wednesday last, at the Edmunds Main Colliery, to a young boy named Thomas Ratcliffe, aged fourteen years. He was engaged ... as a horse-driver, and was following his usual calling when the corves were descending ... when by some means the full ones ran him down and ran over one of his arms, nearly severing it from his body. He was conveyed to his lodging in Howard's Square, Worsbro Dale, and Dr Smith was sent for and found it necessary to amputate the arm; up to yesterday at noon he was still alive but in a very very precarious state. He was an orphan and a native of Lancashire, and has only been at the colliery three weeks.

Barnsley Record, 31 March 1860

The big disasters provided spectacular copy for most newspapers and were reported in great detail. Eyewitness descriptions were used alongside a reporter's interpretation of the scene at the pit head. Journalists compiled and helped each other with a huge amount of oral information and, not surprisingly, there were inaccuracies. Many local newspapers were week-lies, published on Saturdays, so the immediacy of the report depended very much on the disaster day in respect to copy deadlines. Yet some of the larger local newspapers provided a massive amount of detail, even publishing two or more editions, updating their readers with more detail. Fatality lists and lists of injured were hurriedly published, but these should always be checked against other, more official sources whenever possible, as errors involving names and ages understandably occurred. For many early nineteenth-century disasters reporting was limited to regional and national press in the absence of a local newspaper.

The new illustrated periodicals, most notably the *Illustrated London News* (ILN, 1842 onwards), covered many of the larger pit disasters, and prominently so from from the late 1850s. The ILN's main rival, *The Graphic* (1869–1932) is also worth consulting. Shorter-lived examples such as the *Pictorial Times* (1855–72) and *Illustrated Times* (1855–72) are also useful. The periodicals dispatched talented artists to disaster sites within hours of the event. Some sketches and engravings were based on early photographs. Reconstructed images of exploding pits, shattered cages, floods, anxious relatives rushing to the scene and crowded pit-heads made spectacular copy; as did images relating to rescue, recovery of bodies and funeral scenes.

The local newspaper is the obvious place to start your search if you know the date of the disaster. But do check other local, regional and even national newspapers as well. It is not exceptional for a relatively small accident to be

Patrick Johnson was pinned to the ground by a piece of rock weighing over a ton, in partly flooded workings at Skellington Colliery, near Glasgow. Despite frantic efforts, his mates were unable to free him before he drowned in rising water. The dramatic scene was reproduced in the Illustrated Police News *of 17 August 1912.*

From 1857 the larger mining disasters often made the front page of the Illustrated London News. *This example from 1880 shows tenacious explorers descending Seaham pit in a hoppit 'to rescue the men below'. Over sixty men survived but the death toll was horrendous: 164 men and boys killed, after an explosion on 8 September.*

No: 1615. [REGISTERED FOR CIRCULATION IN THE UNITED KINGDOM AND ABROAD.] SATURDAY, JANUARY 26, 1895. Price One Penny.

Images relating to pit disasters had great impact in the Illustrated Police News *as their artists produced montages such as this spectacular example, which relates to the disaster at Diglake Colliery, north Staffordshire, in 1895. An inrush of water from an underground reservoir resulted in the deaths of 77 men and boys.*

reported in a national newspaper; and although news copy was often obtained from a single 'master' report, there may well be extra information included in other newspapers. For many coalfield areas it is the regional and national papers that will be the only news report available for the earlier, say pre-1850, disasters.

> ## Tip
>
> The *Illustrated Police News* (1864–1938) was voted 'the worst newspaper in England' in 1886, because of its often lewd and dramatic images. Nevertheless, its melodramatic pages often included quite detailed reports as well as graphic illustrations of mine disasters. It's a much underused source.

Where to find newspapers

Start by accessing newspapers in the relevant coalfield area in which your ancestor lived and worked, usually in a local studies library or record office. Check online for their holdings. *Local Newspapers 1750–1920 England and Wales, Channel Islands, Isle of Man: A Select Location List* by Jeremy Gibson, Brett Langston and Brenda W. Smith is a very useful index. Reprinted many times by the Federation of Family History Societies, its best to use the third edition, published in 2011. Unfortunately papers with a run of less than four years (and there were many) are not included; and do bear in mind that there may be gaps in some editions as the originals may not have survived. For Scotland see Joan Ferguson's *Directory of Scottish Newspapers and Periodicals 1800–1900* (National Library of Scotland, 1984) but far more up-to-date is the National Library of Scotland's online Guide to Scottish News-papers: http://www.nls.uk/family-history/newspapers; and the database Guide to Scottish Newspaper Indexes: http://www.nls.uk/family-history/indexes.cfm. Also available to search free online is the Scotsman Digital Archive (1817–1950), private subscriptions ranging from £7.95 for a 24-hour 'archive pass' to £159.95 for a year.

It is becoming exceptional to be allowed to use original bound volumes of newspapers as microfilmed (and, increasingly, digitised versions) are now commonly available. Relatively few microfilmed ones are indexed. However, most libraries have cuttings files and these can be extremely useful for mine accidents, disasters, inquests and obituaries. Thanks to the huge Newsplan project (see www.bl.uk/reshelp/bidept/news/newsplan/newsplan.htlm) involving public libraries, the British Library, the National Library of Scotland, the National Library of Wales, the National Library of Ireland and the newspaper industry itself, hundreds of titles have been filmed, details described in their regional reports, published by the British Library. The most relevant coalfield ones are Northern (1989), Yorkshire and Humberside (1990), East Midlands (1989), West Midlands (1990) and Wales (1994).

The British Library's Newspaper Collection (formerly at Colindale in north London, now relocated to Boston Spa, West Yorkshire), is one of the best and biggest in the world. From 2014 researchers will be able to access newspapers and periodicals via a new Newspaper Reading Room at the BL's St Pancras (Euston Road, London) site. The resources guide at httt://www.bl.uk/welcome/newspapers.htlm is the starting point for information on news-papers, periodicals, and visits. For admission/registration details see http://www.bl.uk/reshelp/inrrooms/blnewspapers/newsrr.htlm. Search-Explore the British Library http://explore.bl.uk to find the newspapers and periodicals that are available. Still very useful is the the the BL's 19th-Century Digitalisation project (http://www.newspapers.bl.uk/blc) that allows access to a small sample (currently forty-nine) of newspapers and magazines published between 1800 and c.1900 (about half of them 'local'). Access to the

Penny Illustrated Paper, *The Graphic* and *Illustrated Police News* is free so you can search, view and print coalmining related items from these via your home computer using key words. For viewing the rest you need to pay (£6.99 for a day or £9.99 for a week) but access is free of charge at many subscribing public libraries. Furthermore, by visiting the Newspaper Reading Room in person a huge number and variety of titles – local, regional and national – will be available to view via microfilm or digital means. Titles not yet scanned – providing they are not too fragile for travel – will be supplied from Boston Spa on a 48-hour order basis. UK national newspapers are only available via microfilm and/or digital versions.

A massive digitisation project will transform access to British newspapers over the next few years, and the process is well advanced. This is through a partnership between the British Library and Brightsolid Online Publishing. The first phase is accessible at www.britishnewspaperarchive. co.uk. It's free to search but for home access you need two-day, seven-day and thirty-day packages (for £6.95, £9.95 and £29.95 respectively) or you can subscribe and have unlimited access (for £79.95). The scanned collection (growing daily) is free to search on computer terminals at Colindale/St Pancras.

For mine disasters, some accidents and a variety of other mine-related items, the Guardian and Observer Digital Archive is well worth accessing (http://archive.guardian.co.uk). This large resource currently covers the period 1821–1990 (*Guardian*) and 1791–1990 (*Observer*). The charges are £7.95 (twenty-four hours), £14.95 (three days) and £49.95 (one month) for home computer convenience. Many libraries also subscribe. A 'pay-to-view/use' internet source for most national titles is ukpressonline (www.ukpressonline. co.uk), for an annual fee of £50, but it may also be accessed at subscribing public libraries and institutions.

Wikipedia has a 'List of Online Newspaper Archives' (http://en.wikipedia. org/wiki/Wikipedia:list_of_online_newspaper_archives) that includes UK titles.

Tip

Many of the main public libraries in coalfield regions allow you to register for online reference, and you don't necessarily have to be a local resident. Lancashire Library (www.lancashire.gov.uk/libraries), for instance, provides an excellent online service. It gives free access to the British Library's nineteenth-century newspaper archive and seventeenth–eighteenth-century Burney Collection of early newspapers; and also free use of The Times Digital Archive that would otherwise involve payment. You can also access other useful sources, including the *Dictionary of National Biography*.

Finally, there are many private holdings of newspapers still kept in original or other formats by existing newspapers/newspaper groups, and you can access 'newspapers and publications' via major family history internet sites such as Ancestry.com. Original pages from Victorian illustrated periodicals such as *The Graphic* and *Illustrated London News* are listed for sale on internet auction sites.

Internet sources

The Coalmining History Resource Centre (www.cmhrc.co.uk).
Founded and developed by Ian Winstanley, this is the most detailed and comprehensive website for accidents and deaths in the coal industry of Great Britain. It is now in the care of Raleys, Barnsley-based solicitors with a long record of dealing with miners' compensation claims. Click on the accidents/disasters page and you can freely search the National Database of Mining Deaths [and some injured miners] by surname. If you can also enter the name of the colliery, year of the accident or town/county that will narrow your search. By entering 'Cardwell 1860' the following information was found:

Name:	CARDWELL George
Age:	0
Date:	10/05/1860
Year:	1860
Occupation:	A Boy
Owner:	Earl Fitzwilliam
Town:	Rotherham
County:	Yorkshire
Notes:	Crushed by corves in the mine.

However, despite its huge 164,000-entry database there will be some omissions, understandably so given the number of accidents and the errors, even in official sources. For data protection later twentieth-century injuries and deaths are not accessible.

You can also access, print and if you wish download files relating to UK mining disasters, arranged chronologically from 1707 to 1979. Again, these are based on personal research by Ian, inspection reports, inquest and inquiry reports, and extracts from useful sources such as the *Colliery Guardian* (from 1858).

Durham Mining Museum (www.dmm.org.uk)
This site is especially useful for northern England (County Durham, Northumberland, Cumberland and Westmoreland). It is best to start by searching their Memorial Roll (under 'Disasters'), selecting the first letter of

a surname, and then the second letter to narrow the field. As in the Raley site, basic information, such as age, date of death, date of accident, name of colliery, name of colliery company, occupation of deceased, notes (i.e. basic circumstances of the death) and date of burial, all if available, is provided. For many entries you can also, via 'Quick Links', access a variety of web pages providing further information about the mine – with a useful set of icon codes by way of reference and acknowledgement. Access to the actual entry from the mines inspector's report (and where to find it) is particularly useful. For disasters, again use 'In Memorial' for names and reports, the former via 'Entrance' (under 'Museum') and the latter via 'Reports'. This online resource welcomes further information from family historians and you can upload basic family information that can be viewed by someone researching the same name/person. It is therefore a growing site well worth revisiting from time to time. The site also hosts Pitwork.net, which also has lists of names of those killed and injured in some mine disasters.

Scottish Mining (www.scottishmining.co.uk)
Under 'Mining Accidents' this superb site run by volunteers has lists of c.14,000 'fatality names' compiled from a variety of sources that you can access from indexes from pre-1840 to 1960 onwards for the whole of Scotland. Details from the inspector's report are included where possible and there are also newspaper items and 'extra details'. You can also complete a submission form if you have details of a fatality not recorded. There is also a 'non-fatal accident' listing on a surname basis and a list of 'disasters and major accidents' (1760–1973) includes lists of fatalities in most cases. Do check their Frequently Asked Questions page regarding fatalities and other family history information.

Fife pits, Scotland (www.users.zetnet.co.uk)
Michael Martin's site includes an A-Z Memorial Book of miners killed in accidents, currently containing 2,322 entries, information provided from a variety of contributors, the original held by Fife Council Libraries.

Welsh Coal Mines (www.welshcoalmines.co.uk)
Under its Collieries page this site has a list of disasters (arranged A-Z) where there were five or more fatalities, along with names of the c.6,000 victims. It also has a useful Mines Rescue page.

Healey Hero (www.healeyhero.co.uk)
Fionn Taylor's site in memory of Philip Healey (1928–2000) has a list and details of mine disasters and fatalities and has information regarding mines rescue.

There are many other internet sites that relate to regional or single mining disasters, so just by searching for a particular disaster one or more will usually appear. As with all information from above it is really important not to rely on a single source but to use a variety of records about a particular accident or disaster.

Other useful sources

Mining Deaths in Great Britain 1850–1914

Printed listings of persons who have died as a result of a mining accident can be consulted at the National Coal Mining Museum for England's (NCM's) library. Based on the work of Ian Winstanley, the information is arranged chronologically by (pre-1974) county and there is a good surname index. The name of the colliery and its location is included as well as the occupation and age (where known) of the deceased person. To make an appointment contact the NCM via email: curatorial.librarian@ncm.org.uk or telephone: 01924 848806. Also see Part 2 (regional) section of this book for other repositories.

Coroners' Records (England and Wales only)

Where coroners' records survive they are certainly worth consulting, though bear in mind that newspapers reported inquests in great detail and contain much more contextual information. See Jeremy Gibson and Colin Rodgers, *Coroners' Records in England and Wales*, Family History Partnership, third edition, 2009, for background information and the whereabouts of records. There are legal restrictions on access to records less than seventy-five years old, though you can make a request to view (see Gibson and Rodgers, p. 7). How do you know if an inquest was held? Well, for the civil registration era it should state so in column 7 of the death certificate. Coalfield area family history societies may have items relating to coroners' records either in their journals or publications. Pontefract FHS's *Index to the Inquest Notebooks of Thomas Taylor, Yorkshire County Coroner*, for the years 1844–1885, for example, is an excellent searchable source on CD containing over 11,000 records, many of them relating to mining deaths. 'Accidental death' was by far the most common verdict of inquest juries relating to the coal industry.

Scottish fatal accident records

There is no inquest system for Scotland. Sudden deaths are investigated through an official called the Procurator Fiscal. Fatal Accident Inquiries (FAIs) were held for industrial accidents – such as those in coal mines – only after 1895. For information about pre and post-1895 accidental deaths (including the location of surviving records) see the National Archives of Scotland's guide, printable via http//www.nas.gov.uk/guides/FAI.asp. But again, due to the paucity of pre-1895 records, local newspapers remain the best source.

Compensation and accident records

Compensation records, where they survive (see the reference sections in Part Two of this book), are useful to the family historian as they provide the name of the person, date and cause of the accident, the colliery name, occupation and details of compensation. Many miners took out 'accident insurance' from local companies, paying a penny or two a week. There were also philanthropic associations and friendly societies that provided basic financial help in case of serious accident or death. The miners' associations themselves also operated schemes for its union membership. Paying a penny a week to a burial club also provided reassurance that a basic funeral could take place. There were also specific relief funds (and mayoral funds) established to provide financial assistance to widows and orphans after a disaster. It was the Permanent Relief Funds that attracted the greatest support. Some, like the West Riding Permanent Relief Fund, became well established and old disaster-specific relief funds were often integrated into general accident funds. Newspapers are a good and reliable source relating to accident and relief funds in the first few weeks following an accident, and in the case of major disasters, for many years afterwards. Accident books were kept at collieries but with some exceptions few have survived. The same is true for wages books, which contain references to compensation relating to an accident and any subsequent absence, including hospital care. It is also worth knowing that many responsible colliery companies cooperated with 'butties' (sub-contracted miners) and miners, providing sick pay and widows' allowances, and also help with burial costs.

Public monuments and monumental inscriptions (MIs)

Unlike war memorials there is no national database of mining monument but if your ancestor was killed in a major disaster it is likely that there is some form of public memorial. Many of the historic memorials are 'listed buildings' so will be recorded in some detail (including photographs) by the local authority's planning department database. Local libraries should have some information about the disaster and its aftermath. Disaster memorials were usually financed through public subscription and/or via a benefactor, so information will be found in local newspapers in the weeks and months following the tragedy. In recent years there have been many new memorials established (and re-dedications/restorations) thanks to a great deal of hard work by local groups, including the process of accessing funding sources. In addition, there are many new memorials commemorating *all* deaths at a particular colliery; and in some cases individual names are then inscribed.

Individual memorials and monuments, if they exist or have survived, are of course important to the family historian researching a mining ancestor. Most of my mining ancestors have unmarked graves, as families were unable to afford a headstone. But I found it contextually useful to record a few others relating to the same disaster or from a similar period. Researchers from family history societies have carried out excellent work over many years transcribing monuments in churchyards and cemeteries. 'MIs' are usually available for purchase either in printed form or on CDs, by post, online or at meetings and events such as family history fairs, and may also be accessible in local studies libraries.

Accident and disaster ephemera and mementoes
Anyone researching a major mining disaster will come across a variety of printed material, often hurriedly produced, and sometimes described as souvenirs. It was the Victorians who started the fashion of disaster and death mementoes, but examples continued well into the twentieth century, including:

- Picture postcards
- Poems
- Newspaper supplements
- Serviettes and napkins
- Funeral cards (mass and individual)
- Bibles/prayer books
- Church service programmes
- Fund-raising event programmes

A wartime boy miner's funeral card, produced after his death 'through injuries caused at Bentley Colliery' (near Doncaster) on 23 December 1916.

IN AFFECTIONATE REMEMBRANCE OF

MY DEAR SON,

THOMAS J. McKONE,

WHO DIED THROUGH INJURIES CAUSED
AT BENTLY COLLIERY,

on DECEMBER the 23rd, 1916,

Aged 14 years 4 months.

A typical Warner Gothard montage illustrating the fire at Hamstead Colliery in 1908. It is interesting that a rescue team from as far away as Tankersley, near Barnsley, attended the incident, perhaps due to their specialist knowledge and skills.

Some were sold for a penny or two, or given away free. Perhaps the most innovative and enterprising of the postcard publishers was Warner Gothard, who, with his sons, produced a series of montage-style cards from c.1905–16, from his main studio and works in Barnsley. Known examples are for Barrow (1907), Hoyland Silksone (1907), Washington (1908), Hamstead (1908), Midsomer Norton (1908), Maypole/Wigan (1908), West Stanley (1909) and Wharncliffe Silkstone (1914). Mark Fynn's website www.warnergothard. com provides background information. There were many other notable and enterprising postcard photographers, including Glasgow's W. Benton, who produced a series relating to Senghenydd (see Simon Barnett's US site www.senghenydd.net) in 1913.

Research projects and publications
It is worth checking via regional libraries and record offices whether anyone is undertaking research on mining accidents and deaths. Ray Ditchburn, for example, using sources such as miners' compensation/relief fund records and miners' union minutes, has built up a large database of information on mining fatalities and injuries in Northumberland. He also has details of mining

deaths for Durham. Ray welcomes information from family historians to add to his research and for enquiries can be contacted via rayditchburn@hotmail.co.uk.

For coalmining in the Llanelli area of south Wales see Malcolm V. Symons, *Coal Mining in the Llanelli Area: Sixteenth Century to 1829* (Llanelli Public Library, 1979), which includes collated information from all known accident data, using parish records and newspapers (from 1804). Inevitably this will still represent a minority of actual deaths. Volume 2 (Carmarthen County Council, 2012), covers the period 1830–1871.

Tip

Family historians should check all available sources on accidents and deaths in mining as there are many discrepancies, for example when comparing mines inspectors' reports, newspaper reports and death certificates. For multiple fatalities/disasters do look at several reported viewpoints whenever possible. The information from a rescue worker, eyewitness, manager, interrogated miner at an inquest, and so on, may vary considerably – and do check more than one newspaper account. Also find out if there are any oral history recordings or published memoirs relevant to a particular event via sources held at the national coalmining museums and British Library.

Mines rescue

If your coalmining relative or ancestor was involved in mines rescue (or was a pit 'ambulance man' or 'pit nurse') you may already have some knowledge of this through oral information passed down over several generations. If he was an official member of mines rescue there may be surviving photographs of the team, usually displaying equipment ranging from canaries to breathing apparatus. If he was involved in a twentieth-century disaster then he may be named in reports and/or shown in news photographs. Service awards in the form of badges or certificates may also have survived in family and public archives. However, well into the twentieth century it was far from unusual for what might be called unofficial rescuers to be involved in accidents and disasters: men – and even boys – called upon or self-volunteered into assisting with the rescue operations in several ways, for example in the recovery of bodies.

Like war veterans, several miners that I have interviewed were reluctant to talk in detail about their rescue and recovery experiences; and it was always an emotional response, a great deal of clarity usually emerging, as though the incident had happened the day before and not many years earlier. I'll never forget the testimony of Ron Palmer. When he was aged 16 he was woken in the early hours of the morning on 6 August 1936 and told to rush to his pit, Wharncliffe Woodmoor 1,2 & 3 Colliery, at Carlton near Barnsley. When he arrived, in pouring rain, hundreds of people had assembled in and near the pit yard as an explosion had occurred in the early hours. Scared, he reported to his deputy who instructed him to go down and wait at the pit bottom. His dreadful job was to record the names of the dead bodies as they were stretchered into the cage. Fifty-eight men lost their lives. He was allocated this task as he was 'used to writing production figures' for his deputy in an underground office known as the 'box-hole'. Understandably, Ron was badly affected by this memory for the rest of his life, becoming a passionate union member and union official.

Bentley's 'ambulance man', Tom Hopkinson, was one of the forty-five miners who died as a result of the 1931 disaster. Speaking to me in 1997, his daughter Doris Kitchin recalled the sad day and its aftermath, when she was aged 11:

Dad was at work on his afternoon shift. Granddad and I were playing Ludo. Suddenly he looked up and listened. There was the sound of pit boots on the road ... there had been an explosion at the pit. The street was filled with fearful people who were anxious to gain news of loved ones or friends. Mum and Gran rushed home after hearing the news when out shopping. As the men were brought out dead she scanned each one anxiously, each name chalked up on a board. Dad was the last to be brought out, badly hurt. He had insisted on staying behind to give first aid ... he just managed to say a few words, asked about me but died a few hours later. The whole village was in mourning. All the coffins were placed side by side in St Philip's church and most were buried together in a big grave in Arksey cemetery. Our house bore such grief and sadness and I was bewildered by it all ... many miners who survived never worked there again, it shocked them so much. The piano stood silent in our front room ... no more laughter, no singing ... I cried a lot but when I went to bed I looked through the window at the moon and felt happy because I thought I saw Dad's face and it made me feel safe.

Thomas's widow was presented with the Order of Industrial Heroism award by the *Daily Herald* in 1932.

Tom Hopkinson dressed in his ambulance uniform.

Was your mining relative or ancestor in the mines rescue service?

Miners always rush to help trapped and injured colleagues, risking their own lives, but for much of the nineteenth century there was little or no training given and safety equipment was minimal. It was not until 1902 that the first dedicated mines rescue station was established, at Tankersley, near Barnsley (Yorkshire). Others were built in the major coalfields, at Howe Bridge (Lancashire, 1908); Wath-upon-Dearne (Yorkshire, 1908); Abercam and Crumlin (south Wales, 1909); Mansfield (Nottinghamshire, 1909); Altofts (Yorkshire, 1909); Elswick (Durham, 1909); Cowdenbeath (Fife, 1909); New Tredegar (south Wales, 1910) and Stoke-on-Trent (Staffordshire, 1910). But it was the Coal Mines Act of 1911 that ensured rescue stations had to be provided within 15 miles of most mines. By 1918 there were forty-six Central Rescue Stations, as they were known. Former miner-soldiers involved in tunnelling companies on the Western Front were able to pass on a wealth of experience and a more regimented system of training evolved. The new stations needed to be staffed by a corps of at least six or eight men on a permanent basis, under the leadership of a supervisor. At least one and as many as four (according to the size of the colliery) rescue brigades had to be established at each mine, recruited from its own workforce. The men had to be 'carefully selected on account of their knowledge of underground work, coolness and powers of endurance, and certified medically fit, a majority of whom shall be trained in First Aid . . . ' If you know the approximate period that your mining relative or ancestor worked in mines rescue (usually as a young man under the age of 45) it should be fairly straightforward to build a context file of background information from newspaper reports of accidents and disasters at his colliery and neighbouring pits. There's also a range of memorabilia, photographs and ephemera that are well worth searching for and collecting. Although many rescue stations have been demolished, others have been converted to a variety of uses. In most cases photographs will exist. He may also have received an award, usually a medal for five, ten or fifteen (and exceptionally twenty) years' service, inscribed with his name. Do check the major coalmining museums for examples if you can't find a personal one.

The Philip Healey website www.healeyhero.co.uk provides an overview of the history and development of mines rescue; also useful are Les Hampson's Lancashire-based notes via COLSOL (Communities Online in Salford) at www.lancashireminesrescue.colsol.org; and Philip Clifford's www.heroes-of-mine.co.uk.

The Scottish aristocrat and gas-mask inventor John Scott Haldane (1860–1936) carried out many experiments concerning safety measures for exploring post-explosion underground workings and gas pockets. He even created a special cage for canaries – subsequently known as 'the Haldane' – that had its own oxygen supply to revive the birds, which continued to be used for locating gas pockets right up to the 1980s. Air quality was a major hazard to safe rescue and if your ancestor was in a mines rescue team from the early years of the twentieth century he would have been trained in the use, or certainly aware of, breathing apparatus with trade names such as 'Drager' and 'Meco-Briggs', but it was the 'Proto' brand that became internationally renowned, developed by R.H. Davis (later Sir Robert Davis) for his Siebe-Gorman company. So if your relative or ancestor was in the mines rescue service he would have been either part of a colliery's brigade, basically a volunteer, or a permanent member of a rescue corps at a Central Rescue Station.

The present-day mines rescue service (Mines Rescue Service Limited [MRSL]) is based at Mansfield, Nottinghamshire and functions via seven training sites. For further information visit www.mines rescue.com.

Did your coalmining relative or ancestor receive a bravery or gallantry award?

Great numbers of miners have performed acts of courage in the course of their working lives, and occasionally their bravery was acknowledged by some form of award. The range was considerable, from small commemorative items to substantial monuments. A silver teapot engraved and presented to William Washington 'by 645 admirers at Swaithe Main Pit for heroic daring on 6 December 1875' is a rare surviving Yorkshire example, and remains a family heirloom. A spectacular public example in the same area is the *Gloria Victis* sculpture and obelisk sited at the top of a hill at Kendray, near Barnsley, overlooking the 'valley of tears' where the ill-fated Oaks Colliery once functioned. It was commissioned by local businessman Samuel Joshua Cooper in the wake of the 1912 Cadeby disaster when fifty-three men involved in the search and rescue operations were killed. Retrospectively, however, the monument commemorates the bravery of mining engineer Parkin Jeffcock and 'other heroes of the rescue parties' who lost their lives forty-six years earlier in the 1866 Oaks disaster, and pays tribute to 'the signal bravery' of John Edward Mammatt and Thomas William Embleton when rescuing the sole survivor.

The most prestigious awards for bravery and saving life in the coalmining industry were the Albert and Edward medals.

The *London Gazette* was the official medium through which medal awards were announced. Now digitised, you can search via http://london-gazette.co.uk/search. Do look up local, regional and national newspapers for more information. Here is an early follow-up example from the *Manchester Guardian* of 20 August 1879:

Albert Medal for Abercarn heroes

Last night's Gazette announces that the Queen has been pleased to confer the 'Albert Medal of the First Class' on Henry Davies and John Harris; and the 'Albert Medal of the Second Class' on William Simons, Thomas Herbert, Miles Moseley, Charles Preen, William Walters and Lewis Harris. All the men are employed at the Abercarn Colliery.

On the 11th September, 1878, an explosion of firedamp occurred in the Abercarn Colliery, in the county of Monmouth, whereby 260 persons perished, and on that occasion the greatest possible gallantry was exhibited in saving about 90 lives. The force of the explosion was terrific, doing great damage to the roadways and to the bottom of the shaft; and setting the coal and timber on fire

---

in several places. The men named, without hesitation descended the pit, and although they discovered that the fires were raging in the mine, and that the chance of another explosion was considerable, they remained at their humane work of rescue, not re-ascending the shaft until they had satisfied themselves that no-one was left alive. Henry Davies, after being down the Abercarn pit all the afternoon with those recommended for the second class medal, volunteered to descend the Cwmcarn pit (a shaft two miles distant) with a view of conveying to the explorers who had attempted to enter the workings from that side an order from those in charge of the operations to come out as, in consequence of the fires underground continuing to burn fiercely and large quantities of gas pouring out of the workings, a second explosion was deemed to be inevitable. After being deserted by two men who refused to accompany him further, and when he must have felt that there was little or no chance of his coming alive out of the pit, pursued his course alone for 500 or 600 yards, and heroically accomplished the object of his mission. John Harris went down the pit with those recommended for the second class medal. Having descended to a depth of 295 yards, the progress of the cage was stayed by the damaged state of the shaft. John Harris got off the cage, and sliding down a guide rope reached the bottom, where, although he knew well that at any moment might be his last, he remained for many hours until all who were alive, some of whom were badly burnt and otherwise injured, reached the cage by his assistance, and were taken to the surface in safety.

First instituted in 1861 for gallantry in saving life at sea, the **Albert Medal** was extended to gallantry on land in 1877. The change coincided with what many regard as the most extraordinary rescue in British coalmining history, after the inundation at the Tynewydd Colliery in the Rhondda on 11 April. Its first First Class (gold) recipients were William Beith, Isaac Pride, John Howell and Daniel Thomas, for their courage when rescuing four men and a boy, trapped underground for nine days at Tynewydd. Twenty-one other rescuers received the Second Class (bronze) medal, one withdrawn later. The Albert Medal was last awarded to a living recipient in 1943 and the gold version was abolished six years later, replaced by the **George Cross**. Posthumous bronze medals continued to be issued until the award ceased entirely in 1971.

The Edward Medal for Mines was instituted by Royal warrant on 13 July 1907 in recognition of life-saving in mines and quarries and was of two grades:

First Class (silver) and Second Class (bronze). The name of the recipient was engraved, as was the date (and sometimes the location of the mine) after 1930. The first recipients were Frank Chandler, for his heroics during a boiler explosion in Hoyland Silkstone Colliery, Barnsley on 23 November

Yorkshire miner Frank Chandler (right) being presented with the Edward medal in Buckingham Palace. To his immediate left is the other recipient, Henry Everson, a Glamorganshire pitman. King Edward VII is doing the honours.

The silver (First Class) version of the Edward Medal (for mines).

1907, and Henry Everson, for saving the life of of a workman during the sinking of Penallta Colliery, south Wales, on 12 September 1907. Both got First Class medals. Photographed at the presentation in Buckingham Palace, Chandler sported a beard almost identical to that worn by the King, who had a similar stature, and it is hard to distinguish the two on the official photograph but for Chandler's ceremonial bowing. For years afterwards Frank Chandler enjoyed his 'celebratory' status locally, medal proudly pinned to his jacket, a familiar figure in and around his pit village. The Edward Medal or 'miners' VC' was greatly respected in the coal industry. The First Class version was only awarded on seventy-seven occasions and bronze recipients numbered 320. Living holders were invited to exchange their Edward Medal for the George Cross in 1971 and only a small number declined. A George Cross database can be accessed via http://www.marionhebblethwaite./ gc.index.htm. Kevin Brazier's book *The Complete George Cross* (Pen & Sword Books, 2012) is a new reference guide to the medal and its holders.

The other what might be called official gallantry awards were the **Empire Gallantry Medal** (instituted in 1922 and functioning until 1940 when it was replaced by the George Cross) and the **George Medal** (instituted in 1940, for bravery, but not as outstanding as the George Cross). Further information about gallantry awards can be seen via Philip Clifford's site already referred to above (http://heroes-of-min.co.uk) and there are lists of recipients for several of the awards. D.V. Henderson's books, listed below, are also useful reference guides. Go to http://dmm.org.uk/gallantry/names (Durham Miners' Museum site) and there are lists of named recipients arranged alphabetically by surname; there's also a useful link to Bill Riley's www.pitwork.net where Edward Medal holders are listed by colliery.

The Order of Industrial Heroism (medal and certificate) was instituted by the *Daily Herald* newspaper in 1923 (ceasing when the newspaper closed in 1964). Designed by Eric Gill, this award, usually issued posthumously, is also known as the 'workers' VC' (see further reading below and web sites/links referred to above). In all, 444 'OIH's' were awarded. **The Carnegie Hero Fund Medal** (via the British Carnegie Hero Fund Trust, administered from Dunfermline, Scotland from 1908) was another notable life-saving award relevant to miners. **The Order of St John Life-Saving Medal** was awarded 'for bravery in mines and quarries' and was first awarded in 1875 (see www.orderofstjohn.org). **The Royal Humane Society** (www.royalhumane society.org.uk) also awarded medals to miners for exceptional bravery

The Manvers Main (Yorkshire) mines rescue brigade with a range of their equipment, including breathing apparatus, photographed in February 1926.

in rescuing persons from asphyxia, drowning, etc; and also testimonials and certificates of commendation. Their records are held by the London Metropolitan Archives (accessed online via www.cityoflondon.gov.uk). A less well-known bravery medal was presented by the **Royal and Antediluvian Order of Buffaloes**. In some cases miners received awards from from more than one organisation for the same act of bravery. So it's worth a check.

Examples of medals and awards are housed and catalogued at all British national museums and/or at the mining museums for England, Scotland and Wales. Although relating to Wales, Edward Besly's guide, *For Those In Peril. Civil Decorations and Lifesaving Awards at the National Museums & Galleries of Wales* (National Museum of Wales, 2004), is also useful background for other coalfield regions. In addition to the *London Gazette*, quotations relevant to particular Albert/Edward Medal holders can be checked within the HO45 series at The National Archives. In addition to the reading list below, the annual *Medal Yearbook* (Token Publishing) is the authoritative reference guide to medal values.

Further reading, video and film

Maureen Anderson, *Durham Mining Disasters c.1700–1950* (Wharncliffe, 2008)

Maureen Anderson, *Northumberland & Cumberland Mining Disasters*, (Wharncliffe, 2009)

Keith Armstrong and Peter Dixon, *Still the Sea Rolls On. The Hartley Pit Calamity of 1862* (Northern Voices Community Projects, 2012)

James Beechill, *The Terrible Yorkshire Pit Disaster* (Cadeby Main Colliery Memorial Group, 2012)

Alan Davies, *The Pretoria Disaster. A Centenary Account* (Amberley, 2010)

Helen & Baron Duckham, *Great Pit Disasters. Great Britain 1700 to the Present Day* (David & Charles, 1973)

Julie Dexter and Dennis Chedgy, *Mines, Safety and Rescue in the Somerset Coalfield* (Five Arches Special Issue, November 2002: Radstock, Midsomer Norton and District Museum Society, 2002)

Brian Elliott, *South Yorkshire Mining Disasters, Volume 1. The Nineteenth Century* (Wharncliffe, 2006)

Brian Elliott, *South Yorkshire Mining Disasters, Volume 2. The Twentieth Century* (Wharncliffe, 2009)

W.H. Fevyer, J.W. Wilson and J.C. Cribb, *The Order of Industrial Heroism* (The Orders and Medals Research Society, 2000)

Amanda M. Garaway, *104 men. The William Pit Disaster* (Hayloft, 2007)

Martin Goodman, *Suffer and Survive. Gas Attacks, Canaries, Spacesuits and the Bends: The Extreme Life of Dr J.S. Haldane* (Simon & Schuster, 2007)

Henderson, D.V., *Heroic Endeavour: Complete Register of the Albert, Edward and Empire Gallantry Medals and How They Were Won* (J.B. Hayward, 1988)

Henderson, D.V., *Dragons Can be Defeated: A Complete Record of the George Medal's Progress, 1940–83* (Spink and Son, 1984)

Fred Leigh, *Most Valiant of Men. Short History of North Staffordshire Mines Rescue Service* (Churnet Valley Books, 1993)

Jack Nadin, *Lancashire Mining Disasters 1835–1910* (Wharncliffe, 2006)

Matt O'Neil, *Lanarkshire's Mining Disasters* (Stenlake, 2011)

David Owen, *South Wales Collieries. Volume Six: Mining Disasters* (The History Press, 2005/2010)

Roy Thompson, *Thunder Underground. Northumberland Mine Disasters 1815–1865* (Landmark, 2004)

Lesley Hale, John Colledge and Michael Wileman, *Banded Together. Leicestershire's Worst Mining Disaster in 1898* (Whitwick Historical Group, 1997)

Stanley Williamson, *Gresford: The Anatomy of a Disaster* (Liverpool University Press, 1999)

Ian Winstanley, *Weep Mothers Weep. Wood Pit Explosion, Haydock, 1878* (Landy Publishing 1989)

Ian Winstanley, *With Hearts so Light. The Story of the Queen Pit Explosions at Haydock, 1868 and 1869* (Picks Publishing, 1990)

Ian Winstanley, *Hell under Haydock. The Lyme Pit Explosion, Haydock, Lancashire, 26 February, 1930* (Landy Publishing, 2000)

DVDs/Film

The Brave Don't Cry, [Knockshinnoch, 1950 (Group 3, 1952 [Philip Leacock, Dir]

Escape From the Dark/The Littlest Horse Thieves (Walt Disney Productions, 1976 [Charles Jarrott Dir])

Historical Disasters. Black Christmas [Pretoria, 1910] (Reel Vision Films, 2006)

The Huskar Disaster 1838 (Roggins Local History Group, Silkstone, 2008)

Sneyd Pit Disaster. January 1 1942 (Staffordshire Film Archive, n.d)

The Terrible Price. Gresford 1934 (Panament Cinema, 2004)

Chapter 3

RIGHTS AND STRIKES: ASSOCIATIONS AND UNIONS

From the middle decades of the nineteenth century many coalminers were members of district unions and regional 'associations'. Before 1945 and the formation of the National Union of Mineworkers (NUM) all coalfield areas had a variety of unions, some so local as to represent men at a single colliery or village. Many were short-lived, some merged and others amalgamated or became part of federations.

Do bear in mind that some owners did not allow or like their employees to be union members and it was not unusual for some of the more outspoken miners to be sacked and 'blacklisted'. This chapter provides an overview of the miner and his (and occasionally her) union, which was an integral part of their working life.

In the early days, as with friendly societies, being in a union was a form of family insurance against hard times when illness, injury, handicap or old age reduced or prevented work. Grievances apart, just having someone to talk to at work or the branch (or 'lodge') meeting held in the pub or working men's club was an immensely important social benefit, even in retirement. Mutual support and friendship were the fraternal and symbolic components of the backbone of union membership, as was a vision to change to a more equal and just society. Miners' unions were also of course an integral part of the labour movement as a whole.

'Eddie' Collins (b.Wombwell, Barnsley, 1894), lodge secretary at Denaby Main for twenty years, recalled his union background:

I joined the union when I started work at the pit [Cadeby Main, near Doncaster]. Young lads had only threepence to pay, then it went up to sixpence a week. My father paid a shilling. My father was always in the union. I used to go and pay the union for my father when he worked at New Oaks colliery. They paid it at a Saturday then ... I was a young lad of nine or ten ...

'A.J. Cook' (Arthur James, 1883–1931) as he was generally known, is regarded as one of the most important of all miners' leaders. Somerset-born, Cook rose to prominence as a full-time union official in south Wales after working as a miner in Merthyr Tydfil. A lay Baptist preacher, 'Cookie' was a brilliant speaker. He was elected as General Secretary of the Miners' Federation of Great Britain, serving until his premature death in 1931 and was a key figure during the 1926 General Strike and miners' lock-out.

He was never in arrears ... Eventually, in 1934, when I became branch secretary ... there was just over 1,200 in the union, and we'd about 2,200 workmen, and I thought, 'That's got to be altered,' so I used to be standing at the pit gates and asking them to join the union. I got men to join, and we had above 2,000 members before 1936.

Collins also served as a 'workmen's inspector' under the 1911 Coal Mines Act, representing the miners on safety issues. Politically active, as chair of the Minority Movement in Yorkshire and founder member of the Communist Party of Great Britain, he managed to arrange for the militant socialist and Welsh miners leader Noah Ablett and the charismatic A.J. Cook, Secretary of the Miners' Federation of Great Britain, to speak at the Denaby branch. His final working years were spent as Compensation Agent for the Yorkshire Area NUM in the Miners' offices in Barnsley.

(Jim McFarlane, 'Denaby Main: A South Yorkshire Mining Village', in *Studies in the Yorkshire Coal Industry* [Manchester University Press, 1976].)

Major issues such as pay and working conditions were dealt with through representative negotiation with management and owners. Rates of pay before nationalisation were largely fixed through complicated 'price lists' on a colliery and area basis. In some extreme circumstances miners and their families were evicted from their company-owned houses resulting in exceptional distress. There are several examples, but two of the most astonishing cases of extreme action by owners occurred within a few years in the Yorkshire coalfield, at Denaby Main (1902/03) and Kinsley (1905). The disputes attracted national media coverage as well as parliamentary debate. Keir Hardie, the indefatigable pioneer Labour leader and MP for Merthyr Tydfil, visited Kinsley and, 'banners flying', there was a major demonstration at May Day Green, Barnsley in 1906, with speeches from miners' leaders.

During the twentieth century, and especially after the formation of the NUM in 1945, a wide range of benefits were available for members. Practical help following accidents not only included compensation assistance, but also the provision of convalescence facilities. The long battle to obtain compensation for the long-term respiratory and associated illnesses has continued to the present day, though not without controversy. One other underrated role of the NUM has been the provision of education and training, for example at Day Schools, for its officials and members.

Union development c.1780 onwards

Before the 1830s, small 'associations' of miners lacked any organisation for effective bargaining power and had limited success against the owners and an unstable market for coal. The use of special constables, soldiers and the reading of the Riot Act stamped on protest and underlined the fragmentary ineffectiveness of local combination. In south Wales Richard Lewis (better known as Dic Penderyn) paid the ultimate price in 1831, hanged outside Cardiff gaol for the apparently false accusation of stabbing a soldier in the rising at Merthyr on 3 June. Towards the end of the decade Chartism demonstrated that miners had a common ideology, beyond local and area boundaries. The search for national unity began. It proved to be a very long and rough road, starting at Wakefield in November 1842, with the albeit short-lived Miners' Association of Great Britain and Ireland.

If your coalmining ancestor worked from the 1850s to the 1870s he was probably a member of one of the many district unions. The moderate Miners' National Union (MNU) gradually lost support from most of its affiliated areas, its falling membership concentrated in Durham and Northumberland. However, under the leadership of Alexander McDonald, the MNU played a decisive role campaigning for better conditions of employment and safety through the Coal Mines Regulation Act of 1872. The districts came under great strain after the great fall in coal prices during 1874 and wage reductions sparked off disputes and strikes throughout the coalfields. A variety of contentious 'sliding-scale' pay arrangements were introduced, and the bargaining strength of the miners weakened.

A miners' federation initially comprising the county associations of Yorkshire, Nottinghamshire, Derbyshire, Lancashire, north Wales, Stafford-shire, Warwickshire and Leicestershire was formed in 1889. The Miners' Federation of Great Britain (MFGB) soon attracted affiliation from the Scottish and south Wales miners, and also from Northumberland and Durham. With a membership of 600,000 the MFGB could claim to represent all miners, but the situation remained complex. The deputies and craft unions (winding enginemen, mechanics, firemen etc) remained largely separate and in 1910 there were still seventy-four independent coalmining unions in existence. The South Wales Miners' Federation (founded in 1898 and known as 'The Fed') with 137,553 members became the largest constituent of the MFGB. Durham Miners' Association were not far behind (121,805) and well ahead of third-placed Yorkshire (88,271).

The fragmentary state of coalmining unions hardly helped solidarity during the 1926 strike and its aftermath, including the breakaway 'Spencer Union' in Nottinghamshire. After the Second World War the inauguration of the National Union of Mineworkers (NUM) on 1 January 1945 took place just at the right time, with a new and reforming Labour government coming to power, just two years before the nationalisation of the industry under the National Coal Board. At last the miners had a single voice and a single negotiating partner. The NUM membership was substantial at 533,000; two officials' and deputies' unions had a combined membership of 23,133 and there were a few hundred in a winding enginemen's union.

During the 1960s, when Lord Robens was Chairman of the NCB, about 400 pits were closed and half of all the miners lost their jobs. The massive run down and virtual eclipse of the deep-mining industry following the 1984/85 miners' strike now means that NUM membership has declined from around 180,000 to less than 2,000. Nevertheless, the NUM, with its historic headquarters in Barnsley, continues to operate and represent its members past and present on a federal basis via the main old coalfield areas.

Strikes and lock-outs

Miners were always one of the more radical groups of industrial workers and from the eighteenth century every coalfield had its 'turn-outs', short-term strikes or withdrawals of labour, with the main areas of Northumberland and Durham, south Wales and Yorkshire more prone to longer and more frequent agitation. Disputes were often very local and short-lived, lasting a shift or a few days, but others continued for weeks and months, spreading to other coalfields. 'Lock-outs', where the coal owner or company barred its miners from returning to work were not uncommon. Your mining ancestor is therefore highly likely to have been involved in one or more industrial disputes during a working life.

Tip

Local newspapers are an excellent source of information on industrial disputes and it is well worth taking a sample few years just to get an impression of the 'militancy' of the area in and around where your ancestor lived. Build up a 'context' file and it will help you appreciate what issues may have affected your miner (and of course his family). Reportage of the meetings of the miners' associations is particularly useful and the 'local news' sections may even include information about events at branch/lodge level. Do also check the 'magistrates' court' pages too! One commonsense word of warning about actual strike/lockout accounts: newspaper editorials and reportage varied according to the political slant of the editor/owner. So do read more than one source.

> ## Tip
>
> Personal, eyewitness reports are invaluable even though you may not have anything direct from your own ancestor. And don't forget to include the contributions from women. Autobiographies, published and in typescript, often lodged in local studies and archive libraries, are well worth consulting, as are any relevant oral history recordings or transcripts. For the 1984/85 strike a massive amount of material has emerged into the public domain over the last thirty years. The role of women during and after the strike was exceptionally important. The BBC regional radio stations and the archived main BBC news site (www.bbc.co.uk) make excellent starts; and a search using 'miners' strike' will direct you to many online sources.

Notable strikes and lock-outs

1893: the 'Great Lock-out' affected Yorkshire, Lancashire and the Midlands, from June. Two Yorkshire miners were shot dead (and sixteen injured) in the 'Featherstone Massacre' of 7 September when troops opened fire on a protesting crowd following a reading of the Riot Act. The dispute dragged on until the end of November when, after arbitration via a new National Conciliation Board, the owners' demand for a 30 per cent reduction in miners' wages was reduced to 10 per cent.

1894: in Scotland, June-October.

1898: in south Wales, over five months.

1902/03: Denaby Main, Yorkshire, lockout and evictions.

1905: Kinsley, Yorkshire, lockout and evictions.

1912: arguably the first truly national coalmining strike; over a million men affected, from late February to mid-April; an often bitter dispute over a minimum wage requirement (in an attempt to deal with inconsistencies concerning pay-rates for coal-getting in different coalfields and districts).

1921: a national lockout, from 1 April (to 1 July) following a return to 'district agreements', in effect wage reductions, involving all miners; the Triple Alliance (miners/railwaymen/transport workers) fell apart on Black Friday, 15 April, leaving the miners on their own during a three-month dispute which involved widespread poverty in the coalfields.

1926: a national lock-out from 1 May (and nine-day General Strike from 4 May), following the 'reduced wages' Royal Commission report on the industry which the miners felt favoured the owners. The men remained out but by the autumn many thousands had returned to work including the

Miners' wives and children supporting pickets at Rugely Power Station during the national coal strike, 18 January 1972.

members of George Spencer's Nottinghamshire-based breakaway union. Bitter recriminations continued for many years.

1972: the first national strike for over forty-five years was about pay, a dispute against the NCB and statutory incomes policy of the Heath government. It lasted from 9 January – 28 February and resulted (via a landmark inquiry under Lord Wilberforce) in a substantial improvement in pay and conditions. The strike was noted for co-ordinated and strategic (and so-called 'flying') picketing of sites such as power stations and, most famously, at Saltley Gate coke plant, Birmingham, led by a young Yorkshire miners' leader called Arthur Scargill.

1974: on 9 February, two days before Parliament was dissolved, 82 per cent of the NUM voted for strike action in support of higher wages. The snap General Election on 28 February resulted in a defeat for the Conservative Government of Edward Heath and a Labour minority government under Harold Wilson came to power. The strike ended on 11 March with the award of wage increases and better conditions of work and employment, though some of the injustices still outstanding from 1926 remained.

1984/85: the last and now often referred to as 'great' miners' strike lasted almost a year, starting in South Yorkshire, from March. Often personalised as a battle between Scargill and MacGregor/Thatcher, experts continue to argue over the background and outcomes of what is now generally regarded as the most bitter and most controversial industrial dispute in modern British history. Whatever the analysis, its legacy is undisputed: the miners' demise was a precursor of the virtual destruction of deep coalmining in Britain through post-strike pit closures, especially during 1985–1994.

Strike Memories

Ernest Kaye (b.1917), Birdwell, south Yorkshire

The [1926] strike was clog and boot time if you like, not much to wear, no money at all. There was mother and father, me and my two brothers, one of them dying aged ten. Quite a few people gave food to the community. We went to school as normal ... some wearing just one shoe ... big holes in jumpers ... we used to take our pot to school and go across to Birdwell Club and have our tea there, two jam sandwiches and a bun. At the top of our road there were some allotments and one very knowledgeable man decided to sink a pit. A big hole was dug. All the men, colliers, stood around and they went as far down as to think to get some coal ... My dad was among them. A big bicycle wheel with a rope on and a bucket was set up and they used to shout 'Reight, lower it down'.

Barbara Williams, miner's wife, Maerdy Women's Support Group, south Wales, 2004

The memory doesn't go away. It's as if it was a few weeks ago. We had to form a committee. Somebody said, you need a treasurer and secretary and my friend said, put your hand up and get involved. At the start no one would have envisaged it would have been a year-long strike. We realized there was a fight on, but at the end of the day we were fighting to keep the pit open, for the men to keep their jobs to support their families. I think a lot of women proved there were things they had never, ever done before that we were now capable of doing.

Demonstrations and Galas

Regional gatherings of branches and lodges, leading to an open-air meeting involving speeches and entertainment, became increasingly common from about 1860 and attracted huge crowds. The South Yorkshire Association, for example, held fourteen Demonstrations between 1863–79, mostly at Barnsley, and the neighbouring West Yorkshire union had ten Demonstrations during a similar period (1867–80). After amalgamation in 1881 demonstrations in Yorkshire were held annually (except during 1912–31 and 1940–46). In Derbyshire, the first demonstration was held in 1873. The annual Northumberland Miners' Picnic, which began in 1866, also attracted a large following. Although there are now no deep mines in the area, the famous Durham Miners' Gala or 'Big Meeting' is still held each second Saturday in July, in Durham city. First held in 1871, in its heyday during the 1950s over 300,000 people were in attendance. In Fife the annual celebration held to commemoration the famous eight-hour day victory of 1870, was in 1947 incorporated with the Scottish Miners' Gala Day at Holyrood Park, Edinburgh, inaugurated after the winning the five-day week. By 1953 the attendance at the Gala exceeded 100,000. Demonstrations were always well reported in local and regional newspapers and the programmes, photographs and film of the events are well worth consulting in local studies and national libraries.

Banners

Banners were not only used at demonstrations or galas, but also at funerals, especially after accidents and disasters. In recent years they have have formed the backdrop of a variety of commemorative ceremonies and the unveiling of mining monuments. Surviving miners' banners can be seen in many settings, from working men's clubs and miners' welfares, trade union offices and town halls to regional and national museums. In the North East a particularly good display can be seen at the Woodhorn Museum, near Ashington. The South Wales Miners' Library in Swansea has a collection of thirty-nine relatively modern banners. Samples are usually on display at the national mining museums for Scotland, England and Wales.

The early, hand-made silk or velvet versions are rare, fragile survivals. In most cases the banner you will see is a replacement of one or more earlier versions as they were only expected to have a lifespan of a generation or so. Inauguration was a special occasion. The artwork on the banners includes a variety of social imagery: 'Steps to Socialism' or the achievements of the unions and the Labour Party; 'prosperity and happiness'; 'health and peace'; 'five-day week'; 'nationalisation'; 'family allowances'; and 'social security'. From Keir Hardie and Alexander McDonald to Clem Attlee and Harold Wilson, the heroes of Labour are portrayed on many of the banners, as are the great mining leaders: Tommy Hepburn, Arthur Horner, Peter Lee, A.J. Cook, Herbert Smith and, on several of the new banners, modern leaders such as Lawrence Daley and Arthur Scargill.

Miners' leaders

Was your ancestor a miners' leader? If not he would certainly have known one. Such men were very important in miners' working lives, and were also often prominent in matters relating to welfare. And of course some held public office, locally or regionally. In some respects their relatively well-documented lives can also help us to appreciate what it was like to be a miner, as most had worked in the pits from leaving school.

Levi Lovett (1854–1929), miners' leader

Born at Hugglescote, Leicestershire, his publican parents moved to nearby Swannington where Lovett spent the rest of his life. At the age of 12 he started work at Swannington (No.3) pit but through self-education studied and passed all grades of mining work. Lovett remained as a miner until the age of 32 when he was appointed as checkweighman at Snibston. He helped to form the Coalville and District Miners' Association (later renamed the Leicestershire Miners' Association [LMA]), serving as president from 1887 until 1900. His union activities, however, continued, as he worked as secretary and agent for the LMA and as their representative on the executive of the Miners' Federation of Great Britain. Due to ill-health Lovett resigned as agent in 1923, after thirty-six years of service to the miners of Leicestershire. He had been particularly important in helping miners with their compensation claims. Like most miners' leaders of this era, Lovett was active in local public life, as parish councillor, president of the village horticultural society, governor of Leicester Infirmary and as a magistrate.

Apart from published autobiographies and biographies, by far the best source for miners' leaders is the thirteen-volume *Dictionary of Labour Biography*, a remarkable and ongoing piece of scholarship originated in 1972 by Joyce Bellamy and John Saville (Macmillan Press Ltd) and later by Keith Gildert and David Howell (for Macmillan Palgrave). Most miners' leaders, however, are contained in the first five volumes. If there is a family connection you can then consult the relevant volume for the biographical entry. Greg Rosen's *Dictionary of Labour Biography* (Politico Publishing, 2001) is worth consulting for several of the better-known leaders, as is John Ramsdon's *The Oxford companion to twentieth-century British politics* (OUP, 2002 & 2005). For national figures, the *Dictionary of National Biography* (DNB) is the standard reference work (online via some library services or held at some central libraries). One early but hard-to-find source, containing thirty portraits, is William Hallam's *Miners' Leaders* (Bemrose & Sons, 1894).

Joseph Arthur Hall (1887–1964), miners' leader

'Joe' Hall was born in the small mining community of Lundhill, Wombwell, in south Yorkshire. Here, thirty years earlier, residents experienced one of the worst disasters in British coalmining history when 189 men and boys were killed. By the age of 12 he was working underground, at Darfield Main, replacing burnt-out lamps at the coal face; he then went pony-driving. Moving to Cortonwood, he was set on as a 'trammer', hauling full and empty tubs for his paymaster collier. In 1907, Joe Hall was elected to the Cortonwood branch of the Yorkshire Miners' Association (YMA), progressing to delegate (1910) and secretary (1916). He served as checkweighman at the pit from 1917. By 1925 he became a paid official (financial secretary) of the YMA (which then had a substantial 160,000 membership). In 1930, he was elected as an executive member of the Miners' Federation of Great Britain (MFGB) and was a key figure at the Gresford (north Wales) inquiry following the disaster of 1934; he gave evidence to the resultant Royal Commission on Safety in Mines. The climax of Hall's union career was his election as president of the YMA in 1939, succeeding the great Herbert Smith. Joe remained in office until his retirement in 1952. Affectionately known as 'Our Joe', centre-stage in the Miners' Hall at the NUM headquarters in Barnsley is a stone plaque commemorating his services, especially his 'unceasing efforts to save life at many of the mining disasters in the country'.

Women

Female union membership was very sparse until towards the end of the First World War when women were recruited in significant numbers to work at pit-heads. There were only 290 female miners' union members in

1896 and 1,041 in 1914, but by 1918 their numbers had swollen to 10,000. Female union labour was spread throughout the main coalfields. In Lanarkshire, for example, there were 2,040 women members in December 1908 (out of a total membership of 48,000). They worked as coal-pickers, haulage hands and saw-millers, earning from about 6 to 15 shillings a day including bonuses, far higher rates than in most other industries. Although female membership was welcomed, it was the policy of the union to get rid of female labour 'owing to the conviction in members' minds that their employment about collieries is not suitable'.

Research guide

1. Where to find miners' union records

What survives is scattered across a range of archives. Some union records may be deposited in your local and/or county record office, so it is always worth a check there as a first step. For regions, see Chapter 9. The National Archives (www.nationalarchives.gov.uk/), National Library of Scotland (www.nls.uk) and National Library of Wales (www.llgc.org.uk) also hold mining union records. Here are some of the main specialist libraries and archives, but you will need to make an appointment prior to any visit.

- **National Union of Mineworkers**, 2 Huddersfield Road, Barnsley, S70 2LS [t] 01226 284006; [w] www.num.org.uk. The NUM/MFGB records are not properly catalogued as yet, though there have been discussions about the establishment of a new research centre.
- **The Modern Records Centre** (MRC), University Library, University of Warwick, Coventry, CV4 7AL [t] 024 7652 4219; [e] archives@warwick.ac.uk [w] www2.warwick.ac.uk/services/library/mrc). A major trade union records repository including the archives of the TUC. The Centre has a useful online Family History and Occupational guide. Online catalogue. Holdings include records of the National Association of Colliery Overmen, Deputies & Shotfirers (NACODS) (ref: ODS), from 1962; publications relating to the the Miners' Federation of Great Britain (MFGB) and National Union of Mineworkers (NUM) 1888–1992 (ref MFG) including some constituent MFGB associations; and the NUM Birch Coppice (Warwicks) Branch 1941–68 (ref NUM). There are also online guides on the General Strike (1926) and Miners' Strike (1984–5). Very useful is the current King Coal exhibition webpage (www2.warwick.ac.uk/services/library/mrc/images/coal) which ran alongside the British Film Institute's 'This Working Life' project. This archive does not hold membership records, so you are unlikely to find a miner's individual record, but it is an excellent source for background information.

- **TUC Congress Library Collections**, Holloway Road Learning Centre, 236–250 Holloway Road, London, N7 6PP. [t] 020 7133 3726; [e] tuclib@ londonmet.ac.uk; [w] www. londonmet.ac.uk/services/saslibrary-services/tuc/. A massive source for pamphlets and periodicals especially. Online catalogue and Enquiry Desk.
- **Working Class Movement Library**, Jubilee House, 51 The Crescent, Salford, M5 4WX [t] 0161 7363601; [e] enquiries@wcml.org.uk www.wcml.org.uk; [w] www.wcml.org.uk. Started in the 1950s by union activists Edmund and Ruth Frow. Houses a wonderful collection of books, leaflets, recordings, memorabilia etc. The website has genealogical advice/guidelines. Online catalogue of library and archives includes NUM/MFGB records. A really good place for background information.
- **People's History Museum**, Left Bank, Spinningfields, Manchester, MR3 3ER. [t] 0161 838 9190; [e] info@phm.org.uk; [w] www.phm.org. uk. Ex National Museum of Labour History, reopened in February 2010 after a massive redevelopment. Objects of regional and national importance (online catalogue) include banners and badges; also commemorative items, posters, photographs, pamphlets, tokens and medals. The **Labour History Archive and Study Centre** (LHASC) (online catalogue) complements the objects, allowing access to resources on social, economic and political life. Jack Jones Reading Room for researchers. [e] archive@phm.org.uk .

2. Websites
- **The Union Makes Us Strong** (www.unionhistory.info). This is the important site based on the the TUC Congress Library Collections (London Metropolitan University). Free access to a massive amount of information and images.
- **Trade Union Ancestors** (www.unionancestors.co.uk). Mark Crail's excellent site, well worth consulting, with friendly advice for family history research.

Further reading

Mark Crail, *Tracing Your Labour Movement Ancestors* (Pen & Sword Family History, 2009)

Robert ('Robin') Page Arnot's four-volume histories of the MFGB and the formation of the NUM (1949–79) remain the most detailed general works, published by George Allen & Unwin: *The Miners. A History of the Miners' Federation of Great Britain 1889–1910* (1949); *The Miners. Years of Struggle. A History of the Miners' Federation of Great Britain from 1910 onwards* (1953); *The Miners in Crisis and War. A History of the Miners' Federation of Great Britain from 1930 onwards* (1961); *The Miners. One Union, One Industry 1939–46* (1979)

Union/Labour histories

Robert Page Arnot, *A History of the Scottish Miners* (George Allen & Unwin, 1955)

Robert Page Arnot, *South Wales Miners. A History of the South Wales Miners' Federation 1894–1914* (George Allen & Unwin, 1967)

Robert Page Arnot, *South Wales Miners. A History of the South Wales Miners' Federation 1914–1926* (Cymric Federation Press, 1975)

Carolyn Baylies, *The History of the Yorkshire Miners 1881–1918* (Routledge, 1993)

Alan Campbell, *The Lanarkshire Miners. A Social History of their Trade Unions, 1775–1974* (John Donald, 1979)

Alan Campbell, *The Scottish Miners 1874–1939, Vol. 2, Trade Unions and Politics* (Ashgate Publishing, 2000)

J. Davison, *Northumberland Miners' History 1919–1939* (NUM, 1973)

Hywel Francis and David Smith, *The Fed. A History of the South Wales Miners in the Twentieth Century* (Lawrence and Wishart, 1980)

Alan Ramsey Griffin, *The Miners of Nottinghamshire 1914–1944. A History of the Nottinghamshire Miners' Unions* (George Allen & Unwin, 1962)

Frank Machin, *The Yorkshire Miners. A History*, (NUM, n.d. [c.1958])

Cliff Williams, *A Pictorial History. National Union of Mineworkers Derbyshire Area 1880–1980* (NUM, 1980)

J.E. Williams, *Derbyshire Miners. A Study in Industrial and Social History* (George Allen & Unwin, 1962)

John Wilson, *A History of the Durham Miners' Association 1870–1904* (J.H. Veitch, 1907)

Strikes

V.L. Allen, *The Militancy of British Miners* (The Moor Press, 1981)

R. Church, and Q. Outram, *Strikes & solidarity: coalfield conflict in Britain 1889–1966* (Cambridge UP, 1998)

David Douglass, *Strike, not the end of the story. Reflections on the major coal mining strikes in Britain* (National Coal Mining Museum for England Publications, 2005)

Francis Beckett and David Hencke, *Marching to the Fault Line* (Constable, 2009)

Brian Elliott (ed), *The Miners' Strike Day by Day. The illustrated diary of Yorkshire miner Arthur Wakefield* (Wharncliffe Books, 2002)

Triona Holden, *Queen Coal: Women of the miners' strike* (Sutton Publishing, 2005)

Banners

Derek Gillum, *Banners of Pride. Memories of the Durham miners' gala* (Summerhill Books, 2009)

N. Emery, *Banners of the Durham Coalfield* (Sutton, 1998)

John Gorman, *Banner Bright. An illustrated history of trade union banners* (Scorpion, 1973 & 1986)

W.A. Moyes, *The Banner Book. A study of the lodges of Durham Miners' Association* (Frank Graham, 1974)

Chapter 4

WOMEN AND CHILD MINERS

It would not be too surprising if you found that one or more of your mining ancestors was a woman. Only two generations ago a small number of females were still employed as 'screeners' or 'coal-pickers' – 'pit brow lasses' or 'screen wenches' as the Lancashire versions were famously and derogatorily known. In similar roles were the 'pit-head women' of Cumbria and Scotland, 'tip girls' of south Wales, pit-bank women of Shropshire and south Staffordshire and the 'bal maidens' of Cornish mineral mines.

The last two women workers were retired at Haig Pit, Whitehaven, in 1972, so well into the twenty-first century there are plenty of former female pit-top workers still alive. In 2006, seventeen of the surviving women who worked in dreadful conditions at West Cumbrian mines, sorting and breaking the coal, were presented with framed certificates and given a civic reception in Whitehaven. Annie Ferguson (b.1923), who started working as a screen lass at Haig in 1939, aged 16, was reported as saying:

A lot of people don't realise how hard it was. We worked up a lot of iron steps, and you could look through the gaps and right down into the pit, and when it rained it [dust] would come down and cover you in black. There's still a few that won't admit they worked on the screens . . . but I never bother about it because I was with a group of lasses, and we were glad of the wages.

And Hannah McCarron (b.1921), her friend, said:

When I first saw the screens I went home and said to my mother 'it's not women they want on theer, it's hosses'.

Despite the hardship and social stigma, the Whitehaven women, mostly in their eighties, looked back on their experiences with affection, their stories collected together in an excellent publication: *Ah'd Gaa Back Tomorra!*, part of a four-year project between Haig Pit Mining Museum and the Whitehaven Miners' Memorial and Living History Project (see Further Reading below).

This cartes image from the camera of W. Clayton of Tredegar shows a young unnamed mine tip woman sat on a pile of coal, her pick by her side, preparing to eat from her lunch can, c.1865. Courtesy of Gallery of Costume, Platt Hall, Manchester City Galleries.

'Sal Madge' – 'last of the women colliers'

Whitehaven's most legendary female miner, Sal Madge (Sarah Magin) was born in Penrith, Cumberland and baptised in 1831. From about the age of 9 she worked at several of the Lowther family pits (Wilson, Howgill, Croft and Wellington) on the surface as a very able horse-driver/waggoner. Although she wore a skirt, albeit under a man's jacket, waistcoat and cap, Sal appears to have discarded most feminine attributes, smoking a clay pipe, drinking pints of beer and taking part in wrestling and football at local sports events. Suffering from bronchitis, she continued working to within a few days of her death aged 68 in 1899. Her 'pauper's grave' in Whitehaven Cemetery was marked by a new headstone in 1993, funded by the Friends of Whitehaven Museum. Vandalised in 2010, it has now been replaced by a replica memorial – to one of the most remarkable women of Cumberland. Sarah's details are not easily identified in the censuses though she is listed as a 'colliery wagonner' in 1881.

Studio photograph of 'Sal Madge'.

98

At some Cumberland pits female employment was extremely common. In 1802 124 out of 453 mineworkers at Lowther's Howgill Colliery were women, about six out of ten of them actually working underground. In another of the smaller coalfields, Shropshire, 137 females were employed on the surface in 1900 and eight were still there in 1920.

The annual (c.1854 to 1918) regional HM Mines Inspectors' reports occasionally contain reference to named females who had been injured or killed at collieries. In Shropshire, five females lost their lives by falling down the shaft and children of just 8 or 9 were known to be employed on the surface. Using inspectors' reports for the Wigan area, Alan Davies in the Appendix of his 'Pit Brow Women' book, cited below, found thirty-seven instances of serious and fatal accidents suffered by pit brow women and women who had strayed onto the colliery surface. The most common accidents concerned some form of haulage mishap, involving coal trucks or wagons, and several were struck by stray tubs. The information supplied by the representatives of the coal owners to the inspectors in most coalfields was deliberately vague on occasion, with terms such as 'a girl' or 'poor girl' or 'a female' with – suspiciously – no ages recorded. Fear of prosecution still ruled. As family historians we need to be aware of the context of such entries whenever possible.

Local newspapers are a graphic source of information too, providing details of incidents involving women and children at collieries. Staying in Shropshire, *The Wellington Journal* records that in 1856 Elizabeth Williams, alias Potter, a bankswoman (a skilled and responsible person loading and unloading the cage at the surface) at John Ferriday's pit fell down the shaft. In 1863, 'T. Purslow', described as 'a boy', aged 10, fell down the shaft at the Asterley mine. The engineman, T. Gettins, was sent to prison after the accident was investigated.

This chapter provides background and research information to help you if you have identified a female and/or child miner-ancestor. Furthermore, even if you don't discover a family example it is well worth being aware of the employment situation and conditions for such workers, as your male ancestor may well have worked with or alongside females and children above and below ground.

'Invisible' female miners

For centuries, right back to medieval times, women worked at coal mines (in small-scale workings employing a few hands) but the records of their involvement are scarce. It was usually only when a serious accident occurred that females were recorded. We know that Emma, daughter of William Culhare, was killed by 'le Dampe' (poisonous gas or an explosion) while drawing water from a coal-pit at Morley (Derbyshire) in 1322 – but this is a very rare early example. Where lists of colliery workers survive they show an entirely or predominantly male workforce right up to the start of the nineteenth century. The main exceptions were in parts of Scotland and Lancashire where the hewers provided their own bearers, so often employed wives and children.

As mining developed on a larger scale, women and children worked in family groups alongside their menfolk in some areas, particularly seasonally when other jobs in and around the home and farm, in winter months especially, were less worthwhile. Even the men worked seasonally, balancing work on the land with another craft or trade. An eighteenth-century Barnsley man, Richard Fisher, described himself as 'colyer' in his will made in 1726. But he had several other 'occupations'. Fisher brewed ale commercially, probably running an alehouse with his wife, as he lived in a strategically important part of town, directly overlooking a major routeway, and his probate inventory shows that he had a smallholding that included sixteen sheep, a few geese, basic farm equipment and a store of hay for animal feed. Fisher worked at the pit as and when he could. Interestingly, he left his wife 'those fifteen gines [guineas] that she took out of my pocket ... in whose hands she put them I know not pray God forgive her': an invisible but heartfelt bequest!

Women pit-top workers

For many generations women and girl pit-top workers were employed on deceptively menial or unskilled jobs. This included picking out waste material, grading coal and even breaking coal on the screens or picking tables. Other jobs included the pushing and emptying of tubs of coal via the tipplers and surface haulage and driving horse-wagon loads of coal. It was extremely hard work, dreadful in adverse weather and was noisy, dirty and dangerous. Most females worked for relatively short periods, until getting married or finding alternative employment, but those that continued or were re-employed later faced the kind of long-term ailments and diseases encountered by male miners.

Mary Ann Ralph: 'last of the coal-pickers'
'We just put up with it, we didn't know any better'

Interviewed for the *Barnsley Chronicle* shortly after her 90th birthday in 1986, Mary recalled that for most local girls seeking employment the choice was either the pits or the mills. She spent her teens and early twenties knelt hand-picking the coal from the 'dirt' at Standish, near Wigan. It meant getting up at 6am and walking to work to start a

7am shift, which ended at 5pm. If she heard the pit buzzer going off she would begin running, passing through the pit gates out of breath. There was a half-hour break for 'a slice of toast' at breakfast and an hour off at 2pm when the girls were allowed home for lunch. The day-rate was 7s 6d with 3d deducted for union dues. Mary wore a  blouse, hessian skirt, men's over-trousers, a special bonnet with a cover to protect the back of her neck and wooden-soled and leather-topped clogs. Gloves were a waste of time as they 'cramped the work'. It was noisy and dirty work, the dust 'getting everywhere' and there was no option but to 'go home in my pit muck' [some of the larger companies provide separate pit baths for women]. At bath-time the 'tin' receptacle was carried upstairs into a bedroom and jugs, kettles and pans of water would be heated on the range in the family's two-up and two-down terraced house. After marriage, in the 1920s, Mary and her husband Richard moved to Barnsley 'because there was work in the pits there'. Men 'have got it easy' these days, she concluded with a great smile.

During much of the nineteenth century the women working on the pit-tops in their distinctive garb were regarded by some elements of society as 'curiosities', their appearance perfect copy for newspapers, magazines and especially the new medium of photography.

We know in graphic detail about how the women and girls actually looked, most notably those working at collieries in the Wigan area and part of south Wales. This is because of the survival of a remarkable series of photographs, the earliest examples dating from 1859–60. These images attracted a great deal of public attention, as was soon appreciated by the studios and shops that sold many hundreds of quality cabinet and *carte de visite* versions. Many thousands more were produced and reproduced from the early 1900s with the introduction of the picture postcard. The sight of women wearing trousers and displaying the tools that they used was not only a novelty, but a commercial asset too, appealing to a much wider than local coalfield audience. The cards were sent all over Britain and there was a good trade in photographs. If your female 'mining ancestor' was from the Wigan area, she may have visited one of the leading studios, operated by John Cooper, T.D. Dugdale, Robert Little, Miss Louisa Millard, Thomas Taylor and Herbert Wragg.

A Lancashire Colliery Girl.

Group of Pit Brow Girls.

The Wrench Series. No. 3720

A pair of classic 'pit brow girls' images from the author's collection. The group image, an outdoor shot on the pit bank, shows the young women well arranged and wearing very similar attire; it is by Robert Taylor and the card, by Starrs, was postmarked 14 May 1904. The sender's brief comment was 'How does tha like um[?]'. The carefully-posed 'Lancashire Colliery Girl', one of many cards published by Wrench, was posted in Wigan, on 11 September 1904. Both images probably date from the 1890s.

Much contemporary and later interest in working women during the mid-Victorian period is due to the lifelong observations of an intrepid Londoner, Arthur J. Munby (1828–1910). His diaries, notebooks and sketches contain many entries about the lives and circumstances as well as the appearance of Victorian working women, including what he sometimes called his 'pit wenches'. Try reading extracts relating to Wigan, which he described as 'the picturesque headquarters of rough female labour', and you will see that he had one of the most underrated qualities of any researcher – good observation and listening skills. During his Wigan wanderings he also instigated and collected many photographs of the women. Much maligned by some later writers, his diaries were never meant to be public anyway and his work is of immense social importance today. Here is a typical journal entry, for Monday 10 September 1866, Munby starting his account at Bottom Place Pit, Ince:

It was noon now, and they were just knocking off work on the brow for dinner: girls catching up their jackets to run home, or getting out their dinner cans in the cabin, where I found half a dozen lasses seated, holding in their black hands meat pasties or hunches of bread ... Ann Prescott was there, with her broad shoulders, and a wonderful red and yellow kerchief round her head, setting off the grimy darkness of her handsome face. She had promised to go and be 'draw'd aht' [photographed] at Cooper's; but now she said she dared not, her father had forbidden it. Sarah Fairhurst also, whom I found in the cabin at the sister-pit close by, along with Maggie Taberner and a man, was as

Carte by Little of Wigan showing Ellen Grounds, aged 22, alongside Arthur Munby, taken on 11 September 1873. Courtesy of Library of Trinity College, Cambridge.

unwilling as ever to be photo'd; which is a pity, as she is one of the most robust of her class. She stood up erect against the cabin door, whilst I measured her height; and she is 5 feet nine.

For most women – especially on their own – it must have been quite an ordeal to be posed and photographed in a studio, and this is evident in their facial expressions. Less common were the more informal photographs taken on the pit-tops, though even here a good deal of direction and arrangement is clearly evident.

But what about the women's rights then? Did they exist? The Women's Trade Union League, founded in 1874, was certainly keen to promote the right of women workers to 'combine' or join 'men's unions'. Independent women's friendly societies and clubs emerged. A few miners' unions began to accept women recruits, the Cumberland Miners' Union for example attracting a few female 'screeners'. The Miners' Federation, however, through the Coal Mines Regulation (Amendment) Act of 1885, wanted the complete removal of the estimated 4,450 women employed at pit-heads. In 1886–87, protests from the pit lasses themselves, which included work-clothed deputations to Parliament, were well covered in the press. This wave of feminine agitation stopped legislation to ban them working, much to relief of most of the women; and they were not affected unduly by the 1911 Coal Mines Act. An article in the *Manchester Guardian* (13 May 1886), written during the protesting period, suggested that in Wales a voluntary code had emerged whereby no married woman worked at a pit if the husband was able to earn a living. There was a fear in other areas that the labour of women induced 'idleness' in their men!

During the First World War, when industrial labour suffered due to recruitment into the armed forces, thousands of females joined or rejoined pit-top teams of workers on a 'substituted' or permanent basis. Female miners' union membership peaked at about 10,000 during 1914–18, spread between fifteen local miners' societies, which then represented as much as 92 per cent of all women and girls working at the pit-head. The Lanarkshire Miners' County Union was a typical example, its female members increasing from a few dozen in 1914 to over 2,000 by 1918.

But what did female pit-top women earn? Well, it was certainly not equal pay for equal work. The labouring day-rate varied from 6s 3d (for 'ordinary' workers) to 9s 1d for the best paid 'drawers off' (wagon/tub haulage work) in December 1919; and a typical coal-picker got from 7s 10d to 8s 6d a day. Inclusive of bonuses, male saw millers expected to get about 16s a day, but on average females got 8s or less doing exactly the same, quite skilful, job. So if your ancestor was a female 'miner' at this time she is very likely to have been a local union member too. But she would not have received equal pay for equal work. For the coalowners, women employees

Strung out across a pit lane, a group of shawled and clogged pit-brow women photographed during a coal strike, probably 1912.

were cheap labour; even the better-paid female surface workers were cheap compared with those underground.

The miners' unions continued to press for women not to be employed on pit-top work as a matter of principle, but there was a great reduction of female labour anyway after the war.

Munby's travels in the 1860s included south Wales, where his interests were the 'mine tip girls'. One useful person he apparently missed was the prolific Tredegar photographer W. Clayton, who took a large number of *carte de visite* portraits of the tip girls.

A Welsh mine pit girl, possibly from A. Clayton's studio, c.1860s. She has a tin water bottle in her hand and lunch can under her arm and appears to be well attired from head to foot. Big Pit: National Mining Museum Wales.

Research Tips

- The Munby collection (of diaries, sketches and images) can be viewed by appointment via the archivist and modern manuscript cataloguer at the Trinity College Library, Cambridge, telephone 01223 338579 or use the contact enquiry form via www.trin.cam.uk/library. The indexes for each volume include the names of the working women, though many are referred to anonymously.
- For south Wales, the A. Clayton album (accession no. 2008.40.9.1) containing *carte de visite* images can be seen by appointment at the Gallery of English Costume, Platt Hall near Manchester: telephone 0161 245 7245 or via the enquiry form at www.manchestergalleries. org.
- Many images of women pit-top workers are included in the excellent books by Michael Hiley and Alan Davies listed in the Further Reading section below.
- Occasionally photographs and postcards of pit-brow women can be purchased via internet auction sites and collectors'/postcard fairs, but the better and rarer ones are expensive.

Women and children working underground

The 1842 Act and its implications for family history research

The 1842 Mines and Collieries Act banned females from working underground and boys under the age of 10 years. In theory therefore you should not have a female or young child miner-ancestor who worked underground after this date. In practice this was not always the case, but let's start by examining the impact of the new law on former female miners and their families.

The Act did not go down well with many of the women whose future employment prospects were then severely restricted. The financial impact was particularly bad for the older females and widows, and in family circumstances where, for example, there were no sons to aid a sick or disabled father. Reverend J. Adamson, minister of the parish of Newton, Mid-Lothian, told a mines commissioner in 1844 that two daughters, aged 49 and 50 and their 75-year-old father were left to 'shift for themselves', the women having no prospects of work in domestic service 'after having been for so long a period nothing better than beasts of burden'. In 1845, a 'charitable lady' in England went so far as to send Lord Ashley the sum of £100 to benefit those Scottish 'labouring women' still suffering from the financial effects of exclusion from their collieries. Ashley, the greatest campaigner for the Act, added some of his own cash to Adamson's donation. The money appears to have been used to provide clothing and shoes for

106

forty poor widows. Complaints and protest were numerous in Scottish coalfields where relatively large numbers of females had been employed in mines. The displaced women, many of them reduced to poverty, were even refused parish relief.

As family historians, we need to be aware that some abuse of the Act did take place for both female and boy labour. But there was a phasing period, from the Royal Assent date of 10 August 1842 until 1 March 1843, when absolutely no women were then allowed to work underground. Even so, your female and boy miner-ancestors may well have continued or started to work underground after this date. This is not surprising as compliance was slow and enforcement very difficult, especially in the more remote districts.

The full extent of any abuse of the law is hard to evaluate, but there are numerous official and unofficial reported cases, especially in the immediate post-1842/43 years. Three women, Mary Booth, Jane Helliwell and Jane Moss, were among eight persons killed in an explosion at Burgh Colliery, Coppull, Lancashire in November 1846. The pit's owner, John Hargreaves – incredibly a local magistrate – was held to be responsible for the illegal employment of women. His manager, Joseph Ellis, denied that he had told female workers (believed to be as many as thirty) to wear men's clothes in order to conceal their sex.

Occasional accidents revealed further abuse of the law. A 9-year-old girl hurrier, Patience Wroe, accidentally set her hair on fire when working underground at Caphouse Colliery (now part of the National Mining Museum for England),Yorkshire, in 1847. Martha John, aged 13, fell to her death when being lowered down Moreton Colliery in Pembrokeshire in July 1847.

The first inspector of mines, Hugh Seymour Tremenheere, writing about the state of south Wales mining districts in 1850, stated that 'some of the larger companies ... have failed to exercise their authority in support of the law', stating that 'females were again working below ground' at Blaenavon, Clydach, Nantyglo, Beafort, Blaina and Coalbrook (and also suggesting that 'one or two more' pit owners had turned a blind eye to the Act). Robert Smith, the mineral agent at Blaenavon Colliery, informed Tremenheere that he had 'turned out' seventy women and girls, 'as many as 20 of the latter being not more than eleven or twelve years of age'.

The most extreme case of illegal women miners in British coal mines comes from the pen of one our most respected writers and social commentators. In 1936, after visiting pits and living amongst mining families in Wigan and Barnsley, George Orwell wrote:

There are still living a few very old women who in their youth have worked underground, with a harness around their waists and a chain that passed between their legs, crawling on all fours and dragging tubs of coal.

This remark, on page 30 of the Penguin edition of *The Road to Wigan Pier*, if correct, would certainly refer to illegal female miners, several decades after the 1842 Act. Interestingly, in his recently published diaries (*George Orwell Diaries*, edited by Peter Davison, Penguin Modern Classics, 2009), on 19 March 1936 Orwell refers to 'a very old woman – a Lancashire woman' working 'down the pit, dragging tubs of coal with a harness and chain', saying that the 83-year-old would probably have been doing this in the 1870s. Anecdote and fact may have been blurred for political reasons here, but we do need to be aware of the possibility that at least a small number of women continued to work in mines, maybe in out of the way locations, long after 1842.

The Children's Employment Commission (Mines) and its two Reports 1840–42

As a young Barnsley-area secondary school teacher in the early 1970s one of the first primary sources that I used in the classroom was from the second (regional evidence) commissioners' report covering the employment of children and young persons (and women) in mines. This was thanks largely to extracts reproduced by E. Royston Pike's excellent compilation (see Further Reading, below), which also included some of the graphic illustrations that caused so much shock to Victorian society. Nowadays, the report's findings are much more widely available via the internet and library services and through excellent displays at our national mining museums (see Research Tips, below).

Jane Kerr, aged 12: coal-bearer, Dryden Colliery, Midlothian, Scotland

I get up at three in the morning, and gang [go] to work at four, return at four and five at night. It takes us muckle [much] time to come to the road, and put on our clothes. I work every day, for when father does not work, the master pays me 6d. a day for bearing wood for him.

I never get porridge before my return home, but I bring a bit of oatcake, and get water when thirsty. Sister and I can fill a tub of 4 cwt in two journeys. Sister is 14 years of age. My sister and brothers do not read, but I did once go to school to learn reading when at Sir John's work; have forgotten all the letters.

The Ladder Pit which I work in is gai [very] drippie [wet?], and the air is kind of bad, as the lamps do na burn sa bright as in guid [good, better] air. My father straps me when I do not do his bidding. The work is very sair [hard, sore] and fatiguing. I would like to go to school, but canna wone [go] owing to sair fatigue.

[Sub-Commissioner Franks. The Kerrs, a family of ten, lived in a single room, five of the children huddled in one bed.]

JANE KERR, Age 12, Coal Breaker

Model of Jane Kerr displayed in the Scottish Mining Museum.

The four commissioners and twenty sub-commissioners appointed to find and collect evidence did so with varying attention to detail and skill, but contributed to one of the most important and spectacular documents in modern British parliamentary history. Coverage ranged from Cornwall to Scotland, divided into twenty-four regions. Extracts from the report are essential reading for anyone with ancestors living and working in coalfield areas during (and indeed well before) the early years of the reign of Queen Victoria. The fact that there were so may *named* interviewees – several thousand women and child miners – means that you may even be able to find an example of your ancestor's evidence to the Commission. Initially, the cut-off point for 'boy' and 'girl' was deemed to be 13 years, but from February 1841 young persons up to the age of 18 were included. Exceptionally, it was found that children as young as 4 years old were employed underground, for example as 'trappers', though the starting point for most was between the ages of 6 and 9 (8.8 the mean age of all starters), after which they could be employed as pushers and pullers of carriages of coal from the workings to the pit bottom, described by a variety of regional terms: 'bearers/thrusters' (Scotland); 'trailers' (Cumberland); 'putters' (North East); 'hurriers and 'trammers' (Yorkshire); 'drawers' (Lancashire) and 'hutchers' (Forest of Dean). Being a bearer was one of the most arduous of tasks, usually for a child or young woman who carried corves (baskets) of coal on their back, often along inclines and even up tiers of ladders, especially in Scotland. The pushers and pullers of tubs or sledges on rails fared little better, having to cope with loads of two to three hundredweight per journey.

Pushing and pulling a wagonful of coal was often the job of women and children, as in this engraving from the 1842 report.

Bearing coal was a back-breaking job, especially on inclines and up ladders.

Pulling and pushing a corve or basket of coal on a sledge. The young man wears a leather waistband and a chain attaches him to the load, his only aid being a rope for pulling on. From the 1842 report.

Even by the standards of the time, it was astonishing that the commissioners reported in 1842 that around 5,000 children aged 5–10 toiled underground for up to twelve hours a shift. This meant working and living in virtually complete darkness during the long winter months.

Margaret Leveston, aged 6, coal-bearer, Peeblesshire, Scotland

Been down at coal-carrying six weeks; makes 10 to 14 rakes a day; carries full 56 lbs of coal in a wooden backit [bucket]. The work is na guid [not good]; it is so very sair [hard]. I work with sister Jessie and mother; dinna ken the time we gang [go, walk]; it is gai [very] dark. Get plenty of broth and porridge, and run home ... never been to school; it is so far away.

[Sub-Commissioner Franks]

Mary Davis, aged 7, air-door trapper, south Wales

A very pretty girl, who was fast asleep under a piece of rock near the air-door below ground. Her lamp had gone out for want of oil; and upon waking her, she said the rats or some one had run away with her bread and cheese, so she went to sleep. The oversman, who was with me, thought she was not so old, though he felt sure she had been below near 18 months.

[Sub-Commissioner Franks]

John Saville, aged 7, collier's boy, Intake Colliery, Sheffield

I stand and open and shut the door all day. I'm generally in the dark and sit me down against the door. I like it very well. It doesn't tire me. I stop 12 hours in the pit. I never see daylight now except on Sundays. I fell asleep one day and a corve ran over my leg and made it smart.

[Sub-Commissioner Symonds. This boy could not read or write and had worked at the pit for two weeks at the time of his interview]

Matilda Carr, aged 12, hurrier, Silkstone, near Barnsley

I hurry with my brother. I don't like it but my father can't keep me without going. I think it will continue to tire me after I have been accustomed to it. I go down the shaft at half past five and stop a bit and then begin again. We sit us down and rest and have meat and beer for dinner. They use me well at the pit and don't beat me or call me but I would rather be at school than in the pit.

[Sub-Commissioner Symonds. Matilda had worked at the pit for just one week when interviewed.]

The graphic illustrations that were used, commonly reproduced in the newspapers and periodicals of the day and in many later publications, continue to have impact.

1842 Research Tips

- The Children's Employment Commission Reports (there were two), on Mines – 'Blue Books' as such publications were known – are at The National Archives ([TNA] ZHC 2/79), as are the background parliamentary proceedings (ZHC 2): see National Reference section of this book for complementary records and guides. Entire, regional or abstracted copies may also be found in many other collections, national and regional including the National Mining Museum for England; and via some family history societies: use website internet search facilities or enquiry forms to check availability. Very many books contain abstracts, E. Royston Pike's, R. Page Arnot's, Anthony Burton's and Ray Devlin's being particularly useful (see reading list below). TNA's educational website (www.learningcurve.gov.uk) contains very useful items relating to Victorian mining including women ('Queen Coal').

- Internet sites include Raley's Coal Mining History Resource Centre (www.cmhrc.co.uk) where you can download regional pdf versions of the report. Digital versions may still be obtained from the CMHRC's founder, Ian Winstanley, via ian.winstanley@blueyonder. co.uk (enquire first). Another useful site is http://freepages.genealogy. rootsweb.com/-stenhouse/coal/pbl/coalmain.htm, which is devoted to women in mining. Sample testimony from 'Ashley's Mines Commission' can also be accessed via http://www.victorianweb. org/history/ashley.html and via the North of England Institute of Mining and Mechanical Engineers at www.mininginstitute.org. Using a search engine such as Google with 'Children's Employment Com- mission Mines' or, say, 'Children in Mines' you will find many online sources.

- Recently, new research by Denise Bates on female miners, which is especially valuable when interpreting the 1842 report, has become available in her *Pit Lasses* book (see Further Reading, below).

- As with all other key mining sources, the report is best used in combination with other sources such as censuses and newspapers.

Well before the sub-commissioners started their research, as we have already seen, there was much evidence to show that women and children were employed in British coal mines; but the conditions for women in Scottish mines were particularly bad, as brought to public attention in 1793 by Lord Dundonald. Then in 1812 Robert Bold published his *Inquiry into the Condition of Women who carry Coals under ground in Scotland, known by the name of Bearers* (Edinburgh, 1812). Bold saw the treatment of women as akin to slavery, 'a very bad, old and disgraceful custom'. His report includes some of the most compelling descriptions of the work of women and children, well worth reading if you have Scottish female mining ancestry. Bold explained that it took up to two men to lift baskets of coal on to the backs of a mother and her two daughters. What followed was probably typical of the women bearers: they really were like human pit ponies.

> The mother sets out first, carrying a lighted candle in her teeth; the girls follow, and in this manner they proceed to the pit bottom, and with weary steps and slow, ascend the stairs, halting occasionally to draw breath, till they arrive at the hill or pit-top ... and in this manner they go for eight or ten hours almost without resting.

Conditions in most English and Welsh mines that employed females and very young children were little better. In Tyne and Wear pits, however, women and girls largely ceased to be employed by about 1780. In Cumberland, 'beastly girls' were encountered by Richard Ayton when he descended one of Lord Lonsdale's pits, when he was researching *A Voyage round Great Britain undertaken in the Summer of 1813*, published in 1814.

A 'Mr Tufnell' reported on child labour in Lancashire mines for the Factory Commission of 1833. After descending and exploring the workings of several pits he concluded 'that the hardest labour in the worst room on the worst-conducted factory is less hard, less cruel, and less demoralizing than the labour in the best of coal-mines'.

The commissioners collected evidence from the major coalfields of Britain, concentrating on east Scotland, west Lancashire and south Wales for female miners. Chapters 4 and 5 of Denise Bates' *Pit Lasses* book contains useful overviews of the employment of females in each region and the variety of jobs carried out underground.

Betty Harris, aged 37, drawer, Lancashire

I have a belt round my waist, and a chain passing between my legs, and I go on my hands and feet. The road is very steep, and we have to hold by a rope; and when there is no rope, by anything we can catch hold of. There are six women and six boys in the pit I work in; it is very hard work for a woman. The pit is very wet where I work, and the water comes over our clog-tops always, and I have seen it up to my thighs; it rains in at the roof terribly. My clothes are wet through almost all day long. I have known many a man beat his drawer. I have known men take liberties with drawers, and some of the women have bastards.

[Sub-commisioner Kennedy. Betty Harris was a former weaver, moving to Andrew Knowles' pit at Little Bolton when she was married, aged 23.]

Elizabeth Day, aged 17, hurrier, Hopwood's Pit, Barnsley

We always hurry in trousers as you saw us today when you were in the pit. Generally I work naked down to the waist like the rest. I had my shift on today when I saw you, because I had to wait and was cold; but generally the girls hurry naked down to the waist. It is very hard work for us all. It is harder work than we ought to do a deal. I have been lamed in my anckle, and strained my back; it caused a great lump to rise on my anckle-bone once. The men behave well to us and never insult or ill-use us, I am sure of that ... I have never been at school ... I go to chapel on Sunday night. I can't read at all.

[Sub-Commissioner Symonds. Hopwood's Pit employed six females, Elizabeth one of five hurriers (the other female being a young trapper). Jellinger Cookson Symonds was the only investigator coming across females working topless, or at least reporting the same. His compilations had great attention to detail but unknown to him, on 21 February 1842, a subsequent underground explosion at Hopwood killed four workers, three of them female, one being 15-year-old Mary Day, probably Elizabeth's sister.]

Although the Hopwood accident was missed by the Sub-Commissioner and not included in the published report, sad instances of serious accidents and disasters appear to have influenced the sub-commissioners to visit small and obscure mining communities. In July 1838, a flash flood resulted in an inrush of water at Robert Couldwell Clarke's Huskar Pit at Silkstone, near Barnsley, resulting in the deaths of twenty-six children and young persons aged between 7 and 17, eleven of them girls, the youngest, Sarah Newton, just 8 years old. The disaster may have been a contributory factor in the setting up of the Commission and certainly attracted evidence gathering from Silkstone.

Female miners and the 1841 census

Taken on 6 June 1841, enumerators for the first time recorded names and occupations, a task that took place not long after the sub-Commissioners of the Children's Employment Commission had carried out most of their interviews. The census recorded 2,350 females working underground in British mines, about half of them (1,165) under the age of 20. A further 3,650 women and girls were employed on the pit-tops. Of the 6,000 women and girls identified, 2,240 were employed in Scotland, where some of the larger pits had a hundred or more females on their books [E. Royston Pike, 246].

There are bound to be some omissions and errors but the 6,000 census figure is probably as accurate an indication as we will ever have of the number of females employed in the coalmining industry during the early years of Victoria's reign. Although the total is a small proportion of the c.150,000 miners employed in c.2,000 collieries, the concentration of female mineworkers in a small number of regions, most notably in parts of Scotland and Lancashire, made their presence far more obvious to local investigators, photographers and the media of the day.

If you have a female miner or indeed a male miner in your ancestry it is well worth remembering that many thousands of women in pit communities had homes and young children to look after as well as working. Some toiled under and above ground at pits well into pregnancy. Women were often among the first to appear at the pit-head after disasters. It is easy to get over romantic and too sentimental about 'grieving women/widows' as they were pictured with so much drama in Victorian engravings, but the news of a loved one trapped, lost or killed must have been an horrendous and unforgettable experience. Stories were passed down the generations. It is only from good family history research from a variety of sources – and placed in context – that a full and meaningful picture emerges. The more examples we have, the more we will understand and appreciate our previous generations – and contribute to social history as a whole. Inability to read or write, wearing old clothes and walking home with coal-black faces does not mean that the women had less intellectual ability or were meek and less feminine. Nor were they the coarse or immoral 'wenches' as suggested by some contemporaries. Far from it. They were working-class girls with extraordinary abilities. So, if you have a female miner-ancestor or an ancestor who was a child-miner, be rightly proud of their achievements.

Further reading

Denise Bates, *Pit Lasses. Women and Girls in Coalmining c.1800–1914* (Wharncliffe, 2012)

Ivor J. Brown with Kelvin Lake, *A List of Fatal accidents in Shropshire Mines from 1850–1979 with some details of major incidents* (Shropshire Caving and Mining club, Account No.24: 2005)

Anthony Burton, *History's Most Dangerous Jobs: Miners*, The History Press, 2013

Robert Burlison, 'Fuel for Concern' in *Ancestors* [magazine], July 2007

Roy Church, *The History of the British Coal Industry. Volume 3. 1830–1913 Victorian Pre-Eminence* (Clarenden Press, 1986)

Alan Davies, *The Pit Brow Women of the Wigan Coalfield* (Tempus/The History Press, 2006/09)

Ray Devlin, *Children of the Pits. Child Labour and Child Fatality in the coal mines of Whitehaven and District* (Friends of Whitehaven Museum, 1999)

Barbara Drake, *Women in Trade Unions* (Virago Press 1984 edition [originally published by Labour Research Department, 1920])

Maureen Fisher and Sue Donnelly, *Ah'd Gaa Back Tomorra! Memories of the West Cumbria Screen Lasses* (Whitehaven Miners' Memorial and Living History Project, 2004)

Alan Gallop, *Victoria's Children of the Dark* (The History Press, 2010)

Ken Howarth, *Dark Days. Memories of the Lancashire & Cheshire Coalmining Industry* (Greater Manchester County Council, 1978 & 1985)

Michael Hiley, *Victorian Working Women: Portraits from Life* (Gordon Fraser Gallery Ltd, 1979)

Angela V. John, *Coalmining Women. Victorian Lives and Campaigns* (Cambridge University Press, 1984)

E. Royston Pike, *Human Documents of the Industrial Revolution in Britain* (George Allen & Unwin, 1966)

R. Page Arnot, *A History of the Scottish Miners* (George Allen & Unwin, 1955)

Chapter 5

COALFIELDS AND MINERS AT WAR

Most of us with relatively recent coalmining ancestors will have one or more examples who were involved in some way with the armed forces during the first half of the twentieth century. He may have been one of the many thousands of pitmen who responded to Kitchener's call for volunteers after the start of the First World War. If not he would certainly have known workmates who joined the armed forces at this time, or a year or two later, many never to return to their collieries. Twenty years afterwards, in 1936–37, significant groups of miners voluntarily fought against the growing threat of Fascism during the Spanish Civil War; and of course many others saw active service during the Second World War or joined the Home Guard. Staying with the Home Front, your mining ancestor may have been a recruit of a different kind, a 'Bevin Boy', conscripted to the mines to make up for the shortage of labour during the 'coal crisis'. Whatever the background or situation, discovering the role and contributions of your 'wartime miners' is a very relevant and rewarding part of family history research.

First World War 1914–18

The three men set off deeper into the darkness. It took them five minutes to reach the point where Jack was crouching with his ear to the wall. At the end of the timbered tunnel they could see a ragged hole where German diggers had burst through.

Sebastian Faulks, *Birdsong* (1993)

Physical and mental attributes such as fitness, strength and tenacity had always made mineworkers very useful recruits for the armed forces. Often St John's-trained, miners came into their own for a variety of first-aid duties within the Royal Army Medical Corps, and their strong arms and backs also made them ideal stretcher-bearers. Whether actual or perceived, the miner's smaller stature was also advantageous when he was used in confined spaces, for example when deployed towards the end of the war in tanks (for the Tank Corps). But it was the miner's unique underground and

Detail from the front cover of the souvenir brochure published by Cortonwood Collieries for the unveiling ceremony in memory of their miners killed in the First World War and in honour of those who served in the Forces.

engineering skills that were the most desirable attributes for a variety of strategic situations, no more so when assigned as a 'human mole', tunnelling towards enemy lines on the Western Front (Royal Engineers Corps).

Information and help about tracing your military ancestors is now easily accessible online and via published guides, some of which are listed below. The main theme of this chapter is to provide the context and background for the many thousands of miners who served in the armed forces during the first half of the twentieth century, especially in the First World War. Although some joined the Navy it was the infantry regiments that recruited the vast majority of miners. The use of emergency labour during the Second World War – the so-called 'Bevin Boys' – is also outlined, along with research suggestions.

Why did your miner-ancestor swap the dangers and demands of pit-work for the uncertainties of soldiering? Masses of miners joined up in 1914–15 for very similar reasons to other volunteers, but, patriotism and peer-pressure apart, economic circumstances in the coal industry pushed many into armed service. At the start of the war coal was stockpiled and miners were reduced to part-time work or unemployment. Thus many joined up because they thought that they would be far better off, even feeling it was a safer option. And yet the human carnage in the industry remained very high: 1,753 killed and a staggering 178,962 injured (i.e., requiring at least seven days off work), according to official figures for 1913 alone. The shadow of Senyghenydd, when 439 men and boys were killed in a single disaster, was fresh in the memory, no more so than in south Wales pit communities. Each day an average of four miners were in fact 'killed in action' in British mines.

And yet statistics show that the call to arms in all coalfield areas was extremely successful. Before hostilities started there were 1,116,648 workers employed in British mines. After seven months of war 191,170 miners had enlisted, a figure that increased to an astonishing 250,000 in 1915. A measure of the importance of miner-recruits was that by February 1915 almost 1 in 5 of all military volunteers came from the pit communities of England (18.00%), Wales (18.7%) and Scotland (21.3%). Locally, recruitment into the Territorial Army ('Terriers') also attracted miners; for some miners, attendance here had been a welcome respite from the pit for a few weeks a year, so to enlist 'permanently' was a natural progression.

Coal production for the war effort at home and abroad remained extremely important: for the Navy, for the strategic operation of the Allies, for domestic transport, for munitions, for the supply of TNT (and other strategic products), even, arguably, for the morale of the civilian population. Speaking to a coal-industry conference on 29 July 1915, Lloyd George proclaimed that coal was 'everything for us', the country's life and blood, its 'international coinage'. At the end of the same year manpower in the pits had dropped to

120

953,000. The resulting fall in coal production was so serious that Belgian refugee ex-miners were allowed to work in British mines.

If your miner-ancestor stayed in mining (or was a new miner) during the war his job was harder than ever. Investment by the coal companies in mechanisation was slow or non-existent before 1914 – the typical attitude was why spend money on machines when muscle-power would do? Not surprisingly, given the terrible conditions, absenteeism in the coal industry remained an abiding problem for many years.

Throughout the early war years there was a great employer preoccupation with the shortfall of labour and production. Of course it was the younger, 'more energetic' miners, alongside experienced colliers in their twenties and thirties, who were most missed. The recruiting momentum from some collieries was extremely high and may only have come to light after the war when some form of 'presentation' took place. Of the 900 employees at Thrybergh and Swinton collieries in south Yorkshire, for example, nearly 300 joined the armed services, or one in three of all workmen, at least thirty-one of these paying the ultimate price.

Alarmed coal owners campaigned for urgent 'solutions' to the shortfall in labour, each one vehemently opposed by the mining unions: the abolition of the Eight Hour Act (which limited work-time underground), reduction of holidays, even a lowering of the age limit for the employment of boys underground. What did help was that many more females were employed – mainly as labourers – to work on the surface of collieries. By December 1916 the Government's response to all the pressure was to take the coal industry under state control, starting in south Wales (where industrial relations was poor) and then, from 1 March 1917 (to March 1921), nationwide. This 'nationalisation' really meant controlling output, distribution and wages, for the coal owners continued to receive guaranteed profits as part of the arrangement.

The Military Services Act of 29 January 1916 introduced conscription, initially for British male subjects aged 19–41, but some of the most vital types of mining jobs were exempted. However, volunteers for 'tunnelling corps' continued to be called for and in June the Cabinet authorised the potential release of up to 100,000 miners for enlistment. Although soldiering had lost some of its idealistic attraction, significant numbers of pitmen still enlisted.

The massive response from miners to the call to arms was most obvious in industrial areas where the so-called 'Pals battalions' (part of what soon became the 31st Division of the New Army), were established. Recruits could serve alongside workmates, friends and neighbours. In Accrington, 104 men were accepted for service in the first three hours of recruitment on 14 September 1914, a good number of them miners. Ten days later, the Accrington Pals, or 11th Battalion East Lancashire Regiment, to use their

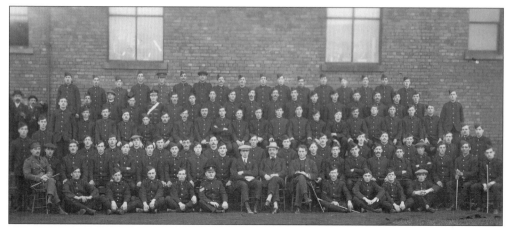

A single colliery was capable of providing a significant number of volunteers for the New Army, as can be seen in this example for the York and Lancasters (Barnsley Pals) Regiment, recruited from my paternal grandfather's pit, Monckton, near Barnsley.

official name, was 'full strength', with 1,100 men. In the Yorkshire coal town of Barnsley, more than a thousand men were recruited for the 13th York and Lancasters in less than two weeks, the town council therefore deciding to support the raising of a second Pals battalion (the 14th York and Lancasters). A similar pattern of recruitment occurred in other coalfield areas including Durham (18th Durham Light Infantry), Leeds (15th West Yorkshires), Manchester (16th Manchesters), Salford (15th Lancashire Fusiliers), Tyneside Scottish (20th Northumberland Fusiliers), Cardiff (11th Welsh Regiment), Swansea (14th Welsh Regiment) and north Wales (13th Royal Welsh Fusiliers). A full listing of Pals battalions can be seen at http:en.wikipedia. org/wiki/List_of_Pals_battalions.

Several of the Pals battalions suffered very heavy casualties during the disastrous Somme offensive of 1916. Of the 720 Accrington Pals who took part in the attack on Serre, 584 were killed, wounded or missing, almost eight out of every ten soldiers. The Leeds Pals lost an astonishing 750 of 900 participants and the Sheffield City Battalion lost about half of its men.

Tip

Andrew Jackson's excellent site www.pals.org.uk, which focuses on the Accrington, Barnsley and Sheffield Pals battalions, includes a research guide and is also useful for information on the First World War as a whole.

Of the other army units that recruited miners several stand out. A 'miners' battalion' was raised by the West Yorkshire Coalowners' Association, very quickly, from 5 September 1914. The 12th (Service) Battalion (Miners) (Pioneers), part of the King's Own Yorkshire Light Infantry (KOYLI), or 't'owd twelfth', was founded in Leeds. Recruits trained in Otley and then Burton Leonard, near Ripon, prior to service overseas, initially Egypt and then on the Western Front in France. The 'Miners' 12th' was the lead battalion of the 31st Division, operational on the first day of the Somme offensive, not only in 'sapping' (strategic excavation) work, but also in attacks with other Yorkshire Pals' battalions.

One of the most extraordinary recruiting successes involving large numbers of miners in Wales and northern England especially were the battalions collectively known as 'Bantams'. Thousands of sturdy and skilled miners ruled out of the initial recruitment through a height restriction of 5ft 3in came forward when this regulation was lifted, following an impressive campaign by the Birkenhead MP Alfred Bigland. Earlier, a group of 'miner rejects' had called on the Cheshire MP to state their case, one of them even offering to 'fight any man' in order to prove his worth as a soldier. From Birkenhead, Bantam battalions soon spread to other coalfield regions, forming two British (35th and 40th) Divisions (twenty-eight battalions in all) and two Canadian battalions. The old mining area of Durham was fairly typical in its response, the momentum of volunteering well described by Sidney Allinson in his tribute book, *The Bantams*:

> Men streamed from collieries at Percy Main and Esh Winning; from Shillbottle where men worked stripped naked because of the heat under-ground; from Washington ... and from pits at Morpeth, Cowpen, and Blaydon Main, and a dozen other coal workings.

But some of the Durham Light Infantry miner-recruits were not in the best of of health:

> Doctors were horrified at the condition of a batch of Bantam miner volunteers from Monkwearmouth Colliery, whose bodies were covered with carbuncles and huge open sores caused by years of working in hot salt water seeping down from the North Sea far above the mine tunnels.

War service, at least in theory, brought an improvement in health.

For many small Welsh miners it was, at last, a chance to demonstrate their strength and skills and even earn a bob or two, summed up in a wonderful quote by Albert Lewis, in Allinson's book:

> We were miners in our late teens, and we set out to join the new Tunnelling Companies that were being formed by the Royal Engineers. An agent had come to the pit and told us we could work as Army

Moles, digging under the German lines, and be paid as much as five shillings a day. That was big wages in those days, so we set off to make our fortunes!

As well as tunnelling, the Bantams proved to be highly adept in the confined space of the new tanks, as well as in many other awkward but strategic

'Their old work in a new guise' was the magazine caption used under this contemporary illustration showing a pair of tunnellers. These two ex-Durham miners were said to be 'preparing a practice sap'.

situations. But it was at a massive human cost, as they were to be involved in some of the hardest battles of the war, at Arras and Bourlon Wood in particular.

It is only relatively recently that the role of former miners, or so-called 'clay-kickers' – the First World War tunnellers – has been appreciated more widely by the British public, and worldwide, helped in part by the extraordinary success of Sebastian Faulks' best-selling novel *Birdsong* (first published in 1993 and adapted for the stage and television in 2010–12), and through well-researched military books (see below). The accounts of tunnelling by ex-miners and the use of reminiscences make these sources particularly valuable for family historians.

Sapper William Hackett VC (1873–1916)

Hackett was a 'coal miner's filler' according to the 1901 census, living at Denaby Main, a south Yorkshire mining village named after its pit. Desperate for work, he had walked to Denaby from Nottingham at the age of 18, and after a twenty-three-year stint got a job at nearby Manvers Main Colliery, near Mexborough, moving there in about 1914. Hackett was therefore an experienced miner, strong and robust despite his build and stature (less than 5 feet 3 inches tall and only 118lbs) when war broke out. Keen to enlist, he was rejected on three occasions by the York and Lancasters due to his age – and an apparent heart condition – but was welcomed as a 42-year-old volunteer with the Royal Engineers in October 1915. After just two weeks' training he was in France with 254th Tunnelling Company, Corps of Royal Engineers.

Sapper Hackett's extraordinary act of bravery took place between 22–23 June 1916 when, with four other men, he was digging a tunnel 40ft below ground towards enemy lines near Givenchy when a mine exploded above them. Buried by debris, Hackett managed to help three of his mates to safety through a hole that had been excavated by rescuers after twenty hours, but he insisted on staying with a badly injured man, Private Thomas Collins from Swansea. Unfortunately after four days the tunnel and the shaft collapsed and both men lost their lives. Their bodies were not recovered.

William Hackett was awarded the Victoria Cross, the first (and only) First World War tunneller to receive the award, albeit posthumously. His wife, Alice, received a pension of 21 shillings for herself and her now two dependant children. Sapper Hackett's medal is displayed in the Royal Engineers Museum at Gillingham.

Detail of the plaque commemorating 'Sapper' William Hackett, now placed alongside the war memorial at Mexborough in South Yorkshire.

Specialist mining units of the Corps of Royal Engineers were established to excavate tunnels under no man's land and enemy lines. By February 1915 eight tunnelling companies had been formed and in the summer of 1915 the British Army had at least 20,000 men experienced and active in underground warfare, mostly former miners. The miner-sappers had minimal military training and were subject to far more dangerous situations than mining at home, often sustaining heavy casualties. It was the most extreme form of mining, health and safety virtually non existent at times; but 'Proto' breathing apparatus and the miner's old friends, canaries and mice, were used for rescue and gas detection. Matters improved after mines rescue bases were established.

Underground armed conflict and huge explosions apart, the working conditions – often with just candles for light – were extraordinarily bad. When carefully chipping through chalk, in shift rotation, some men suffered from snow blindness due to the glare from the rock. But tunnelling became a very sophisticated engineering process. The Germans, however, responded with equal ingenuity, tenacity and bravery. As time progressed the stalemate situation led to deeper and more extensive tunnels, massive detonations of mines or camouflets, and British and German 'moles' became increasingly sensitive to each other's strategies in the fields of France and Flanders. 'Listening duty' was an integral and essential part of subterranean tactics. From Hill 60 to the battles on the Somme, Vimy Ridge and Arras, tunnelling was widespread; but the most spectacular example on the Western Front occurred during the Second Army attack on Messines Ridge on 7 June 1917, when nineteen deep mines were fired in timed succession, the blasts heard as far away as London. As many as 10,000 German casualties accrued, with only a few from the assaulting troops. The scenes of military tunnelling resulted in massive craters still bearing testimony to the actions, the largest, Lochnager, now a recognised historic battlefield site.

Casualties, honours and gallantry awards

It is individual stories and circumstances, often unearthed by local, family and military historians during the course of their research, that provide us with the most meaningful appreciation of the soldier-miners' honours and the losses. It is also worth bearing in mind that there were over 6,600 miners 'killed in action' in their home pits during 1914–18, whilst producing coal in various forms for home and overseas consumption. Around 120,000 soldiers were discharged from the armed forces at the end of the war to return to the pits where they were previously employed.

The illustrated extract relating to the death of Corporal W. Clarke (a Cortonwood Colliery miner) appeared in the *South Yorkshire Times* on 10 July 1915. 'Soldiers Died' on Ancestry.com confirms that William Clarke, A/Sgt (308) 2nd Battalion Lancashire Fusiliers was killed in action on 29 June 1915. Clarke was born at Blyth, Nottinghamshire,

WOMBWELL D.C.M. KILLED.

Death of Corporal W. Clarke.

News has been received with profound regret at Wombwell of the death in action in France of Corporal W. Clarke, D.C.M., 2nd Lancashire Fusiliers. In a recent letter to his wife, who resides at 61, Concrete Cottages, Wombwell, Corporal Clarke said he was just recovering from a nasty dose of German gas, and it had left him in a very weak condition. It was getting very hard for the soldiers who had been out since the outbreak of the war, but he had hopes that a couple of months would see the end of the war, and he would then be able to rest on his laurels. The sad news of Corporal Clarke's death is conveyed to the wife through Lance-Corporal Ernest W. Grainger, of the same company, who writes:—"I am very sorry to have to send you bad news. Your husband was killed in action on Tuesday evening. He was looking over the parapet of the trench in order to fire when he was shot through the head. I thought it might be some consolation to you to know that his death was instantaneous and quite painless.

He was a plucky young man, and what he did he did well. He took an interest in his work, and no one in the company will be more missed than he is. I hope you will do your best to bear up in your trouble." Prior to the outbreak of the war Corpl. Clarke was a reservist, and worked at the Cortonwood Colliery. The news of his promotion and the stories of his valour were received with pride by his fellow-workmen. Mrs. Clarke received the sad intimation on the birthday of her only child.

This interesting local newspaper feature, relating to the Lancashire Fusilier Corporal W. Clarke, is from the South Yorkshire Times, *10 July 1915. After major battles such as the Somme the papers were flooded with accounts of casualties and gallantry stories, often illustrated with small head-and-shoulder portrait photographs.* South Yorkshire Times.

and enlisted at Strensall, Yorkshire. The Commonwealth War Graves website gives his age as 30, and that he was the son of George William Clarke, of 5 Coronation Avenue, Dinnington, Rotherham; and husband of Harriet Dodds (formerly Clarke), of 61 Concrete Cottages, Wombwell, near Barnsley.

Tip

Do check through local newspapers as they are a rich source of information regarding casualties, honours and awards. Collect examples for the period that your ancestor served, from his regiment, and from other soldier-miners, as well as any specific references. It's a far better approach, providing proper context – then you can use primary and other sources to enhance what you have found.

Tip

Colliery companies and their workmen were proud and informative about the number of their colleagues or employees recruited into the armed forces, some of them commissioning awards, medals and memorials; and the miners themselves usually contributed to this process. A trawl through local newspapers will reveal reported examples, and it is worthwhile extending your search through to about 1920, or even a little later, as 'presentations' and 'tributes' were made well after the end of the war.

For some larger collieries, the names of 'fallen miners' were inscribed separately on war memorials; indeed, some newly-commissioned memorials were dedicated entirely to pit workers who died/served in the war. This was the case at Cortonwood Colliery, where a 'miners' memorial' was unveiled in front of the colliery's offices on 27 September 1919. It is not surprising that a dedicated pitmen's memorial was required here. Cortonwood had provided 665 enlistees, mainly for the infantry, ninety-four of whom (including William Clarke referred to above) lost their lives. All of their names are inscribed on the cenotaph-style memorial, which was made even more striking by the addition of sculptured figures of a soldier and a miner.

Where the listings of names on war memorials in former pit villages and small towns have been researched and published in some form or other they provide very useful information about individuals and their backgrounds. Do search via the internet, your local library or family history society for relevant deposits/uploads. The war memorial at Rawmarsh, near Rotherham, in south Yorkshire, one of the last in Britain to be unveiled in 1928, is a good example, researched by a local man, Mick Busby. It has over 320 names inscribed for the First World War (with about sixty missing). Miners accounted for around nine out of ten of all fatalities, a situation not uncommon in many pit villages. Here are abbreviated details of just one name from the memorial researched by Mick:

Private Joseph ('Joe') William Silkstone (1st/5th Battalion York and Lancaster Regiment: Gassed on the Somme.

Joe Silkstone was born at Dalton, near Rotherham in 1889, the son of Albert George and Alice, residing at 36 Carlton Terrace, Rawmarsh. After leaving school Joe went to work with his father at Aldwarke Main Colliery. In 1913, he married Annie Hinds, living at 6 House, 18 Court, Wellgate, Rotherham. Private Silkstone died of gas poisoning when the Germans first released phosgene gas into the British lines near Ypres on 19 December 1915, when he was aged 27. His widow was left with a one-year-old daughter, Eileen. Private Joseph Silkstone is buried at Bard Cot Military Cemetery, Boesinghe, Belgium (Grave I.J.4).

A variety of honours and awards were presented, including posthumously, to miners who served in the First World War, ranging from 'pit war service medals' or mementoes to the most outstanding bravery award of all: the Victoria Cross. Two hundred of the 'soldier-miners' at Thrybergh and Swinton collieries, already referred to above, were presented with inscribed silver watches and medals at a special ceremony in the church hall, and the occasion was extended so as to include presentations to relatives of the thirty-one men 'who had fallen'. Not far away, the Wath Main Colliery Company issued 700 inscribed medals in honour of their employees' war service, and neighbouring Mitchells Main Colliery commissioned solid gold medals, 'by the company officials & workmen for war services'.

Even the most outstanding of First World War miner-soldiers may have been forgotten, but for the research of local and family historians. Mike Gomersall has uncovered a remarkable example: Thomas Bryan, a 35-year-old Yorkshire miner and Northumberland Fusilier (25th Service Battalion [2nd Tyneside Irish]). During the battle of Arras, on 9 April 1917, Bryan destroyed a German machine-gun post which had stopped the British advance. He was presented with his Victoria Cross by King George V in front of a 40,000 crowd at St James' Park football ground, Newcastle, on 17 June. Six days later, on 23 June, to the strains of *See The Conquering Hero Comes*, he was given a huge welcome in his home town of Castleford, West Yorkshire. On 24 June 2012 a ceremony of remembrance organised by the Victoria Cross

Trust took place at his graveside, in Arksey Cemetery, near Doncaster, where he was buried in 1945.

Thomas Bryan's VC is part of the Lord Ashcroft collection at the Imperial War Museum, London.

A similar ceremony took place in my birth village of Royston, near Barnsley, in 2008, courtesy of the Royal British Legion, when a plaque was unveiled to the memory of another remarkable miner-VC recipient, Albert Shepherd. The 20-year-old private got his award following an outstanding act of battlefield bravery at Villers Plouich in northern France on 20 November 1917. The young rifleman attacked and disabled a German machine-gun post, killed two Germans in the action and took command of his company when the last officer and NCO had become casualties. Albert's achievement is also celebrated at the Royal Green Jackets (Rifles) Museum in Winchester, Hampshire.

Company Sergeant Major John 'Jack' Henry Williams (1886–1953) VC DCM MM & Bar

Nantyglo (Monmouthshire)-born John Henry Williams is the most decorated non-commissioned officer in Welsh army history. In 1906 Jack enlisted in the South Wales Borderers, but bought himself out after a short time. He is described as a colliery blacksmith (probably at Marine Colliery in the village of Cwm) in the 1911 census. Williams enlisted again, as a private in the 10th Battalion South Wales Borderers in November 1914, and his leadership quality was such that within three months he was promoted to sergeant. On the Somme, 10–12 July 1916, Williams's 'conspicuous gallantry in action' during the capture of Mametz Wood was recognised in the award of the Distinguished Conduct Medal (DCM). Not long afterwards, at Pilckem Ridge, on 31 July 1917 during the third battle of Ypres, he gained another gallantry award, the Military Medal (MM). After rescuing – under fire – a wounded colleague at Armentières on 30 October 1917 Williams was granted a Bar to his

MM. The climax of the man's extraordinary gallantry record occurred towards the end of the war. Here is his VC citation from the *London Gazette*:

For most conspicuous bravery, initiative and devotion to duty on the night of 7th-8th October 1918, when, during the attack on Villers Outreaux, when, observing that his company was suffering heavy casualties from an enemy machine gun, he ordered a Lewis Gun to engage it, and went forward, under heavy fire, to the flank of the enemy post which he rushed single-handed, capturing fifteen of the enemy. These prisoners, realising that Williams was alone, turned on him and one of them gripped his rifle. He succeeded in breaking away and bayonetting five enemy, whereupon the remainder again surrendered. By this gallant action and total disregard of personal danger, he was the means of enabling not only his own company but those on the flanks to advance.

Severely wounded by shrapnel in the right arm and leg, CSM Williams was discharged from the army on medical grounds on 17 October 1918. He was subsequently decorated with the Médaille Militaire by the French and at Buckingham Palace, in February 1919, George V presented him with four British bravery awards, separately, a unique occurrence. Jack's medals can be seen at the South Wales Borderers and Monmouthshire Regiment Museum at Brecon, Powys.

Spanish Civil War 1936–39

Although direct involvement was small compared with the First World War, the role of miners as part of the British Battalion of the International Brigades in the Spanish Civil War should not be ignored. Miners, most notably from Wales, were a significant part of the 2,500 British recruits. Over 500 British were killed. A file list of British and Irish volunteers killed in Spain can be downloaded via http://www.international-brigades.org.uk/british_volunteers/. Many others found themselves in Franco's prisons. They were very idealistic volunteers, fighting against the rise of Fascism, continuing to participate right up to the end of the conflict. In May 1938 the Miners' Federation of Great Britain raised a levy of 2s 6d in support of 'miner comrades' in Spain. A number of prominent miners' union officials campaigned, recruited miners and took part, especially those with Welsh backgrounds and influence. The most famous were Will Paynter (b. Cardiff 1903), and Arthur Horner (b. Merthyr Tydfil 1894), who was president of the South Wales Miners' Federation; both leaders were also prominent Communists.

> ## *Research Tips*
>
> If you have an miner-ancestor who was involved in the Spanish Civil War the International Brigade Memorial Trust is worth visiting for background information (www.international-brigades.org). The International Brigade Archive is lodged in the Marx Memorial Library, London (www.marx-memorial-library.org). George Orwell's *Homage to Catalonia* (1938) remains a superb personal account. Two well-researched modern publications are listed in the Sources/Further Reading section below. Spartacus Educational (www.schoolnet.co.uk) also has very useful background information and primary sources relating to the Spanish Civil War, plus biographies of Horner and Paynter.

Second World War: 'We'll do the fighting if you get the coal'

The patriotism that most miners had at the start of the new war was mingled with despondency, if not bitterness. Wages in the industry had two unmistakable characteristics: they were extremely low and extremely complex; and by 1943 thousands of men were leaving their pits for better paid and safer jobs. The Welsh miner-author B.L. Coombes spoke for many miners in his writings at this time, though his feature in *Picture Post* calling for more young miners was published just after the Government had introduced an option for young conscripts to go into mines rather than the Armed Forces, a strategy that became far more effective when a balloted (or Bevin Boy) system was introduced:

> Last week, outside our colliery, I saw a poster placed there by the Ministry of Fuel and Power. It showed a soldier striding over some conquered country, and on it was an appeal: 'We need coal to help us. We'll do the fighting if you'll get the coal.' That pictured face had a resemblance to many of the lads who went to the Army from these areas, and they are too near akin for us to have any intention of letting them down. We know that, after all the the theorists have finished, it will be the man in khaki who will have to do the fighting. We know also that, after all the armchair suggestions have tired, it will be left for the man with the mandrel and the dust-grimed face to get the coal ... What we do feel is that for your sake, for our sake, for our country's sake, mining must go on. Its man-power is draining away at a rate of nearly 30,000 a year. Young men and boys must come to replace them, and they must be trained before it is too late.

132

Even before the outbreak of war hundreds of miners were leaving the industry, some joining the Armed Forces, and others were soon drafted into the Territorials or New Militia. But the scale of recruitment was far more limited and subdued compared to 1914–16. And yet, despite the complex reserved status of coalmining a significant number of mineworkers simply handed in their notice and joined the military or civil defence service – or munitions: as many as 27,000 within two weeks of the declaration of war in 1939. My uncle, Lawrence Elliott, left the pit for the Army but spent most of the war as a prisoner of war. His younger brother, my father Fred Elliott, stayed at his colliery and, like many of his mates, served in the Home Guard. My mother, Agnes Elliott née Stone, was one of many thousands of young women in mining communities who joined the NAAFI (Navy, Army and Air Force Institutes), working in a canteen serving tea and meals to billeted soldiers for the duration of the war.

Some coalfield areas, such as the North East and south Wales, suffered badly due to the war, the air raids and shipping disruptions resulting in pits working part-time or closed. Miners' pay was so depressed that they were ranked 81st (out of 100) in the industrial wages league. In 1938 the average miner only received £2 15s 9d a week, way below most industrial occupations.

Access to your ancestor's Second World War service records are only available through the personnel themselves or their proven next-of-kin (see one or more of the research guides below and/or use one of the many available online via national and regional record offices/archives [see regional and national research sections of this book]; and also for casualty and operational records

DECORATED BY "MONTY"

Denaby Corporal's Gallantry

Corporal T. Waters, son of Mr. and Mrs. A. Waters, of 80, Cliff View, Denaby Main, according to the B.B.C. European News, has been decorated on the field by General Mongomery for bravery and a splendid example to comrades which he set on D-Day.

Cpl. Waters is attached to the Signal Section of the 6th Airborne Division Parachute Brigade. He was engaged in fixing communic a t i o n wires on D-Day and some time later found there was no communication and that the wire had been cut. He repaired the wire under great difficulty and it was cut again and again. This happened seven times and at last Cpl. Waters decided to wait and watch the wire. He hid near a bush and saw a German soldier crawling along to cut the communications. He fired, killed the enemy and saved the communications. For this brave act he was awarded the Military Medal Cpl. Waters is 29° and before enlistment was employed underground on the haulage at Cadeby Colliery. He has been in the Army nine years and has seen 7½ years' service in Burma with two years' jungle service. He came home in 1943 and after a furlough joined the Paratroops. Mr. Waters (father of Cpl. Waters), served in the last war under General Montgomery (then Lieut. Montgomery), in the Warwickshire Regiment.

A 'regular' soldier, Corporal T. Waters, an ex-Cadeby Main miner, was 'decorated in the field' by General Montgomery in 1944. Details of his gallantry duly featured in the South Yorkshire Times, 22 July 1944. *South Yorkshire Times.*

Local newspapers are an invaluable source of information on Army personnel, local events, casualties and gallantry awards (see illustrated example to Corporal Waters, page 133).

'Killed in action'

Between 1939 and 1945 almost 5,400 miners were killed at work and 205,000 injured. Many thousands more died from respiratory diseases.

The 'underground front': Bevin Boys

The workforce in the coal industry declined from 784,000 at the start of the war to 690,000 in the spring of 1941. The 'coal crisis' as it became known resulted in the Essential Work (Coal Mining Industry) Order of 15 May 1941 whereby miners were not allowed to leave or be dismissed from their employment without the permission of a National Service office. In effect miners were now tied to their mines by law.

Your ancestor may have been one of about 48,000 recruits conscripted into the coalmining industry rather than the Armed Forces. Bevin appealed for men to return to the pits, including those that had joined the forces, as a workforce of 720,000 was thought to be essential for wartime coal production. But production continued to decline, not helped by absenteeism and ad hoc strikes. In September 1942 men under the age of 25 registered for military service were given the option of underground work in the mines. Hardly surprisingly, this scheme resulted in fewer than 3,000 'optants' entering mining by June 1943, far short of what was needed.

Compulsory recruitment then began. Men aged 18–25, on being available for call-up, were chosen by ballot for pit work, the first draw – for one conscript in ten – taking place on 14 December 1943. The 'lucky' ones became known as 'Bevin Boys' after the speech made by Ernest Bevin MP when he announced the scheme.

Joe Hartley (b.1925) Bevin Boy

Joe was a Yorkshire Bevin Boy conscript and was instructed to report for training at Askern Colliery. Here are his recollections:

I was shocked when I found out. There were lads from all over the country, including Cockneys. We had a week underground

---

and were shown how to couple a tub safely and how to gear a horse up for pony driving. We also did physical training, stripping down to shorts and vests and ran around the countryside and did marching, wearing pit boots. I remember the Bevin Boys' anthem, which went something like:

> *We had to join up*
> *We had to join up*
> *We had to join up old Bevin's army*
> *Fifty bob a week*
> *Wife and kids to keep*
> *Hob-nailed boots and blisters on your feet*
> *We had to join up*
> *We had to join up*
> *We had to join old Bevin's army*
> *If it wasn't for war*
> *We'd be where we were before*
> *Old Bevin you're barmy!*

I was sent to Darfield Main but passed three pits on the way there! I was 17 and the only Bevin Boy. I worked in the pit bottom, by the chair, dealing with full and empty tubs and helped with the haulage. I wore an old boiler suit. One lad came wearing a butcher's smock! He would feed the ponies with pickled onions from his pocket. There were no pit baths so I came home in my pit muck. When you travelled on the pit bus you got some looks; passengers wanted to keep well away.

(Interviewed by the author)

After the end of the war Joe decided to stay in mining, working at Manvers Main Colliery where he progressed to be a senior overman, retiring in 1983.

By the end of the war the Bevin Boys scheme had provided about 21,800 young men for the mines. The much-quoted figure of 48,000 includes the conscripted 'optants' referred to above, taken over a slightly longer period, to 1948. A small number of conscripts refused to be part of the scheme. Within months over a hundred objectors were prosecuted and thirty-two were sent to prisons, though nineteen of these were released when they changed their views, reluctantly joining the industry.

The conscripts were dispatched to one of several regional training collieries for a few weeks' basic training, living in a hostel or in lodgings;

Former Bevin Boy Joe Hartley had mixed memories of his wartime mining experiences, but stayed in the industry, becoming a senior official at Manvers Main.

and then dispatched to a local pit. Fortunately recorded memories and writings of the Bevin Boys provide us with many first-hand accounts of the training process and the understandable shock of compulsory pit-work in the very worst circumstances imaginable.

On commencement of work the Bevin Boys were given overalls, a safety helmet and working boots, but they had to buy their own tools. Work-wise, they were mainly employed on haulage roads, though some helped colliers on coalfaces and even hewed coal. The loading and transporting of coal and materials was far from easy work, in fact it was one of the most arduous and most dangerous jobs in mining, and especially so for beginners. Furthermore, by all accounts they were not always well regarded by other miners, for a variety of reasons. Although some, like Joe Hartley, stayed in mining after the war, the majority of miner-conscripts were pleased to leave the industry.

Mel Harris, south Wales Bevin Boy, 1944–47

Mel describes his work alongside a collier at Cwm Colliery:

> As the days passed, I watched him him at work, noticing how neat and careful he was in everything he did ... Although working hard with Mr David – never called him anything else – my feeling about coal mining did not change. All my friends wore the uniform of one of the Forces ... whilst I was in civilian clothes with no uniform except boots and helmet. I was on meagre rations, a very small wage and open to accusations of cowardice.

(Extracted courtesy of *GLO*, Big Pit/Museum of Wales magazine, 2005)

Following various campaigns, Bevin Boys were deservedly recognised for their war service, albeit decades later. It was not until 1995 that the 'forgotten conscripts' were officially acknowledged in a speech made by HM The Queen, but they had to wait a further nine years to be allowed to march in the Remembrance Day service at Whitehall. In 2007, Bevin Boys were allowed to apply for a specially commissioned commemorative badge produced by the Government in honour of their war service. A moving ceremony took place on 7 May 2013 at the

National Memorial Arboretum in Staffordshire when a tearful Countess of Wessex unveiled a memorial to the 'forgotten heroes' of the war, assisted by Harry Parkes and a few of his surviving Bevin Boy colleagues. Sadly, the official Bevin Boys Association (www.bevinboysassociation.co.uk) has a fast dwindling membership, as most of the veterans are in now in their mid-to-late 80s.

Miners' opinions (Penallta Colliery, south Wales)

These Bevin Boys, they didn't trouble, not one bit. They would rather have gone to the services. (Ivor Davies)

We had quite a number of them. A lot of them to be honest were a waste of time. You'd put a shovel in their hand and and it was like a snake in their hand. But some of them were all right. Some even stopped there after the war. (Vince Court)

(*GLO*, Big Pit/Museum of Wales magazine, 2005.)

Research Tips

If your ancestor was a Bevin Boy or was a miner who trained or worked with Bevin Boys it is well worth accessing one or more of the excellent published autobiographical accounts (see below for several recent titles). Other useful sources included deposited and displayed material (including some recordings) held at the national mining museums. In 2005, the Museum of Wales and Big Pit published an excellent collection of Bevin Boy information and related reminiscences in their *GLO* magazine, well worth reading for other coalfield areas too. For the Midlands area the Imperial War Museum has a complete list of ballotees and optants (1943–47), as well as related documents/photographs: Dept. Documents [Misc. 2834]. As you would expect primary material is also lodged in The National Archives: keyword 'Bevin Boys' in your search.

Selective sources and further reading

Books

Sydney Allinson, *The Bantams* (Pen and Sword Books, 2009)

Alexander Barrie, *War Underground. The Tunnellers of the Great War* (Tom Donovan, 1961)

Peter Barton, Peter Doyle and Johan Vanderwalle, *Beneath Flanders Fields. The Tunnellers' War* (Spellmount, 2004)

Richard Baxell, *British Volunteers in the Spanish Civil War: The British Battalion in the International Brigades, 1936–1939* (Routledge, 2004)

Simon Fowler, *Tracing Your Army Ancestors* (Pen and Sword Books, 2013)

Simon Fowler, *Tracing Your First World War Ancestors* (Pen & Sword Books, 2013)

Hywel Francis, *Miners Against Fascism: Wales and the Spanish Civil War* (Lawrence and Wishart, 1984)

Mike Gomersall, *Thomas Bryan. The Forgotten V.C. of Whitwood & Castleford* (Mike Gomersall, 2012)

Tom Hickman, *Called Up, Sent Down. The Bevin Boys' War* (The History Press, 2008)

Derek Hollows, *As I Recall. A Bevin Boy's Story* (Brewin Books, 2007)

Philip Robinson and Nigel Cave, *The Underground War. Volume 1: Vimy Ridge to Arras* (Pen & Sword Books, 2011)

Reg Taylor, *Bevin Boy. A Reluctant Miner* (Athena Press, 2004)

Warwick Taylor, *The Forgotten Conscript. A History of the Bevin Boys* (Pentland Press, 1995 & 2003)

Film/DVDs

Peter Barton, *The Somme: Secret Tunnel Wars* (BBC4 documentary, 2013)

Miners at War (Puddle Productions DVD)

One of Our Mines is Missing! (Durand Group's investigation of the Broadmarsh and Durand mines (Fougasse Films)

The First World War From Above (BBC documentary)

Their Finest Hour. The Underground Army [Bevin Boys DVD]

Internet

www.victoriacross.org.uk (Ian Stewart's VC burial locations listings)

Military medals/records can be searched via Ancestry.com

Tours

There are many Battlefield Tours available for you to see places where your miner-ancestor may have served; just use your search engine to access up-to-date details. Some recommended sites (and advice) relating to the tunnellers are well described in Robinson and Cave's book (cited above).

Chapter 6

USING THE CENSUS

Incomers and Miner-Households: a case study of Treeton, near Rotherham in south Yorkshire (1891)

Pits were sometimes sunk with little or no fuss, especially in the earlier days of mining, say before c.1830. However, when larger collieries were commissioned and planned it became almost a standard procedure for the occasion to be marked by a ceremonious 'cutting of the sod'. Dignitaries watched as a VIP, often a lady of some social or public standing, carried out the task using a special spade. The Victorians and Edwardians were wonderful exponents of such commemorative occasions.

Commemorative colliery pulley wheel and Miners' Welfare Scheme plaque, Wood Lane, Treeton.

Tip

If your miner-ancestor was one the first workers at a new colliery it's a good idea to check for any report of the ceremonial start of sinking in local newspapers, as the entire proceedings were often reported in considerable detail. From the late nineteenth century, and certainly later, the text was usually enhanced by spectacular images of the event, and occasionally postcards were produced by opportunistic local photographers. 'Pioneer' pitmen, in other words experienced miners from neighbouring or distant coalfields, soon to be living nearby, were often included in the ceremonial party, and might be captured on film.

On a fine autumn morning in 1875, on 13 October, a Mrs Jaffray, wife of the chairman of the Rothervale Colliery Company Limited, did the honours, with a glittering ceremonial spade, placing the sod in an equally grand wheelbarrow, then pushed along a plank of timber. A large marquee provided shelter for visitors to enjoy celebratory refreshments, and for dignitaries, the occasion was further marked by a banquet in the Royal Victoria Hotel in Sheffield, attended by a variety of worthies, including the Master Cutler. The reporter for the *Rotherham Advertiser* included a very down-to-earth comment, contrasting the sunny day and 'charming landscape, which was soon to be disfigured by colliery headgear and huge chimneys'. Locals were well aware of the impact that a new coal mine might have, as two other collieries, Orgreave and Fence, had been established nearby in 1851 and 1863 respectively, both now part of the expanding Rothervale enterprise.

And so the life of Treeton Colliery, near Rotherham, on land owned by the Duke of Norfolk, began, but it was not plain sailing. Development work via the two new shafts was suspended in September 1878 due to financial and economic problems. However, a resumption of work in 1882 ran alongside a significant transformation of the village from a small rural community of just 137 inhabited houses and 383 people in 1871, to 335 separate occupiers and a population of 1,969 in 1901.

The colliery company had facilitated its demand for labour through a building programme that remains impressive even by modern-day standards. According to *White's Directory of Sheffield and Rotherham* (for 1902) some 400 houses had been erected in the township since 1881. This is probably an exaggeration, but distinctive groups of properties are evident on the larger scale OS maps, at Well Lane (Bole Hill Row and New Bole Hill), Wood Lane and Mill Lane. Several of the grander Wood Lane properties, locally known

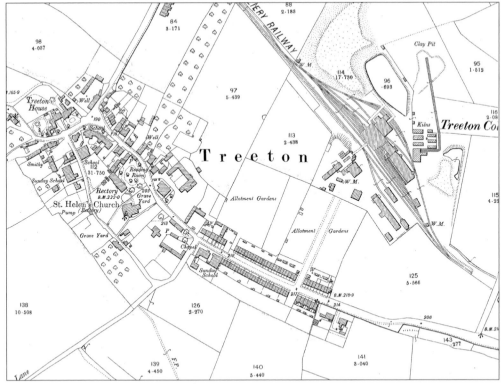

Treeton village and colliery, from the 1:2500 OS map for 1903. The rows of miners' houses SW of the mine are along Wood Lane. Courtesy of the Ordnance Survey.

as The Big Six, were reserved for officials, contrasting with the basic 'colliers' houses' further along the street and those down Mill Lane. The 1891 census has the the pit's first manager, a Scot, Walter Baxter, aged 38, residing at 69 and 70 Wood Lane with his Welsh-born wife Barbara, seven young children,

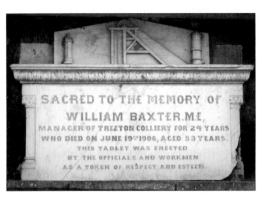

and a 14-year-old servant girl. A Scottish aunt was visiting on census night. The Baxters' older children were born in a distant mining area, Hednesford, in the Cannock Chase coalfield of Staffordshire, prior to their move to Bewdley in Worcestershire, before migrating

Plaque commemorating William Baxter, Treeton Colliery's first manager.

to Treeton in around 1882. Baxter died relatively young, aged 53, and his service to the colliery was commemorated in a specially commissioned plaque, which can now be seen set high in a wall near the community centre, off Wood Lane.

Rothervale's company secretary, John Howard Keep, lived more grandly at Treeton Hall, in the old village, whilst its Staffordshire-born managing director, Frederick John Jones (1853–1936), resided in detached rural splendour at Treeton Grange, with his wife, two young children and two servants. Educated at Repton and Trinity College, Cambridge, Sir Frederick (as he became) was the first chairman of Treeton Parish Council, and had a country seat at Grantham, Lincolnshire. A distinguished mining engineer, Jones was twice President of the Mining Association of Great Britain and also had business interests in several coal-related industries: coke and chemicals; and iron and steel.

Treeton Colliery was able to open with a workforce of 1,043, comprising 835 underground workers and 563 surface workers. By 1908 the total employed there was well over 2,000, making it one of the larger south Yorkshire pits. The landscape and human impact on the locality was enormous: a previously quiet backwater south of Rotherham was transformed into a thriving rural-industrial community within a single generation; and about three out of every four houses were occupied by miners and their families, mostly 'imported' from other coalfields.

Treeton Colliery was sunk by Rothervale Collieries Limited between 1875–77. Although its narrow valley site at the bottom of Spa Hill was unsuited to very large-scale development, the mine was well served by important railways (North Midland and Sheffield District) and a colliery branch line that also linked with its sister pit, Orgreave Colliery. Rothervale became part of the new United Steel company in 1918 and improvement both above and below ground took place in the years before nationalisation. During the NCB era several major developments took place and annual output peaked at 652,000 tons in 1969–70. Treeton's underground link to its sister pit, Orgreave Colliery, was curtailed in 1981, following the latter's closure, the connection to neighbouring Thurcroft Colliery having ended about ten years earlier. A major (£20 million) development of Treeton Colliery occurred in 1976 with the construction of a new drift and underground coal transport scheme. Following geological faulting problems, coal extraction was deemed to be 'uneconomic' and production ceased in December 1990, 115 years after its ceremonial origin.

Among the Treeton censuses (1841–1911), the 1891 returns are the most revealing from a family *and* local history point of view since they provide us with the best snapshot of an emerging pit village. Incomers, and as we have seen there were many, were newly settled and their pit jobs, domestic situations and backgrounds are clearly evident.

The 1891 census includes:

- road, street name of the house
- house number (or name)
- number of rooms (if less than five)
- name of head of household
- relationship to head
- marital status
- age at last birthday
- profession or occupation: employer or employee (or neither)
- where born (place and county)
- disability status i.e. 'if deaf-and-dumb, blind or a lunatic, imbecile or idiot'

Contrary to some impressions and sources, miners' families were not especially large compared with other industrial groups of workers. However, their *households* often were. And this is understandable. Despite the efforts of colliery companies and private builders there was just not enough accommodation for all migrant workers. It was quite common anyway for single men and some married couples (even with young children) to find lodgings in miners' households.

Tip

It is useful when researching the census to appreciate that 'lodgers' and 'boarders' (in reality there was little or no difference in these terms, used interchangeably by the enumerators) were often relatives or at the very least had some previous connection with their 'landlord'. So don't entirely dismiss lodgers/boarders as strangers!

In 1891, the average size of miners' households in Treeton was 7.09. More than half of these, however (55.6%), had 7–10 occupants and a fairly significant number, 17 (12%), accommodated upwards of 11 (to 16) people in what must have been extremely cramped, awkward conditions. There were at least eighty-seven lodgers placed in miners' households, about two-thirds of them under the age of 30. As many as one hundred sons of miners, mostly aged between 13 and 20, listed as 'coal miners' or with mine-related occupations, also lived in parental households. In addition, eleven households had identifiable close relatives residing with them: four brothers, three stepsons, and a brother-in-law, nephew, father and even grandfather, all pit workers. Extended mining families were therefore not uncommon and again this is not surprising given the housing shortage. A few young miners also found accommodation in 'non-mining' households. But even here there may have been some familial link. Colliery shunter John Broughton, aged 22 and born in Warwickshire, lived in the post office at Front Street, where Martha Foers, a 69-year-old widow, was listed as head of the household. Martha also supplemented her income (or maybe helped on social grounds, or both) via another boarder, 22-year-old railway signalman Ernest Tunnicliffe, who came from Staffordshire. Both young men clearly had railway-related skills. In another interesting example, quarryman Thomas Mercer, a widower, living at Upper Bole Hill, provided accommodation for a young married couple: Alexander Tinkler, aged 27, who was banksman at the colliery, and his 21-year-old wife, Harriet.

Head of household George Mallinder, a 'coal miner', aged 31, lived with his wife Alice and two school-age children, in a small property at 1 Mill Lane, but still managed to accommodate three colliery labourers: Charles Lindley, 47, and his sons Henry and Edwin, aged 17 and 16 respectively. The Mallinders and Lindleys came to Treeton from Killamarsh, in north Derbyshire, so there was probably a personal if not family connection.

Even quite large miner-family households could find space for lodgers, especially where there were personal links. Jonah Kyte, a 56-year-old coal-miner, and his wife Mary Ann, 52, like the Mallinders mentioned above living at Mill Lane, had seven children; three of the males (aged 28, 25, and 14) also worked at the colliery. Income was presumably supplemented via three lodgers who also worked at the pit. Goodness knows what bath night was like when they were on the same homecoming shift! The Kytes came to Treeton from Staffordshire, as did two of their lodgers, the other one from Warwickshire.

Another incoming family, the Johnsons, from Derbyshire and Nottingham-shire, demonstrate how mining was such a dominant part of their livelihood and way of life. Coalminer Edwin Johnson, aged 48, and his wife Emma (52), had four work-age sons at home, aged 14–21, each seemingly working with their father at the colliery.

The cottages erected along Mill Lane by the colliery company were quite small and would certainly have been very basic in their facilities. And yet

145

several households were large, none more so than where the Bishops lived, whose abstracted details from the enumerators' returns are shown below:

Henry Bishop, Head, Married, 43, Colliery Banksman, Employed, Brighton

Fanny Bishop, Wife, Married, 41, Nutley, Sussex

Gertrude Bishop, Dau, 19, Mother's Help, Employed, Brighton

Adeline Bishop, Dau, 14, Gen Dom Servant, Employed, Wimblebury, Staffs

Thomas Bishop, Son, 11, Scholar, Wimblebury

John Bishop, Son, 9, Scholar, Wimblebury

Lydia Bishop, Dau, 7, Scholar, Wimblebury

Ernest Bishop, Son, 5, Scholar, Littleworth, Staffs

Frances Bishop, Dau, 3, Treeton

Jacob Bishop, Son, 9 mths, Treeton

Philip Bungay, Lodger, Single, 21, Colliery Labourer, Employed, Brighton

Charles Carr, Lodger, Single, 21, Colliery Labourer, Employed, Nutley, Sussex

John Carr, Lodger, Single, 19, Colliery Labourer, Employed, Nutley

George Fuller, Lodger, Single, 21, Colliery Labourer, Employed, Brighton

Alfred Osborne, Lodger, Single, 21, Colliery Labourer, Employed, Brighton

Horace Wraxall, Lodger, Single, 19, Colliery Labourer, Employed, Brighton

The Bishop family were somewhat unusual in that they originated in Brighton and rural Sussex, far removed of course from any coalmining area. However, the census shows that they had migrated to Wimblebury, in the Cannock Chase area of Staffordshire – a noted mining area – where four children were born c.1877–84. A move to neighbouring Littleworth appears to have taken place by 1886, when another child was born. The great shift to Treeton occurred not long afterwards, coinciding with the development of the colliery, a daughter, Frances, soon born; and then their youngest child, Jacob, a few months before census night. The family income was presumably assisted by the extraordinary presence of six Sussex-born male lodgers, aged 19–21, all of them working at the colliery. What a cramped and

Administrative County of ___ of Treeton

The undermentioned Houses are situate within the Boundaries of the —

Town-or-Village or—Hamlet of Treeton | Rural Sanitary District of Rotherham | Parliamentary Borough or Division of Rotherham | Ecclesiastical Parish or District of Sheffield District of Treeton

No. of Schedule	ROAD, STREET, &c., and No. or NAME of HOUSE	Inhabited	Uninhabited	Number of rooms if less than five	NAME and Surname of each Person	RELATION to Head of Family	CONDITION as to Marriage	AGE Male	AGE Female	PROFESSION or OCCUPATION	Employer	Employed	Neither Employer nor Employed	WHERE BORN	(1) Deaf-and-Dumb (2) Blind (3) Lunatic, Imbecile or Idiot
15	9 Mill Lane	1			John Nadin	Head	M	41		Beer Retailer		X		Sheffield	
					Eliza Do	Wife	M		35					Derby Woodhouse	
					Thomas Do	Son		17		Nathr Wesley Bank		X		Do	
					Henry Do	Son				Scholar				York Treeton	
					John Do	Son				Do				do do	
					Frank Do	Son								do	
					Elizabeth Grant	Niece								Derby Gt Colon	
16	10 Do	1			Fred Redfern	Head	M	39		Colliery Engine Tenter (Station)	X			Notts Wathnall	
					Lucy Redfern	Wife	M		40	Dressmaker				Derby Heanor	
					Joshua Do	Son	S	19		Coal Miner		X		Do New Mill	
					Emily Do	Daur	S		10	Scholar				Do Eckington	
					George A Do	Son	S	7		Do				York Tipton	
17	11 Do	1			William Davis	Head	M	64		Colliery Labourer		X		Rutland Shribs	
					Ellen E Do	Wife	M		46					Lincoln Shillington	
					William H Do	Boarder	S	21		Coal Miner		X		Leicester Slabeb	
					John Cutler	Boarder	S			Do		X		Derby Tamworth	
18	12 Do	1			Charles Radford Sr	Head	M	60		Do		X		Worcester Tamworth	
					Ann Do	Wife	M		33	Do				Do Alverton	
					Henry Do	Son	S			Do				Stafford Lichfield	
					Lily A Do	Daur	S							Do Linthwood Mill	
					George Hindon Boarder		S	26		General Labourer		X		Notts Retford	
					Fred Do	Boarder	S	22		Do		X		Do	
19	13 Do	1			William Radford	Head	M	37		Deputy in Coal Mine		X		Stafford Tall	
					Susan Do	Wife	M		33					Lancs Capel Hill	
20	14 Do	1			William M Gregg	Head	M	44		Colliery Deputy		X		York Barugh	
					Amelia Do	Daur	S		14					Do Do	
					George H Do	Son				Colly Pit Labourer		X		Do Alveston	
					William M Do	Son				Hookworker Pit Bank		X		Do	
					Albert Do	Son		5						Do Higham	
6	Total of Houses and of Tenements with less than Five Rooms	6					Total of Males and Females	20	10						

Extract from the 1891 census showing miners' households, numbers 9–14 Mill Lane. Ancestry.com

147

Former miners' cottages along Mill Lane.

busy household it must have been, sixteen adults and children in a small terraced cottage. Spare a thought for how Mrs Fanny Bishop coped with all the back-breaking and never-ending work, harder than a double shift at the pit I would think.

That big new pits pulled workers from neighbouring areas is not unexpected, but more distant migration, particularly 'mass movement' (often on foot!) from particular areas is less easy to understand. What does seem clear is that 'word of mouth', individuals and families responding either at the same time (or not long afterwards) was an important mobility factor. At the same time, however, the colliery companies themselves were actively and deliberately recruiting in areas where they – the directors, agents and managers – had experience and expertise. That is one reason why significant groups of miners, especially experienced men, often moved from one coalfield to another, despite the distance involved. Local pit closures and economic circumstances apart, the migration of miners and their families from one region to another is a fascinating – but complex – part of local and family history research. Your own research may well contribute to a better, that is more meaningful, interpretation of the migratory process.

The miners and their families brought with them a culture, including accent and dialect, humour, even they way they greeted each other, into a locality, contributing to a rapidly changing community through several generations. The new Board School (1880) and Reading Room (1888), Wesleyan chapel (1892) and restored parish church (1892) were the new hubs of family interaction. To cap it all Treeton was 'illuminated' in 1897 when it became the first village in England to have electric street lighting, the power courtesy of the Rothervale Colliery Company.

Analysis of the place of birth of 142 coalmining male heads of household recorded in the 1891 Treeton census provides us with overwhelming evidence of the importance of migration into Treeton from other coalfield areas:

Derbyshire	34
Staffordshire	22
Nottinghamshire	20
Warwicks/Worc	13
Shropshire	5 (Forest of Dean)
Leicestershire	3
Gloucestershire	3
Durham/Northumberland	3
Lancashire	1
Somerset	1

The above shows that around three out of every four coalmining heads of household (74%) were incomers, most notably directly from Derbyshire and Nottinghamshire (38%) and a significant number (almost 25%) from Black Country counties, particularly Staffordshire. More detailed analysis shows that migration was particularly strong from north Derbyshire (Coal Aston, Staveley, Killamarsh and other nearby mining villages) and Stafford-shire (Hednesford, Moseley, Cannock and Dudley). Only 23 (16%) coal-mining heads of household were born in south Yorkshire, and perhaps even more surprising was that just six of these (4%) came from Treeton or adjacent hamlets.

There were fewer than ten coalmining heads of household born in non-coalmining counties, mostly rural areas such as Lincolnshire, Norfolk and Hampshire.

About 76% of households where the head was employed in coalmining had either a son or sons in mining, or lodgers (or had both miner sons and lodgers).

The occupational part of census returns also provides a fair indication of the range of job 'titles' used by coal industry-related heads of household (or the enumerators' interpretations of the same). Typically, the generic 'coal miner' was used in most cases (77%) but an interesting mix of managerial, craft and miscellaneous terms are listed for the others. In number order they are: deputy (8), labourer (7), banksman (4), engine driver (3), weigh clerk (3), enginewright (3), carpenter (2), manager (2), fireman (1), horse-keeper (1), salesman (1), shunter (1), stoker (1), tipper (1), under viewer (1) and loco driver (1).

There was a similar pattern of 'job description' for miners' sons working at Treeton (or a nearby) colliery. Again, 'coal miner' was the biggest category, though not quite as dominant in usage as for heads of household (60%). The others were: labourer (10), pony driver (8), coal-picker/worker at pit bank (7), banksman (5), carpenter (1), corve runner [haulage worker] (1), errand boy (1), fitter (1), joiner (1), lamp cleaner (1), office boy (1) and clerk (1). Two of the sons were only 12 years old; fourteen were aged 13 and twenty-two 14–15. The largest 'age category' of miners' sons was 16–20 years, accounting for almost half (49) of all the listings, mostly described as 'coal miners'.

What happened at Treeton occurred with understandable variations at many other new mining communities. The census is a wonderful source of information for researching our coalmining ancestry, especially if it is used in context and alongside other material. Just to extract your particular ancestor's details misses out on placing the family in its social and economic setting.

Tips

- Take a wider sweep when using census returns: look at neighbouring properties, the whole village or district if you can and it will be worthwhile, certainly more meaningful; and you may find family links which otherwise would have been hidden.
- Check to see if there is a village/local history society website for background information; some families may have photographs and ancestry details posted there. Names and places on censuses then become real local people, even if they are not on your family tree. And you can reciprocate.
- Do make use of the larger-scale OS maps when using the census. If there is a Godfrey Edition (as there is for Treeton) covering part or the whole area of interest it will be an abiding aid to your research (www.alangodfreymaps.co.uk).
- Take some time to walk around the area, preferably with a camera, map and notebook. To me, this is what makes local and family history so rewarding. The pit site may be eradicated from the local landscape but many miners' houses, facilities and public and private memorials may well be present. And do have a chat with

local people if you get the chance. I have always found this immensely beneficial; it is surprising how it can result in some remarkable findings and connections that would otherwise be unavailable from any source.

Further Treeton sources

wwwtreetonweb.co.uk

Alan Godfrey, Old Ordnance Survey Maps: Treeton & Orgreave 1901 (Yorkshire Sheet 295.07)

Alan Hill, *The South Yorkshire Coalfield. A History and Development* (Tempus Publishing/ The History Press), 2001

Rotherham Archives and Local Studies Library

The census and its usage

These days the census is mostly accessed online via commercial sites such as www.ancestry.com and www.findmypast.co.uk, but most record offices and libraries will have microfiche versions of the 1841–1891 censuses for their areas. Transcripts may also be available locally or online, for example at www.freecen.org.uk; and it's well worth checking what may be available on local history society sites. On usage there's background information in many general books on family history research, for example Simon Fowler's *Tracing Your Ancestors* (Pen & Sword Books, 2011). Specific guides include Stuart Raymond's *Census 1801–1911: A Guide for the Internet Era* (Family History Partnerships, 2009).

Chapter 7

MAKING USE OF OBJECTS AND EPHEMERA

Among my most treasured possessions are a variety of memorabilia once used or associated with my mining ancestors and late mining friends. In many respects such items can be as meaningful and important as any of the usual family history sources. What's more, I believe that family history research is not just about about discovering aspects of our ancestral past, but also about passing on information, stories – and artefacts – to the next generation or more. When I have talked about coal-mining to primary school children the best reaction (and probably the most effective learning experience) was when I involved them handling and trying a variety of authentic materials, from old helmets, lamps and clogs to more modern pitman's gear. Take that a stage further, with role play set in and around a particular event such as a disaster, and the experience widens to involve the whole curriculum and local community.

If you can acquire some personal items they can not only help 'tell the story' of that individual's work but also remain as concrete links to the past. These days, through popular internet auction sites and antique and collectors' fairs, it is easy (except for very rare items) to build up a small collection of relevant items, supplementing any that you already have from family, friends and contacts. The following examples are only suggestions as the range is considerable. More detailed background information is available via sites run by enthusiasts, for instance, the National Mining Memorabilia Association (www.mining-memorabilia.co.uk).

Pit checks

New starters at pits were routinely issued with small numbered personal identification disks, generally known as checks. They were usually thinly cut, using metals such as brass, zinc or aluminium, and had a small hole drilled near the upper edge to facilitate storage. The numbers were often hand-stamped on the obverse side and had embossed or inscribed identification details of the colliery/owners on the other. Routinely, the miner would hand in his check to the banksman at the pit top before descending the cage

Studio photograph of Tony Banks, a coalmining veteran with thirty-eight years' work experience in the industry. A member of Wakefield Family History Society, Tony can trace his mining ancestry through five or six generations, including his son, who worked at the Selby complex. Aged 15, Tony started work at Manor Colliery near Wakefield in 1957, a 'family pit' where his great-great-grandfather had also worked. Later moving to Lofthouse Colliery (the scene of the 1973 flooding disaster), he completed his mining work at Selby, having to retire following the effects of carbon monoxide poisoning in 1995. Dressed in his old NCB suit and with pit deputy items, Tony helps to present mining films to schools and local groups and has a great interest in local mining history. He is often involved in commemorative community events.

of a deep mine, keeping another with him throughout his shift. On completion of his work the miner then handed in his remaining check to the banksman when he reached the surface. This was vital information for use in accidents and disasters, and of course provided management with an accurate record of who and how many workers were underground at any time. This simple but effective manual process continued right up to the 1990s when swipe cards were introduced. Checks were also provided for the issue and return of lamps. The checks were suspended on a numbered tally board in the lamp room or time office. Checks and tokens were in widespread use by the late nineteenth century and – with safety in mind – the system became mandatory for British mines in 1913. Many mines also issued numbered pay checks or tokens for the use of miners when they collected their wages; and there were numerous other types of checks or tokens used at collieries. After nationalisation in 1947 the National Coal Board (NCB) issued its own new checks, though, due to the large number of collieries and miners, some older checks were simply re-stamped. But it is the pre-1947 ones that are the most interesting, though more expensive to buy, particularly rare and early examples. If purchasing, obtain from a trusted dealer or site as forgeries are becoming more common.

Pit check for Comrie Colliery, Scotland dating from the NCB era. This Fife area pit functioned from 1936–1986, employing 1,498 men at its peak in 1963.

Checks were issued in a variety of forms, as can be seen in these examples from Deep Navigation Colliery (oblong, pre-1947, South Wales), Hatfield Main (coffin-shape, Yorkshire, NCB) and New Monckton Collieries (round, pre-1947, Yorkshire, where my paternal grandfather worked).

Early miners' union badges

A large variety of miners' union or association badges were issued – usually in metal – from the mid-nineteenth century, and they were often more creatively designed than most pit checks. They were issued to denote membership and/or record that a subscription had been duly paid. The early ones are particularly interesting. The measure of their former importance

Miners' association badges for the Barrow Branch of the Yorkshire Miners' Association and North Staffordshire Miners' Federation (the latter featuring its well-known leader Enoch Edwards, 1852–1912).

Shield-style union badge for the Hylton Branch of the Durham Miners' Association.

can be seen when worn by miners – pinned to lapels – on old photographs, each one having pin holes for this purpose. Often found via online auction sites, they are also occasionally discovered by metal detectors.

Later miners' union, strike and commemorative badges

A considerable number of NUM branch or area badges, usually in metal and often enamelled, were issued and are meaningful small mementoes of a mining ancestor's union membership. Was he in the 1984–85 strike? The year-long dispute resulted in many hundreds of official and privately commissioned enamel badges. On picketing and social occasions these were exchanged between miners from different pits and areas. After the strike many more appeared on a commemorative basis, relating to individuals, pits, events and anniversaries. Many former miners or voluntary groups also

Orgreave picket badge (Scotland), 1984–85.

Women Against Pit Closures badge, 1984–85.

Tin 'Support the Miners' badge for Dinnington Colliery in South Yorkshire.

commissioned badges to commemorate the closure of a particular pit or as a tribute or fundraising aid for colleagues killed in accidents or a particular disaster. Badges were also issued in respect of galas and demonstrations. In 2008, former miner Brian Witts published *Enamel Badges of the National Union of Mineworkers*, a substantial colour-printed guide well worth seeking. More ephemeral and larger tin and paper badges were also produced for individual collieries as well as for the 1984/85 strike.

Safety lamps

The safety lamp is perhaps the most iconic of all mining memorabilia. To have your father's, grandfather's, or great-grandfather's actual lamp is a great heirloom. Failing that you may wish to obtain a typical example. There are a lot to choose from! Original brass and gauze oil lamps of the style created by

A mid-nineteenth century Davy-style lamp from the author's collection.

A modern flame safety lamp by The Protector Lamp & Lighting Company, presented to the author in 2002.

Davy, Stephenson, Clanny and others are expensive to buy because of their scarcity and the great demand from collectors. Early 'naked flame' lamps such as Spedding's steel or flint mill and small 'tea-pot' wick lamps made of tin or brass (often attached to a hat or cap), popular in Scotland, are less common, as are the 'peg and ball' cap lamps used in Welsh and Forest of Dean mines. Carbide lamps were once used in 'gas-free' workings of adit or drift mines, right up to the 1940s. Modern lamps produced by firms such as The Protector Lamp & Lighting Company (of Eccles, Lancashire) and Wolf (Sheffield) are more easily obtained. Companies such as CEAG Ltd (of Barnsley) pioneered the use of electric safety lamps, cap lamps, inspection lamps and torches, making them to a very high specification right up to 2005, so many examples still survive. Websites for collectors (and to assist identification) of lamps include David Barrie's The Wand of Science (www.thewandofscience.net).

Ceramics and glassware

A large and wide range of commemorative pottery was produced from the mid-nineteenth century onwards. Early examples, usually in the form of plates, mugs and jugs (often marking pit disasters) are quite rare and therefore expensive to obtain, but pieces are usually on display, viewable virtually or on display at mining and other museums. There was a great resurgence of commemorative pottery production after the 1984–85 miners'

This attractive modern plate was one of many similar 'pit closure' examples created by Pear Tree Pottery, a small art pottery in the village of Laughton-en-le-Morthen, near Rotherham. A limited edition of 250, it commemorates the closure of Kiveton Park Colliery. The reverse contains a short history of the mine. A useful souvenir for anyone whose ancestor or relative worked at the colliery, which functioned from 1866 to 1994.

One of two (now rare) transfer-printed commemorative plates produced by Wardle & Sons of Middlesbrough and Stoke for the 6 December 1875 disaster at Swaithe Main, near Barnsley. This example also commemorates the late Yorkshire miners' leader John Normansell, who died on Christmas Eve the same year, its edge surrounded by the names of sixty (of 143) disaster victims. The other version has the name of coal owner Joseph Mitchell in the centrepiece. Mitchell died a few weeks after Normansell, on 24 January 1876. In a very scarce third example the black design at the centre of the plate is overlain with gold lustre.

A much larger 'Edwardian bone china' Swaithe disaster plate was issued in a limited edition by E.J. & J.A. Downes in 1994, with all the deceased miners named, along with their ages and general places of residence. A central image of an underground scene shows rescue workers attending to the victims. Printed on the reverse is a short account of the disaster and an extract from a poem.

strike, either for the dispute itself, or to pay tribute to the closure of a particular colliery. Also very interesting are 'union pieces', commissioned and produced by the NUM and its regional offices; and also items relating to demonstrations. The modern plates in particular often have quite detailed and useful summaries on the backs and are much more easy to obtain.

Commemorative glassware is far less common but became fashionable in Victorian and Edwardian times (and to a lesser extent in later decades), especially in the North East, where everyday items such as tumblers, pub glasses and tankards were hand-engraved. Families were able to commemorate the loss of life of an individual miner in an accident or obtain a disaster souvenir for events at, for example, Hartley, East Hetton, Seaham, West Stanley, Whitburn and Woodhorn collieries. Again, there are examples kept or displayed in museums, and occasionally one will come on the market for purchase.

Small metalware

A variety of small everyday and highly personal metal objects are well worth obtaining. One example is a miner's lunch or sandwich box, known regionally by a variety of terms: snap tin, bait tin, piece tin, for example; although I recall my father taking his sandwiches, usually beef dripping or jam, skilfully wrapped by mum, in 'Mother's Pride' (or other brand) loaf wrappings. The Acme tin was the purpose-made metal version often used, offering some security from rats, mice – and clever pit ponies! Metal bottles of various sizes and shapes were used for containing drinking water. The flat, round versions, known as dudleys, were popular in some areas. Again, my father tended to either use a flask (despite the fragility) or reuse a glass 'pop' bottle.

Small pocket-portable tobacco tins were often used by miners, the 'twist' (chewing tobacco) providing some relief when working in hot and dry underground conditions. The little tins would be topped up from larger containers kept at home or from twist bought from local shops. The tins, round and oval mainly, were made by the local tinsmith, pit blacksmith or the miner himself. What makes so many of them interesting is that they were often personalised, rather like a piece of trench art, with a variety of patterns and/or pictures; and maybe the name of the miner, his colliery and

A typical ACME snap tin.

A Welsh miner's tobacco tin, made of brass and dated 1899. It is inscribed 'Alfred Jenkins. 17 Amelia Terrace. Llwynypia'. The house, not far from Tonypandy in South Wales, still exists.

even his home address, a family historian's dream find. There are some very attractive examples from south Wales.

Ephemera

A very wide range of mine-related paper items will enhance standard family history sources, if you can find or obtain them. Some may have survived within families over several generations, though sadly many will have been lost or destroyed. As with other items, it is still possible to build up a small collection from a variety of outlets, though having extant pieces directly from or relating to your miner is preferable for most of us. Personal examples include pay/wages slips, printed price lists (rates of pay for particular jobs), compensation records, Mineworkers' Pension Scheme items, certificates of competence or qualification, official letters, union cards and summer school/convalescence home ephemera. As with other family history keepsakes, obituary news cuttings, funeral cards and other bereavement items are also important mementoes. Paper items relating to the colliery or collieries where your miner worked are also well worth collecting: NCB brochures, open-day literature, social and retirement events, coal wagon tickets/labels, posters and notices.

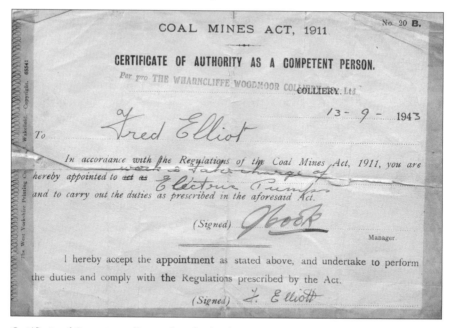

Certificate of Competence ('to work and take charge of electric pumps') issued to my father, Fred Elliott, when he was employed by the Wharncliffe Woodmoor Colliery Ltd. Fred's general employment title was that of an underground fitter.

Price List (agreed wage rate booklet) for Askern Main Colliery (Doncaster area), c.1938.

Payslip for underground piecework for miner 123 (A.K.Clayton) employed by the Newton Chambers Company Limited (at Rockingham Colliery), dated 1 February 1938.

NCB (and NUM/ NACODS) invitation to a 'Christmas Treat', 7 December 1972.

Postcards and studio photographs

Many thousands of 'real photo' postcards were published relating to mines and miners, especially between c.1903–1930. There is a reasonable chance, therefore, that you will be able to obtain a postcard image of the colliery or collieries where your ancestor miner or miners worked; but the originals are expensive, depending of course on rarity and condition. Reproductions, however, will cost a fraction of the cost of originals and can be ordered from archives, libraries and picture collections. Apart from collieries, popular mining subjects include strikes, disasters, rescue and first aid teams and social events such as galas, and views of associated buildings such as

A small group of South Wales miners (and an impressive dog) outside an unnamed colliery during a strike in 1910, photographer unknown. The pit may well have been Aberaman Colliery in the Cynon Valley, which was bought by the Powell Duffryn Steam Coal company in 1866 and the dispute the so-called 'block strike' rather than the more famous Cambrian Combine strike in the Rhondda. About 1,700 men were employed at Aberaman in 1908.

162

institutes, welfares and houses may be found. Sporting teams, colliery brass bands and images of pastimes such as pigeon and greyhound racing were also popular, photographers appreciating their commercial appeal.

Studio photographs, where the miner or miners appear 'as if for work', wearing their pit clothes and displaying lamps and hand tools (as against the usual formal portrait or family group composition) are quite rare. One regional exception, for the Wigan coalfield, are those taken by enterprising studios from the middle decades of the nineteenth century showing 'pit brow' female miners, produced for 'tourists' as well as locals. Again, surviving originals will be both hard to find and expensive to obtain (unless via picture collection services), though Wigan pit lasses also featured on postcards, some of which can be purchased for a few pounds.

Awards

Bravery and gallantry awards have already been discussed in Chapter 2, but a variety of other medals and certificates were presented to miners. Those men who worked in the mines rescue service received long-service medals for every five years of their involvement, certainly from the NCB era. Earlier, one-off medals of recognition in the service were also issued on a regional basis. Occasionally these can be seen on internet auction sites or at collectors' fairs, or are available from specialist medal/coin dealers.

Returning 'soldier-miners' were often honoured by both workmen and companies through the award of a medal (particularly those that survived the First World War) and such events were usually reported in local newspapers. The number of medals awarded per pit could be large; several hundred in many cases. Surviving examples are much sought after by collectors, but a priceless treasure if you already have one as a family history heirloom. It is worth checking out extant examples – virtually and actually –

Brass and enamel mines rescue medal issued by Nottinghamshire and Derbyshire collieries, inscribed 'T.S. Vardy 1914' on the obverse. A check through military records shows that Thomas S. Vardy went on to serve in the Royal Army Medical Corps (RAMC), and was of sergeant rank, though there are no extant service or pension papers. He appears in the 1901 census, aged 18, born at South Normanton, Derbyshire, the son of a miner. In the 1911 census, aged 28, he was living at 44 Lincoln Street, Tibshelf, Derbyshire and is listed as married with one child, his profession or occupation that of 'stationary engineman (down the coal mine)'. So Vardy was a relatively mature and experienced miner aged about 31 when he received his mines rescue medal.

Silver fifteen-year service NCB mines rescue medal presented to A. Gunn, Rotherham Rescue Station, c.1951.

at local, regional and national museums. The quality of these medals was often high, many being struck in silver and gold, and most are inscribed with the recipient's name. Medals, certificates and trophies were also presented after first aid competitions and a photographic record was often made of a successful team (and more rarely of an individual award winner). Again, these are – or should be – treasured family history items. Very many NCB awards and certificates were presented, including those won in recreational and sporting contexts: pigeon racing, horticultural pursuits, football, cricket and athletics. I still have small card certificates won by my father at NCB cage bird shows. For long service, the NCB also presented (or gave out) certificates, and one or more of these may survive among family papers.

Clothing and equipment

Before c.1930 most miners wore old clothes and even dispensed with these when at work in hot and cramped conditions. A cloth cap was the most common head wear. Basic tools such as picks, wedges and shovels had to be bought and were inscribed for recognition and ownership. After 1947 and nationalisation a more formal system and uniform gradually emerged, to the point where miners were perhaps the most visible of workers both underground and on the surface. Carrying items via a leather belt around the waist such as cap lamp battery, safety lamp and self-rescuer added to the weight of other safety and work gear and produced an almost astronaut-like appearance. The more modern items are fairly easy to obtain, even clothing, though old picks and shovels will probably be confined to the garden shed or garage.

Chapter 8

COLLIERIES AND COALFIELDS

Coalfields post-1947

If your mining ancestor worked after nationalisation in 1947 it is important to be aware of the new administrative structure of the industry as this information may help with research, and certainly make the process much more understandable when placing him in context via official publications. On the morning of 1 January 1947 (known as Vesting Day), during what became one of the worst winters on record, posters appeared at every pit, declaring: 'This colliery is now managed by the National Coal Board on behalf of the people.' Nationalisation concerned about 950 directly operated mines and 480 small mines employing fewer than thirty workers, which were allowed to functioned privately under license. A variety of other assets included large numbers of houses for miners and officials. Lord Hyndley, the NCB's first chairman, and nine directors established eight Divisional Boards to administer the industry from headquarters at Hobart House in London. The new Divisions were as follows:

Scotland

Northern (Durham, Northumberland and Cumberland)

North-Eastern (Yorkshire)

North-Western (Lancashire, Cheshire and North Wales)

East Midlands (north Derbyshire, Nottinghamshire, south Derbyshire and Leicestershire)

West Midlands (north Staffordshire, south Staffordshire, Shropshire, Cannock Chase and Warwickshire)

South-Western (south Wales, Forest of Dean, Bristol and Somerset)

Kent

The new NCB Divisions were divided into forty-eight smaller units known as Areas. The collieries, however, remained as basic operational units, with the managers responsible under the Coal Mines Acts for the safety and conduct of their pits. Despite its decline, in 1947 the coalmining industry remained the biggest single employer of labour in the UK, with about 800,000 workers; and had an annual turnover (from the pits alone) of £480m (roughly £12.45m today).

As a result of the rapid run-down of the industry from the 1960s, Areas and Divisions were amalgamated and allocated new names and/or numbers, until the **British Coal Corporation** (BCC) succeeded the NCB in 1987. When the **Coal Authority** took over from BCC in 1994 there were fewer than twenty deep mines still at work.

Lists of coal mines

Which pit or pits did he work at? Finding the name and location of mines where your ancestor worked (and indeed the coal owner, for record purposes) are crucial research requirements. But from the nineteenth century there were many thousands of pits, ranging from small 'day-holes' and drift mines lasting a few months or years, to large colliery complexes working for more than a century. The Coal Authority estimates that there are at least 168,000 old 'mine entries' known, an astonishing figure. Names also changed, especially through changes of ownership and mergers. Many pits were also known locally by slang or even comic names, wonderful allocations which especially occur in oral testimonies. I once interviewed an old miner who worked at 'Bob's Oyle', which was Kilnhurst Colliery, situated near Rotherham in south Yorkshire, but the pit was known as Thrybergh Hall Colliery before nationalisation. Take care with the 'life of pit' dates. Sinking could take place over several years due to geological problems and wartime delays. Also, some pits continued for many months *after* official production closure, before total abandonment. Unfortunately some mines were included in official mineral statistics after they had closed. So care is needed. If your mining ancestor lived a short distance from a particular colliery, don't assume that he worked there! Even in 'one-pit towns' such as Ashington, miners, for a variety of reasons might travel five, ten or more miles to work. This mobility increased with the development of both tram and special rail services during the early twentieth century; some colliery companies or enterprising carriers ran services especially for miners living away from their pit. As a first step it's not a bad idea to check mine entries in trade directories, especially from the last quarter of the nineteenth century.

The extent of this book does not allow for complete listings but some of the most useful online and printed sources are:

- **Victoria County Histories (VCH)** (www.victoriacountyhistory.ac.uk). Colliery names and background information may be worth checking for your area – if available. The relevant published/part-published volumes include Cumberland, Derbyshire, Durham, Lancashire, Leicestershire, Nottinghamshire, Somerset, Staffordshire, and Warwickshire. The VCH is based at the Institute of Historical Research,

University of London. The online information about Derbyshire includes a downloadable list of collieries operational from 1854–1881, taken from mineral statistics compiled by the Geological Survey. Digital versions of the VCH can also be accessed via the British History Online site (www.british-history.ac.uk).

- **British Geological Survey (BGS)** (www.bgs.ac.uk). The BGS produced annual lists of mines (by county, including owners etc) from 1854–1881 and these can be consulted at their Keyworth library by prior appointment (a: BGS, Keyworth, Nottingham NG12 5GG; t: 0115 936 3205; em: libuser@bgs.ac.uk). Information about current active mines is via a purchasable database on the Minerals UK website, see http://www.bgs.ac.uk/mineralsuk/mines/dmq.htlm.
- **Hunt's Mineral Statistics.** The 1854–1871 volumes (*Memoirs of the Geological Survey of Great Britain*) are available free on Google Books. Some libraries will house them, certainly national ones. **HM Inspectorates' Annual Reports.** Official lists of mines were published from 1872 (to 1882) and are generally reliable though Hunt's Mineral Statistics do contain omitted data. Ideally both should be consulted.
- **Mining and Mineral Statistics**, published annually for 1882–1896, as mine listings appear in the 1883–1887 volumes. A separate annual publication, the **List of Mines**, covers 1888–1938 and for some later dates.
- **Colliery Yearbook and Coal Trades Directory.** For 1922–47 (pre-nationalisation) and 1948–64 (NCB Divisions and Areas).
- **Guide to Coalfields** [London Colliery Guardian Co. Ltd]. Lists of collieries by NCB Divisions and Areas (including useful small location maps of mines and administrative headquarters), from 1948–1980s.

Official statistical sources were published as Command Papers by Parliament and are therefore held in Parliamentary Papers in many research libraries. They can be accessed online at http://parlpapers.chadwyk.co.uk/home.do usually via the subscribing organisation. A list of primary mining statistical sources and where some can be found can be seen by reference to http://people.exeter.ac.uk/pfclaugh/mhinf/location.htm.

- **The Coalmining History Resource Centre** (www.cmhrc.co.uk) has an A-Z list of mines relating to all NCB divisional maps.
- **The Durham Mining Museum** (www.dmm.org.uk) has mine lists for Northumberland and Durham, Cumberland, Westmoreland, Yorkshire (North Riding) and part of Lancashire, for the years 1888, 1902, 1914, 1921, 1930, 1934, 1940, 1947, 1950, 1960, 1970, 1980 and

1991. The site links to Ian Winstanley's old coalmining history website (via rootsweb/ancestry.com free pages) for complete listings for all coalfield regions for 1869, 1880, 1908, 1918, 1938, 1945. Also linked are the online lists for 1896, produced by the Peak District Mines Historical Society (see below). The DMM's lists are very useful because the detail may include pit locations, addresses, and names of managers, owners, seams – and the number of men employed.

- **The Peak District Mining History Society Museum** (www.pdmhs. com/MiningMuseum.asp), under 'Resources', currently has a mines index for 1896 for Derbyshire, Scotland, Wales, South of England, Midlands, North of England, compiled from the annual mines inspectors' reports. The list has the mine name, situation, owner and postal address, manager and under manager's name, number of workers employed and main coal seam worked.

- **Colin Jackson's mine database.** Pit check collectors often have an encyclopaedic knowledge of colliery names, before and after nationalisation (1947). Colin Jackson's latest (2002) *A-Z List of Colliery Names*, lists 5,822 collieries, includes the pre-1947 owner, coalfield situation and dates of sinking and closing (where known). This is an excellent reference compilation. It can be purchased from the bookshop at the National Coal Mining Museum for England (t: 01924 848806).

- **Royal Commissions on Ancient Monuments Publications.** The three Royal Commissions responsible for recording the built heritage in England (RCHME/English Heritage), Scotland (RCAHMS) and Wales (RCAHMW) embarked upon emergency programmes to record fast-disappearing mine sites. Three useful publications are: A. Ayris, and S. Gould, *Colliery Landscapes. An aerial survey of the deep-mined coal industry in England* (English Heritage, 1995) which usefully includes grid references and reference to the National Library of Air Photographs (part of the National Monuments Record); Welsh collieries are covered in Stephen Hughes, et al, *Collieries of Wales*, RCAHMW (1995); and for Scotland see M.A. Oglethorpe's comprehensive *Scottish Collieries. An Inventory of the Scottish Coal Industry in the Nationalised Era* (RCAHMS, 2006), which has a county-by-county gazetteer of nationalised collieries with a site number linking each to the the RCAHMS database – and, remarkably, there's a photograph of every colliery.

- **National Coal Mine Museum for Wales (The Big Pit).** An impressive list of c.1,500 Welsh mines can be seen if you visit the main exhibition at The Big Pit (National Coal Museum: www.museumwales.ac. uk/ en/bigpit)

Printed maps and plans

Maps for family history are often underused or even ignored. Not to obtain a detailed map showing the colliery where your mining ancestor and his mates worked, his route to work, and the adjacent or nearby village where he lived, would be a missed opportunity. Especially so since maps are fairly easily found, particularly from the second half of the nineteenth century. Which ones are the most useful? The Old Series (1805–73) of the old one inch to one mile Ordnance Survey maps, subsequent editions of the New Series and the modern 2 cm to 1 km [1:50,000] Landranger series record relatively few collieries/colliery sites. A recent 'Pin the Pits' campaign has gained some support for former, usually regenerated, pit sites to be marked with a suitable symbol on the popular/leisure OS maps, though space would surely limit inclusion to the larger collieries. The 2½ inch (1:25,000 Pathfinder) maps are more detailed, especially the early editions. Better still are the large-scale six-inch (1:10,000) and 25-inch maps, first issued on a county basis from 1856–1893. These will show the pit buildings, railway sidings, associated features such as coke ovens, brickworks, aerial flights, muckstacks and of course nearby streets and individual houses. Most central libraries and certainly county record offices will stock some originals which you can have copied quite cheaply – though it can be frustrating when your colliery falls between two or more sheets! Several companies also publish facsimile and scale-adapted OS maps. The growing series from Alan Godfrey (www.alangodfrey.co.uk) is particularly useful even though coverage, from c.1900, is not yet complete for the coalfields; do check this site on a regular basis as additions are made on a monthly basis. The Godfrey maps have the benefit of a short description, by a local historian, of the area; and as a further bonus usually reproduce extracts from a local trade directory, and therefore are of tremendous value for the family historian. Heritage Cartography (www.victoriantownmaps) may also be worth checking as they are producing high-quality town and village maps based on the early large-scale surveys of the OS which commenced in the 1840s. You can also view online OS maps of different periods via www.old-maps.co.uk and purchase from the same. Cassini (www.cassinimaps.com) have in recent years reproduced historical OS one-inch maps enlarged and re-projected to exactly match the modern Landranger versions. The Charles Close Society for the Study of Ordnance Survey Maps (www.charlesclose society.org) is the authoritative site on British mapping and well worth consulting.

Mid-twentieth-century published town plans such as those produced by Geographia are also useful for showing the sites of the larger collieries. In the 1970s an 82-year-old retired mining engineer who attended one of my WEA local history classes plotted sixty colliery sites (as well as providing index card reference details for each pit) on a folded Geographia map. There are of course many kinds of regional and local geological maps and plans that may also be useful. From 1850, Inspection of Coal Mines Acts required the inspectors to ensure that plans of coal mines were available and effective. An accurate plan of any abandoned mine had to be deposited with the Secretary of State. Mine abandonment plans are now housed at the Coal Authority's Mining Records Office in Mansfield (www.coal.gov.uk; t: 01623 637 233; em: thecoalauthority@coal.gov.uk) and there is a downloadable brochure regarding their services. Do check with them prior to making an appointment.

Very useful is The National Archives' Maps for Family and Local History online guide which has links to the other British national archive sites and several English counties: www.nationalarchives.gov.uk/maps/maps-family-local-history.htm.

Further reading

Charles Masters, *Essential Maps for Family Historians* (Countryside Books, 2009)
Richard Oliver, *Ordnance Survey Maps. A Concise Guide for Historians* (The Charles Close Society, 1993)
—— *The Historian's Guide to Ordnance Survey Maps* (The National Council for Social Service, 1964)

Colliery names

It's worthwhile considering the origin of the name (or names) of the colliery where your ancestor worked. Many are descriptive, after a geographic or geological name or landmark, or the type of mine, for example Greencroft Tower Drift (N. Durham). Others are named after the owner or a famous person or event: Balaklava (W.Yorkshire). Euphemistic names are not uncommon, as well as the use of female christian names: California (Wigan); Isabella (Northumberland). Where the word 'Main' is used (especially in Yorkshire), it refers to the famous Barnsley seam as the primary coal worked (or once worked).

Part 2

WHERE TO FIND INFORMATION

The Scottish Mining Museum, on the site of the former Lady Victoria Colliery.

Chapter 9

REGIONAL SOURCES

'Start local' is good advice for anyone beginning to research their mining ancestors. Most local libraries in former coalfield areas will have some general information about coalmining on their shelves and in their collections. The archives and libraries featured here contain some of the more important mining sources or have particular items of local interest. Do bear in mind that relatively few individual collieries are well documented (indeed record-keeping in the industry as a whole was not good prior to nationalisation in 1947). However, it is possible to compile a reasonably accurate local picture by reference to a variety of sources. Maps (and sometimes plans and aerial views) showing the location of pits are often available and should be made use of whenever possible, as should other somewhat neglected sources such as oral history recordings, estate papers and business records. You may not be able to find a photographic image of your miner in a local collection, but there are some superb and easily accessible local and regional picture libraries for images of collieries and communities – and of the miners themselves. Use of the moving image is also a surprisingly overlooked source, and yet there are many wonderful clips and documentary films available, viewable via regional film archives. The most basic and most detailed source for most mining matters is found in local and regional newspapers, which are becoming more and more accessible and searchable through digitisation projects.

Prior to visiting the archives listed and described in this guide you will usually need to make an appointment and/or obtain a reader's ticket. The same may be true for a local study centre, museum library and certainly for an independent facility. It is always best to check the visitor guidelines posted on the archive's/library's website beforehand, where you will also be able to find out about opening times and other requirements, and also information on disabled access/facilities. Although much preliminary work can be done using online catalogues and online information some records may not yet be digitally available, or not yet catalogued, and there may be new accessions. Despite the convenience of the internet there is nothing better than actually visiting and using a variety of records in an archive or library where professional help is at hand.

Do remember that you may not necessarily have to reside in the local authority's library service area in order to access material online or in person. Joining the library in person (and sometimes quite easily online) will provide you with an enormous amount of research potential via your own computer/device and at library terminals. If for whatever reason you are unable to visit in person most libraries and archives offer a paid enquiry and/or research service.

Some university libraries and their special archive collections contain important coalmining records, which are perhaps underused for family and local history

British coalfields c.1900, from T.H. Cockin's An Elemental Class-Book of Practical Coal-Mining.

research. You do not need to be a university student or academic to access these, but do contact the librarian/archivist beforehand before visiting.

Joining a family history society in the area or areas where your mining ancestor lived and worked is bound to assist your research as you will not only have access to a variety of source material, actually and online, but will also be able to make friendly contact with individuals who may be able to share and/or provide advice.

Although increasingly collections of objects are being placed online, actually visiting relevant museums, heritage centres and places of interest in a coalfield region will always add a new and meaningful dimension to your research, helping to build up a contextual picture of the life and times of your coalminer ancestor; and in some places you can even gain some insight into what it was like to be miner through a guided tour or 'underground experience'.

I have tried to be as up-to-date and as accurate as possible regarding the contact details of the places in this regional guide and have indicated where some archives/libraries were in the course of moving to new headquarters or merging with partner organisations. Do check websites for the latest information. Updates and the very latest information from most large libraries and archives are now also available via their entries on Facebook and Twitter.

This guide covers all of the former coalfield regions of Britain. Each regional research section is preceded by a brief geographical/historical/administrative overview of the area and is then arranged as follows:

- Archives and libraries
- Places to visit
- Family history societies
- Online sources
- Useful books, film and video

SCOTLAND

The coalfields of Scotland

Most of the Scottish coalfields occupied the broad lowland stretching from the Firth of Forth to the Firth of Clyde, an area of about 90 miles by 20 miles. There were four main fields. In order of production (c.1913) these were: Lanark (Lanark, Dumbarton, Renfrew, Linlithgow, Stirling and Clackmannan); Fife (Fife and Kinross); Ayr; and Lothian (Edinburgh, Haddington, Peebles). Small, detached fields also existed at Argyle, Dumfries and Sutherland.

Day-to-day accidents were reported frequently in local newspapers. Apart from Nitshill in 1851 (sixty-one fatalities) Scotland escaped the massive disasters that took place in the main English coalfields during the middle years of Victoria's reign, but at least 207 men and boys lost their lives in explosions at Blantyre, Lanarkshire in 1877. Another twenty-eight Blantyre miners were killed two years later and there were major disasters at Udsen (seventy-three dead) and Mauricewood (sixty-three dead) in 1887 and 1889 respectively.

In 1913, just before the start of the First World War, there were about 150,000 persons employed in Scottish pits, compared with only 88,000 in 1895, an indication of rapid development. At the start of nationalisation in 1947 the Scottish Division of the National Coal Board had responsibility for 275 collieries formerly run by 120 separate companies but seventy-nine of these, small drift mines, were granted licenses to operate privately. The situation was fairly grim as the industry had been in long-term decline since at least 1920. Many near redundant and redundant Scottish miners migrated to 'safer' coalfields such as Yorkshire.

By the early 1950s there were 185 Scottish collieries accounting for about 12 per cent of the Britain's total output (only 3 per cent less than in 1913). But the labour force had shrunk to its 1890s level, about 85,000. Fife and Clackmannan, with large reserves near the coast and under the sea, had the most potential. The Lothian coalfield also had rich reserves, 'with the best mining conditions in Scotland', according to the NCB. The Central coalfield, much of Lanarkshire, had become exhausted and the Ayr/Dumfries fields were run down. The relatively shallow seams led the Scottish NCB to invest in the opening of numerous short-life drift mines. In addition several so-called 'superpits' (Bilston Glen, Killoch, Monktonhall and Seafield) were sunk. The showpiece Rothes Colliery, in production from 1957, closed only five years later, despite the massive efforts of the miners. The severe pit closures of the 1960s left fewer than fifty mines in Scotland and this number was reduced to just fourteen at the start of the 1984 miners' strike. Deep mining in Scotland ended with the closure of Monktonhall (Midlothian, opened 1967) in 1997, the even shorter-lived Castlebridge Colliery (Clackmannanshire, opened 1979) in 1999; and finally when the Longannet Complex (Fife, opened 1969) closed in 2002 following a catastrophic flood.

The Scottish coalfields were administered by the Scottish Divisional Coal Board from headquarters in Edinburgh. There were eight areas: West Fife, Lothians, Central West, Central East, West Ayr, Alloa, East Fife and East Ayr.

Regional source material for Scottish mining is to be found in a variety of locations, from municipal archives and academic institutions to local studies libraries, museums and heritage centres. A summary of the main Scottish archives can be seen online at www.scan.org.uk (Scottish Archive Network).

Archives and libraries
Ayrshire

Ayrshire Archives
Watson Peat Building, SAC Auchincruive, Ayr, KA6 5HW
t. 01292 521 819   e. archives@south-ayrshire.gov.uk
www.ayrshirearchives.org.uk

Online guide. Oral history collection includes coalminers. Ayrshire coalmining resource/research pack contains documents, maps, extracts from sound archive, bibliography and sources. Ayrshire Archives is incorporated into the **Burns Monument Centre** (Kilmarnock) and the Heritage Centre in Saltcoats (see below), both having both archival and local history materials. Although a separate council department, family and local history material is also held at the Carnegie Library in Ayr; see immediately below for contact and content details.

South Ayrshire Libraries Local Studies: Carnegie Library
12 Main Street, Ayr, KA8 8EB
t. 01292 272 231   e. localhistory@south-ayrshire.gov.uk
www.south-ayrshire.gov.uk/libraries/localhistory

Wide range of publications relating to mining in Scotland and Ayrshire. Relevant monographs by local history societies include a reprint of a 1913 report on conditions in Ayrshire miners' rows. MI's. OS maps from 1856. Large photographic collection, arranged by locality, includes some mining images. Local newspapers from 1803 on microfilm; card index to *The Ayrshire Post* 1920–1960 includes many mining references. 'Coalmining in Ayrshire' resource pack produced jointly by Ayrshire Sound Archive and Ayrshire Federation of Historical Societies, 1988. HM Mines Inspector's Report on Knockshinnoch Castle Colliery accident 1950.

East Ayrshire Libraries
t. 01563 554300 (general enquiries)   e. elibraries@east-ayrshire
http://www.east-ayrshire.gov.uk/CommunityLifeAndLeisure/
LibrariesAndArchives.

Use of online catalogue via keywords will achieve many coal-related results. Local and special collections include The Keir Hardie Collection. Local history and family history items are housed at the **Burns Monument Centre**, Kay Park, Kilmarnock, East Ayrshire, KA3 7RU (t. 01563 576695; e. info@burnsmonumentcentre.com). Also see Ayrshire Achives (above) and www.coalcollections.org.

North Ayrshire Archives/Heritage Centres
Manse Street, Saltcoats, Ayrshire, KA21 5AA
t. 01294 464 174   e. naheritage@north-ayrshire.gov.uk
www.ers.north-ayrshire.gov.uk

Stevenson Coal Company (Cunninghame of Auchenharvie Papers). Ayrshire Sound Archive (Ayrshire Federation of Historical Societies tapes and illustrations). Local newspapers e.g. *Ardrosssan & Saltcoats Herald* 1857–2012. Printed sources include *Auchenharvie Colliery History* (Three Towns Local History Group) and Janet Retter's *Drongan: the story of a mining village*. Also see www.coalcollections.org.

Clackmannanshire

Clackmannanshire Archives and Local Studies Service
Archives contact: Lime Tree House, Castle Street, Alloa, FK10 1EX
t. 01259 452 272
http://www.clacksweb.org.uk/culture/archives

Alloa Library (archives can also be ordered for consultation here):
Spiers Centre, 29 Primrose Street, Alloa, FK10 1JJ
t. 01259 452 262   e. libraries@clacks.gov.uk
http://www.clacksweb.org.uk/culture/localhistoryandlocalstudies

Online library catalogue. Local Studies/Archive listings soon online. The Walter Murray Local Studies has many family history resources including local newspapers, photographs. Devon Valley Colliery and Glenochil Mine plans. Devon Colliery 1897 disaster report. Alloa & Hillfoots Searchlite (miners' newspaper) microfilm 10/1925 to 6/1026.

Dunbartonshire
East Dunbartonshire Information and Archives
The William Patrick Library, 2–4 West High Street, Kirkintilloch, G66 1AD
t. 0141 777 3143 (local studies) 0141 777 3142 (archives)
e. libraries@eastdunbarton.gov.uk or archives@eastdunbarton.gov.uk
http://www.edlc.co.uk/libraries.aspx

Covers the 'old' counties of Dunbartonshire, Stirlingshire and Lanarkshire. Browse archive collections online and search archive collection via online catalogue: use keywords such as 'mining', 'coal', 'colliery/colliery name' and 'mine' for many results eg, Summburgh Mining Co. (GD101/14/179); Miners' Relief Fund 1928–32 (BK/15/5): Woodhall Esate (GDC01): list of colliery employees (Meiklehill, GD52/2); Cardowen Colliery closure (GD112/1); Miners' Welfare (GD49/6). Local and family history collections mainly at William Patrick Library and Brookwood Library (Bearsden). Extensive mining photograph collection relating to local collieries; local newspapers (*Kirkintilloch Herald* 1886-to date; *Milngavie & Bearsden Herald* 1901-to date) and newspaper index/cuttings files; Cadder Valley Colliery Disaster Report; mining books and printed material including maps and plans: search by keyword as above.

West Dunbartonshire Libraries and Archives
Strathleven Place, Dumbarton, G82 1BD
t. 01389 608 965   e. dumbarton.library@west-dunbarton.gov.uk
www.west-dunbarton.gov.uk/arts-culture-and-libraries/libraries/branches/
dumbarton

Dumbarton Heritage Centre has information on the history of the Dumbarton and Vale of Leven areas. Local studies and archives are located at Clydebank (0141 5622 434) and Dumbarton libraries (01389 608 965).

East Lothian
John Gray Centre (East Lothian Council)
New heritage centre combining library, museum gallery, Local History Centre and East Lothian Archives
15 Lodge Street, Haddington, East Lothian, EH41 3DX
t. 01620 820695 (local history/archives) 01620 820 680 (library)
e. jgc@eastlothian.gov.uk   www.johngraycentre.org

Genealogy book collection. Newspapers, printed material, photographs etc.

Fife
Dunfermline Carnegie Library
1 Abbot Street, Dunfermline, KY12 7NL
t. 01383 602 365   e. dunfermline.library@fife.gov.uk
www.fifedirect.org.uk

Extensive local and family history resources. Mining items searchable via archive online catalogue. HM Mines Inspectors' Reports Scotland 1854–55, 1910–13, 1930,

1950 and East of Scotland: 1856–1909. Oral history 'mining memories' mini disk recordings. Mining Memorial Book (updated at www.users.zetnet.co.uk/mmartin/ fifepits [see useful online sources below]).

Kirkcaldy Central Library
War Memorial Grounds, Kirkcaldy, KY1 1YG
t. 01592 412 879   e. kirkcaldy.library@fife.gov.uk
www.fifedirect.org.uk

Fife Council Libraries also have ephemera from the 1984/85 strike in Kirkcaldy and Cowdenbeath areas.

Glasgow

The Mitchell Library (Glasgow City Libraries)
North Street, Glasgow, G3 7DN
(Archives is on Level 2; Family History Centre is on Level 3)
t. 0141 287 2999   e. historyandglasgow@glasgowlife.org.uk
www.glasgowlife.org.uk/libraries/the-mitchell-library/Pages/home.aspx

'One of the largest libraries in Europe' and a 'one-stop shop' for family history research. Online catalogue. Special Collections and City Archives. Courses for research and tours.

List of resources e.g. family and estate archives. Virtual Mitchell (see online sources below). Graham papers (Bargeddie, Old Monkland, Barrowfield, Calton, Bredisholm and Old M collieries); Armitage Shanks Ltd (Ayrshire colliery plans); plans of Sculliongour, Balgass and Woodhead coal and lime workings. Sound archive. Also see www.coalcollections.org.

University of Glasgow Library and Archives
Library: Hillhead Street, Glasgow, G12 8QE
Archives: 13 Thurso Street, Glasgow, G11 6PE
www.gla.ac.uk/library
t. 0141 330 6704   e. library@lib.gla.ac.uk
t. 0141 330 5515   e. enquiries@archives.gla.ac.uk

Ardenrigg Coal Company records (N. Lanarkshire); Ayrshire Coal Owners Association; Bairds & Dalmellington; Coalmasters of Scotland; Gladsmuir Collier; Glencairn Coal Co.; Halbeath Colliery; Lanarkshire Coal Masters' Association; Mining Association of Great Britain archive; William Baird papers. HM Mines Inspectors' Reports Scottish Division 1957–1975.

Lanarkshire

Airdrie Library Discovery Room
Wellwynd, Airdre, ML6 0AG
t. 01236 758 070   e. online form   www.northlanarkshire.gov.uk

North Lanarkshire Heritage Centre
1 High Road, Motherwell, ML1 3HU
t. 01698 524 712   e. online form   www.northlanarkshire.gov.uk

178

Archives: records of John Alson & Son (U2); coal company records: Blackbands (U2/5/02); Burnbank (U2/5/03); Gartness (U2/5/09); Monkland Glen (U2/5/16); Leaend (U2/5/26; Chapel Miners' Welfare and Community Society 1851–1994 (U25); Wm Dixon iron & coal masters, Coatbridge 1810–1911 (U47); Stanrigg Disaster Relief Fund 1918–1928 (U52); Anderson Boyes & Co. coal-cutting machine-makers 1904–1994; estate papers of Carrick-Buchanan 1560–1960 (U1); Baird papers (relating to local mining). Large photographic collection includes miners, cottages, miners' welfare, collieries etc. Oral history collection includes several miners. Local history room (e. museums@northlan.gov.uk) holds a wide variety of information on coal-mining and miners. Report of housing, 1910. Reports on disasters e.g. Blantyre and Stanrigg. Local newspapers: *Motherwell Times* and *Wishaw Press* indexed by surname. Ephemera collection includes strike items, list of names of on-cost workers at Cleland Colliery 1849–1865.

Hamilton Town House Library
102 Cadzow Street, Hamilton, ML3 6HH
t. 01698 452122   e. libhc@library.s-lanark.org.uk
http://slleisureandculture.co.uk/info/87/hamilton_town_house_library

Library has extensive reference and local history collection, plus family history resources.

Lanark Library
6 Hope Street, Lanark, ML11 7LZ
t. 01555 661 144   e. libin@library.s-lanark.org
http://slleisureandculture.co.uk/info/89/lanark_library

Local history collection and general family history resources. Photographic collection for Coalburn village (c.1880–1930) and 'Coalburn Chronicles' – papers of Jim Hamilton, 1980s–1990s).

Midlothian

Midlothian Libraries and Archives
9 Clerk Street, Loanhead, Midlothian, EH20 9DR
t. 0131 271 3980   e. library.hq@midlothian.gov.uk

Online library catalogue. Nine local libraries. Local newspaper: *Dalkeith Advertiser* (from 1869).

Stirlingshire

Stirling Libraries and Archives
Libraries: Central Library, Corn Exchange Road, Stirling, FK8 2HX
t. 01786 432 107   e. centrallibrary@stirling.gov.uk

Archives: 5 Borrowmeadow Road, Stirling, FK7 7UW
t. 01786 450745   e. archive@stirling.gov.uk
www.stirling.gov.uk/services/community-life-and-leisure/libraries-and-archives

Central library and sixteen branch libraries. Online catalogue: SEDAR. Local and special collections: local history and heritage and researching your family history. Local newspapers e.g. *Stirling Journal & Advertiser* (for disasters and strikes

179

especially) and also Valuation Rolls, which show the head of each household and occupation (therefore good for miners' rows).

Falkirk Community Trust Libraries and Archives
Library: Victoria Buildings, Queen Street, Falkirk, FK2 7AF
t. 01324 506 800   e. libraries@falkirkcommunitytrust.org

Archives: Callendar House, Falkirk, FK1 1YR
t. 01324 503 779   e. archives@falkirkcommunitytrust.org
www.falkirkcommunitytrust.org/heritage/archives

Online library catalogue. Eight libraries. Local history collection includes a large number of coal and coalmining items: books, pamphlets, photographs, resource packs, cuttings; also information on the Redding and Herbertshire pit disasters. The *Falkirk Herald* is indexed from 1845 and Falkirk Death Notices indexed from 1845–1910. Archives can be searched for via the Collection Browser; the collection includes coal company records for local collieries. The Russell and Aitken archive contains many colliery plans. Oral history collection includes recordings of several former mineworkers, including Kinneil Colliery. Redding pit disaster. Useful family history advice pages.

West Lothian

West Lothian Libraries and Archives
Local History Library: County Buildings, High Street, Linlithgow, EH49 7EZ
t. 01506 282 491   e. localhistory@westlothian.gov.uk
www.westlothian.gov.uk/tourism/LocalHistory

Archives and Records Centre:
9 Dunlop Square, Deans Industrial Estate, Livingston, EH54 8SB
t. 01506 773 770   e. archive@westlothian.gov.uk
www.westlothian.gov.uk

Online library catalogue. Fourteen community libraries. Photographic collection on Flickr photostream includes mining. Family history resources. Local newspapers e.g. *West Lothian Courier* (from 1873) is indexed (http://wlhas.westlothian.gov.uk). Downloadable introduction to archives. Lothian Lives project; Black Collection: coal mining in the Lothians (view at Penicuik Library or at the WL Archives). Valuation Rolls 1855 onwards. Mining Deaths in Great Britain 1850–1914 (Winstanley). United Collieries Active Service Rolls 1914–18. Catalogue of plans of abandoned mines. List of local mines and their nicknames. Novels of ex-miner Tom Hanlin of Armadale, 1930s-1950s.

Edinburgh

Edinburgh Central Library and City Archives
Library: 7–9 George IV Bridge, Edinburgh, EH1 1EG
t. 0131 242 8000   e. libraries@edinburgh.gov.uk
www.edinburgh.gov.uk/libraries

Archives: Level 1, City Chambers, 253 High Street, Edinburgh, EH1 1YJ
t. 0131 529 4616   e. archives@edinburgh.gov.uk
www.edinburgh.gov.uk/archives

Online catalogue. Card indexes for coal mining items. Online sources for family historians. Capital Collections image library.

National Archives of Scotland – see national sources
National Library of Scotland – see national sources
Scottish Mining Museum – see national sources

Places to visit
Doon Valley Museum
Dalmellington, KA6 7QY
t. 01292 550 633e.   e. elaine.mackie@east-ayrshire.gov.uk
www.visiteastayrshire.com or www.east-ayrshire.gov.uk

Community museum and art gallery with a 'research lab'. Large collection of old photographs and maps available for family and local history research. Permanent displays feature coalmining and its effect on local communities. Doon Valley FHS meet there.

Prestongrange Industrial Heritage Museum
Morrison's Haven, Prestonpans, East Lothian, EH32 9RY
t. 0131 653 2904   e. online form
www.prestongrange.org

Managed by East Lothian Council Museums, the industrial heritage site includes the old colliery, which functioned from c.1830 to 1962, and its Cornish beam engine. Site is open all year but visitor centre, with exhibitions, from April to October. Guided tours, events and trails.

Scottish Mining Museum – see national sources

Summerlee Museum of Industrial Life
Heritage Way, Coatbridge, North Lanarkshire, ML5 1QD
t. 01236 638 460   e. museums@northlan.gov.uk
http://www.museumsgalleriesscotland.org.uk/member/sumerlee-
museum-of-industrial-life

Large site of former ironworks located by Monkland Canal branch. The museum features include Cardowen Colliery winding engine. A working tram takes visitors down a reconstructed drift mine. Miners' cottages, saw mill and wood-shed. Industrial/social collections include many mining and personal items. Electric tramway. North Lanarkshire Council Museums & Heritage Museum collection includes a range of artefacts relating to mining in Scotland and North Lanarkshire especially.

Smaller displays of coalmining artefacts, images and information about local coalmining can be seen when visiting many other Scottish museums and heritage centres and/or viewing their online collection catalogues. Some regional examples are: Auld Kirk Museum (Kirkintilloch, http://museumsgalleriesscotland.org.uk/member/

auld-kirk-museum); The Baird Institute (Cumnock, www.visiteast ayrshire. com); Clackmannanshire Museums Service (www.clacksweb.org.uk); Dick Institute (Kilmarnock, www.visiteastayrshire.com); John Gray Centre (Haddington, www.johngraycentre.org); Kirkaldy Museum (Kirkcaldy, www.fife.gov.uk) and Whitworth Community Museum within Whitburn Library (www.westlothian. gov.uk).

Family history societies

Visit http://www.safhs.org.uk/members.asp for a complete listing of the members of The Scottish Association of Family History Societies. Most have research facilities and a wide variety of online resources, forums and publications. Coalfield area examples include:

Alloway and Southern Ayrshire FHS www.asafhs.co.uk
Borders FHS www.bordersfhs.org.uk
Central Scotland FHS www.csfhs.org.uk
Dumfries and Galloway FHS www.dgfhs.org.uk
East Ayrshire FHS www.eastaryshirefhs.co.uk
Fife Family History Society www.eastaryshirefhs.co.uk
Lanarkshire FHS www.lanarkshirefhs.org.uk
Lothians FHS www.lothiansfhs.org.uk
Renfrewshire FHS www.renfrewshirefhs.co.uk
West Fife Family History Group www.dunfermlineheritage.org.uk
West Lothian FHS www.wlfhs.org.uk

Online sources

Ayrshire Ancestors www.ayrshireancestors.com

Genealogical help site via subscription with some free services.

Ayrshire History www.ayrshirehistory.org.uk

David McClure's site includes the local history of Ayrshire's parishes, towns and villages and Ayrshire miners' rows.

Ayrshire Roots www.ayrshireroots.com and ayrshireroots.co.uk

Large site tailored to help you research your Ayrshire ancestry. Use 'coal miner' etc as key words – or a family name or place.

Dunfermline Heritage Roots www.dunfermlineheritage.org.uk

Part of Dunfermline Heritage Community Projects (DHCP). Living in the Past area has a history of local coalmining. Useful family and local history information.

Fife Mining Heritage Society www.fifeminingheritage.org.uk

David Reid's 'Preserving mining memories for future generations' site. Registered charity founded in 1995. Information – text and images – about the Fife coalfield and collieries. Includes items of wider interest, e.g. Bevin Boys.

Fife Pits   www.users.zetnet.co.uk/mmartin/fifepits

Michael Martin's excellent site is a comprehensive online source for Fife mining and miners. Navigate via four menus and the Memorial Book contains over 2,300 entries.

Future Museum.co.uk South West Scotland   www.futuremuseum.co.uk

Search museum collections. Features include mining and quarrying (Life and Work key industries area) and coal.

Genuki: Scotland genealogy – see national sources

Lothian Lives   www.lothianlives.org.uk

Records and stories taken from the city of Edinburgh, East, Mid and West Lothian archives. Browse menu. Black Collection includes scrapbook about coal and ironstone mining in the Lothians and Isabella Somerville 'the oldest pit woman in the world'.

Miners Voices   www.miners-voices.homecall.co.uk

Excellent site originated by ex-miner Johnny Temperton in 2007 and dedicated 'to the living history of the Ayrshire miners'. Oral history recordings, documents and photographs. Miners' strikes and disasters. Alex Mills 'union man'.

Scottish Coal Collections – see national sources
Scotland on Film (Mines) – see national sources
ScotlandsPeople – see national sources
Scottish Mining – see national sources
Scottish Screen Archive – see national sources

Sorbie family/Lanarkshire Mining
www.sorbie.net/lanarkshire_mining_industry.htm

History of mining in Lanarkshire.

Virtual Mitchell   www.mitchelllibrary.org/virtualmitchell

Glasgow's Mitchell Library's online image library.

Useful books, film and video

R. Page Arnot, *A History of the Scottish Miners From the Earliest of Times* (George Allen & Unwin, 1955)

R.H. Campbell, *The Scottish Miners, 1874–1939, Volume I: Industry, Work and Community* (Ashgate, 2000)

R.H. Campbell, *The Scottish Miners, 1874–1939, Volume II: Trade Unions and Politics* (Ashgate, 2000)

Baron Duckham, *A History of the Scottish Coal Industry, Vol. I, 1700–1815* (David & Charles, 1970)

Robert Duncan, *The Mineworkers* [of Scotland] (Birlinn, 2005)

Graham Holton, *Discover Your Scottish Ancestry: Internet and Traditional Resources* (Edinburgh University Press, 2009)

Guthrie Hutton, *Fife – The Mining Kingdom* (Stenlake, 1999)

Guthrie Hutton, *Lanarkshire's Mining Legacy* (Stenlake, 1997)

Guthrie Hutton, *Mining Ayrshire's Lost Industry* (Stenlake, 1996)

Guthrie Hutton, *Mining the Lothians* (Stenlake, 1998)

Guthrie Hutton, *Mining From Kirkintilloch to Clackmannan & Stirling to Slamannan* (Stenlake, 2000)

Guthrie Hutton, *Scotland's Black Diamonds* (Stenlake/Scottish Mining Museum, 2001)

Ian Maxwell, *Tracing Your Scottish Ancestors* (Pen & Sword, 2009)

Miles K. Oglethorpe, *Scottish Collieries. An Inventory of the Scottish Coal Industry in the Nationalised Era* (RCAHMS, 2006)

National Archives of Scotland, *Tracing Your Scottish Ancestors. The Official Guide* (Birlinn, 2011)

*　　*　　*

Coalmining in Central Scotland [Kingshill colliery] (DVD: Scottish Screen Archive, 1939)

Memories of Mining in Scotland (DVD: Scottish Screen Archive: www.ssa.nls.uk)

Scottish Miners' Gala Day (DVD: Scottish Screen Archive, 1953)

The Brave Don't Cry [film based on Knockshinnoch Colliery disaster] (Associated British Film Distributors, 1952), Prod. J. Grierson; Dir. P. Laycock

Valleyfield Colliery [Fife] (DVD: Scottish Screen Archive, 1965)

ENGLAND

Northumberland and Durham coalfield

Historically known as the 'Great Northern' or 'Northern', the Northumberland and Durham coalfield was the first in the world to be developed on a large scale. Its nearness to the sea was a tremendous economic advantage over relatively landlocked areas elsewhere, enabling coal to be shipped in bulk. From pithead to waterway staithes and ports, entrepreneurs and engineers developed a system of wagonways, precursors to a dense network of colliery and mainline railways.

The coalfield extended from the river Coquet and Warworth in the north to the port of Hartlepool in the south. Its width varied from a few miles in the north to about 30 miles towards the centre and south. Coastal collieries at Seaham, Ryhope, Monkwearmouth, Horden and Easington worked seams for several miles under the sea. Permian rock strata (Magnesian Limestone) overlaid the older coal measures in the south-east of the area. The western, exposed coal measures covered an area of about 600 square miles and the concealed area accounted for a further 125 square miles. Despite the depth, pit sinking through the overlay was quite early, South Hetton, for example, dating from the 1830s.

In 1915, Professor Jevons (in *The British Coal Trade*) described the northern pitmen as 'some of the finest manual workers in the country'.

The coalfield was plagued by major disasters during the nineteenth century, most notably at Wallsend (1835), Haswell (1844), New Hartley (1862) and Seaham (1880).

Durham's last major pit, Monkwearmouth Colliery, closed in 1993, its site now occupied by Sunderland AFC's Stadium of Light football ground. Both the stadium name and an impressive Davy lamp monument are reminders of a proud mining heritage. Deep mining continued in Northumberland until 2005, when UK Coal closed Ellington Colliery following the serious flooding of an underground development.

184

'Big E' had been exploiting seams off the coast of Northumberland since production began in 1911.

Durham was by far the more productive of the two areas. In 1912, it produced 37.9 million tons of saleable coal compared with 14.8 in Northumberland. John Bowes and Partners Ltd had seventeen mines in 1896 employing 7,189 men. Its operations concentrated on nine or ten collieries after the First World War. However, the typical ownership/operational arrangement in the coalfield was small-scale, just one or two, often quite aged pits employing a few hundred men. In 1898, Northumberland had 112 mines, operated by eighty independent companies. Durham had far more, 246 mines, but owned by ninety-one companies. The thin seams were worked with an increasing number of mechanical coal-cutters, only Scotland having a greater usage. At its peak in 1912 there were more than 250,000 persons employed in the coal-field. By 1947 the number of pits had reduced to seventy-nine in Northumberland (and thirty-eight companies) and 152 in Durham (fifty-five companies). From its Newcastle headquarters in the 1950s the NCB administered over 120 collieries in Durham and fifty-nine in Northumberland. The two Divisions accounted for about eighteen per cent of Britain's output of coal.

This coalfield was one of the first to experience significant pit closures after the First World War, many miners and their families having to seek work in other regions. So if you have an early twentieth-century north-east England mining ancestor there's a good chance he worked at several pits and may have migrated elsewhere.

Archives and libraries

Beamish: The Living Museum of the North
Regional Resource Centre (RRC)

Beamish Museum, Beamish, County Durham, DH9 0RG

t. 0191 370 4000   e. museum@beamish.org.uk   www.beamish.org.ukw.

Archives and collections of the RRC include a vast amount of material of interest to family history research: manuscripts, oral history recordings, photographs and images, as well as printed items from books and newspapers to trade catalogues and ephemera. Its increasingly digitised People's Collection can be searched at http// collections.beamish.org.uk and via 'Photo Archive', 'Objects', 'Catalogues', 'Books', 'Audio' or 'Everything'. Photographs can also be browsed online by map location. Aiden Doyle's book, *The Great Northern Coalfield: Mining Collections at Museum* (Northumbria University Press, 2005) is available at the museum or from other sources. Also see places to visit (below).

Blyth Library

Bridge Street, Blyth, Northumberland, NE24 2DJ

t. 01670 361352   e. Blythlibrary@northumberland.gov.uk

www.northumberland.gov.uk

Online search via 'my library' includes 'Family History'. Northumberland Coal Owners Mutual Protection Association Index 1898–1947 (microfiche). Card index to coalmining items.

185

Durham Clayport Library
Millennium Place, Durham, DH1 1WA
t. 0191 386 4003   e. DurhamClayportLibrary@durham.gov.uk

Modern purpose-built library, part of the Durham Millennium City Project. Online library catalogue. Huge local studies collection and family history resources. Newspapers e.g. *Durham Advertiser* (1814–to date), *Durham Chronicle* 1820–1951.

Durham County Record Office
County Hall, Durham, DH1 5UL
t. 0191 383 3253   e. record.office@durham.gov.uk
www.durhamrecordoffice.org.uk

'A mine of information'. The official record office for County Durham and Darlington. A major holder of coalmining records. The Durham Collieries database can be searched online via keywords such as a place-name or colliery name (see online sources below). Subject Guide 7: Colliery Personnel Records. Mining Hidden Depths database has over 140,000 personnel from the Durham Miners' Association records (see online sources below). Search the online catalogue by selecting Public Records (for NCB), Trade Union and Employers' Association Records and Estate and Family Records. Family History online guide: http://www.durhamrecordoffice.or.uk/Pages/familyhistory.aspx

Durham University Library Archives & Special Collections
Palace Green, Durham, DH1 3RN
t. 0191 334 2932   e. pg.library@durham.ac.uk
www.dur.ac.uk/library/asc/

Large and extensive holdings searchable via online catalogue. Coal company/estates: papers relating to Durham Bishopric, Bishopric Halmote Court Baker, Shipperdson, Grey, Shafto (Beamish), Clayton & Gibson; Mickleton and Spearman MSS, Additional Manuscripts, Durham Cathedral Muniments, Land Tax Records. Reports of HM Inspectors of Mines. Grey Papers, Jack Lawson Papers, Keith Armstrong Collection. Colliery histories. Newspaper and periodicals e.g. *Coal News*. Family History guide.

Darlington Library (Centre for Local Studies)
Crown Street, Darlington, Durham, DL1 1ND
t. 01325 349630   e. Centre.forLocalStudies@darlington.gov.uk
www.darlington.gov.uk/library/localstudies

Mining Deaths in Great Britain (Winstanley) database 1850–1914. Reports of HM Inspectors of Mines 1874–1883 (& 1887). Durham Coal Owners' Association and Proceedings of Joint Committee 1872–1921. Durham Coal Board arbitration 1875–77, 1879–82, 1891, 1908. Durham Miners' Association Joint Committee Decisions etc 1875–1923. Durham Miners' Association Ascertainments 1933, 1935. Reid's *Handy Colliery Guide for Northumberland, Durham, Yorkshire, Cumberland and Westmorland 1923, 1930 & 1938. Colliery Guardian* 1878. Local newspapers e.g. The *Northern Echo* 1870–to date; *Darlington & Stockton Times* 1847–to date.

Gateshead Library

Central Library, Prince Consort Road, Gateshead, NE8 4LN
t. 0191 433 8430   e. libraries@gateshead.gov.uk
http://www.localhistorygateshead.com/local-and-family-history

Bulk of research material relating to the coalfield housed at the main library. Maps, newspapers, trade directories, recordings and transcripts of miners and their families recalling the 1926 strike. Transactions of North of England Institute of Mining Engineers 1852–1947. Archive sources via Tyne & Wear Archives (see below). The St Mary's Heritage Centre holds family history surgeries (http://www.localhistory gateshead.com/about-us/st-marys-heritage-centre).

Newcastle City and Local Studies Library

City Library, Charles Avison Building, 33 New Bridge Street West,
Newcastle upon Tyne, NE1 8AX
t. 0191 2774100   e. information@newcastle.gov.uk
www.newcastle.gov.uk/libraries

'Largest collection of local and family history material in the North East'. Searchable online catalogue and virtual library. Newcastle Collection. Fact sheets include family history, Newcastle history, local maps and newspapers. West Newcastle Picture History Collection (via West End Library: Condercum Road NE4 9JH e: wnls@ btinternet.com). Nineteenth-century newspapers accessible remotely for library cardholders and major family history resources available at terminals across the library service.

Newcastle University (Robinson) Library

Jesmond Road West, Newcastle upon Tyne, NE2 4HQ
t. 0191 222 7662   www.ncl.ac.uk/library/specialcollections

Online catalogue. Special Collection includes many coalmining items.

North East England Mining Archive and Research Centre (NEEMARC)

Level 3, The Murray Library, Chester Road, Sunderland, SR3 1SD
t. 0191 515 2905   e. neemarc@sunderland.ac.uk   www.neemarc.com

NEEMARC is part of the Special Collections at the University of Sunderland. Three important resources with excellent online family history advice (http://library. sunderland.ac.uk/resources/special%20collections/neemarc/articles/miningforfamily historyandneemarc): (1) Records of the National Union of Mineworkers (NUM) Durham Area; (2) The North of England Institute of Mining and Mechanical Engineers (NEIMME: also see separate listing, below) and (3) Durham branch of National Association of Colliery Overmen, Deputies and Shotfirers (NACODS). Some former NCB records. Downloadable leaflets: Mining Your Family History 1, Mining Your Family History 2. Online catalogue: (http://leetar.sunderland.ac.uk/CalmView).

North of England Institute of Mining and Mechanical Engineers (NEIMME)

Neville Hall, Westgate Road, Newcastle upon Tyne, NE1 1SE
t. 0191 232 2201   e. librarian@mininginstitute.org.uk
www.mininginstitute.org.uk

Registered charity. Formed in 1852, the Nicholas Wood Memorial Library is probably the largest mining library in the world. Searchable online library catalogue. Maps and plans. Special Collection includes Buddle, Watson, Forster and Easton papers. HM Inspector of Mines reports 1851–1867, 1869–1917, 1920–1923, 1925–1977. Mine disaster reports, c.1877-c1980s. Colliery histories. Newspapers and periodicals include *Colliery Guardian, Mining Journal, Iron & Coal Trade Review, Colliery Guardian Annual Guide to Coalfields, Coal News, Transactions of North of England Institute of Mining and Mechanical Engineers, Transactions of Institute of Mining Engineers/Mining Engineer.* For more details, other periodicals, date runs etc, consult website and online catalogue. Regular exhibitions and events. New website will include a family history sources page.

North Tyneside Central Library
Howard House, 54a Saville Street, North Shields, Tyne & Wear, NE30 1NT
(temporary address pending refurbishment and proposed establishment of the North Shields Customer First Centre: see website for updates).
t. 0191 643 5270   e. central.library@northtyneside.gov.uk
www.northtyneside.gov.uk

Branch libraries in former coalmining communities (contact details on website). Online catalogue. Although designed for schools, the Tyne Lives project (www. tynelives.org.uk) includes useful information about coalmining at Wallsend.

Northumberland Archives at Woodhorn
Woodhorn, QEII Country Park, Ashington, Northumberland, NE63 9YF
t. 01670 528 080   e. collections@woodhorn.org.uk
www.experiencewoodhorn.org.uk

Major archive and study centre housed in the new Cutter building. Searchable online collection catalogue. Mining records include occupational registers, truck/fine books, training ledgers (post-1947), stoppages registers, estate papers, pit housing records, indemnity books, union records, pay bills, disaster and fatality records, compensation records, superannuation records, HM Mines Inspectorate (post-1921), Woodhorn (1916) and Montague (1925) disaster reports. A 3D collection includes mining items relating to accidents and disasters, strikes, memorials, artworks, banners and samples; and implements. Downloadable user guides include Coal Mining Records for Family Historians, Coroners' Records, Northumberland Family History and Newspapers (see http//www.experiencewoodhorn.com/user-guides-and-forms/ for complete listing). Also see places to visit (below).

Northumberland Libraries
www.northumberland.gov.uk

Northumberland County Council. Use 'my library' via the main website to access contact details of thirty-four local libraries, many in former coalmining areas; also online local and family history sections and searchable book catalogue. Also see Woodhorn and Blyth (below).

South Tyneside Central Library
Prince George Square, South Shields, NE33 2PE
t. 0191 427 1818   e. localstudies.library@southtyneside.gov.uk
www.southtyneside.gov.uk

Serves several former mining communities where there are branch libraries (see main website for contact details). Online catalogue.

Sunderland City Library and Arts Centre
Fawcett Street, Sunderland, SR1 1RE
t. 0191 514 8439   e. localstudies@sunderland.gov.uk
www.sunderland.gov.uk

Local studies material includes newspapers (1831 onwards), maps and trade directories. Local heritage factsheet; Washington F Pit (download). See http//www.sunderland. gov.uk/index.aspx?articleid+1092 for local history and heritage.

Tyne & Wear Archives
Blandford House, Blandford Square, Newcastle upon Tyne, NE1 4JA
t. 0191 277 2248 (searchroom) 0191 232 6789 (switchboard)
e. archives@twmuseums.org.uk   www.tyneandweararchives.org.uk

Covers all North East area and a major source for local and family history research. Online catalogue. User guides include 19A: Coal Industry (general sources, public records, business records, industrial relations; welfare and safety; maps and plans; film and miscellaneous and 19B Collieries (individual colliery records); also useful is 16: Trade Unions, Employers and Professional Associations. HM Inspector of Mines reports 1864–1866: Children's Employment Commission (TWAM L/3983). HM Inspector of Mines Northern District Dec 1859–Dec 1860 (TWAM DF.WF/38). For mine disaster reports search catalogue, e.g. Hartley (1862), Montague (1925). Miners' Permanent Relief Fund available on microfilm and CD.

Places to visit
Beamish The Living Museum of the North
Beamish, County Durham, DH9 0RG
t. 0191 370 4000   e. museum@beamish.org.uk   www.beamish.org.uk

Multi award-winning 'open-air' museum of great interest to anyone with coalmining ancestry. Pit Village (Pit Cottages, Board School and Methodist Chapel); Colliery and Colliery Yard; Mahogany Drift Mine (guided tours with ex-miners); Lamp Cabin; Engine House; Pockerley Waggonway and many mining exhibits. Also see archives, libraries & local studies centres (above).

Bellingham Heritage Centre
Station Yard, Woodburn Road, Bellingham, Northumberland, NE48 2DF
t. 01434 220 050   e. info@bellingham-heritage.org.uk
www.bellingham-heritage.org.uk

Volunteer-run local history museum and registered charity. Collections include an excellent mining heritage exhibition relating to the North Tyne and Redesdale.

Bowes Railway
Springwell Village, Gateshead, Tyne and Wear, NE9 7QJ
t. 0191 416 1847   www.bowesrailway.co.uk

Registered charity. Designed by George Stephenson for John Bowes et al in 1826, for hauling coal from local collieries to boats on the Tyne. Such colliery railways were once common in the North East. The section that remains is the only surviving and preserved operational rope-hauled railway in the world.

Durham Mining Museum
Spennymoor Town Hall, Spennymoor, County Durham, DL16 6DG
t. 0757 701 2822

Mining artefacts and information. Display rooms are open on weekdays (12–4) and Saturdays (10–2). Also see online sources (below).

Segedunum Roman Fort, Baths and Museum
(Tyne & Wear Archives & Museums)
Buddle Street, Wallsend, NE28 6HR
t. 0191 236 9347   htttp//www.twmuseums.org.uk/segedunum

Interactive museum that also houses coalmining artefacts; history of Wallsend Colliery. A recent exhibition was 'Into the Mouth of Hell' relating to four major pit disasters on Tyneside, including the 1862 Hartley disaster. New permanent exhibition on the evolution of the local landscape includes the coal trade.

Washington F Pit Museum
Albany Way, Washington, NE37 1BJ
t. 0191 553 2323   http://www.twmuseums.org.uk/washington

Owned by Sunderland City Council and managed by Tyne & Wear Archives & Museums. Superb Victorian winding engine, engine house and pit headgear. This important colliery site dates back to the sinking of the pit in 1777. Washington colliery was closed by the NCB in 1968 and a museum established in 1976.

Woodhorn Colliery Museum
Woodhorn, Ashington, Northumberland, NE63 9YF
t. 01670 528 080   www.experiencewoodhorn.com

Historic site of Woodhorn Colliery, one of the Ashington pits. Preserved Heapstead, Winding House, Fan Room, Engine House, Workshops, Stables. Guided tour/Darkside Tour. Coal Town (interactive galleries in the modern Cutter building). Unique Pitman Painters (Ashington Group of miner-artists) exhibition; pit banner display. Country Park setting and a superb visitor experience.

Mining artifacts and smaller exhibitions can also be seen at many other North East museums, for example South Shields Museum (http://twmuseums.org.uk/southshields), Sunderland Museum (http://www.twmuseums.org.uk/sunderland) and Wheatley Hill Heritage Centre (www.wheatleyhillheritagecentre.btck.co.uk).

Family history societies

Northumberland & Durham FHS www.ndfhs.org.uk
Cleveland (North Yorkshire and South Durham) FHS www.clevelandfhs.org.uk
Newton Aycliffe FHS www.nafhs.com/newton_aycliffe.php
Elvet Local and Family History Group e. margot@hallgarthstreet@plus.net

Online sources

Durham In Time www.durhamintime.org.uk

The Community Archive links collections from local and family history groups, and other groups. Project websites include Durham Miner and Coal Mining Oral History Project. Digital archive. Run by Adult Learning and Skills Service of Durham CC.

Durham Miners' Gala

Many sites but for an overview see the Wikipedia entry en.wikipedia.or/wiki/ Durham_Miners'_Gala. Video clips on youtube. Artist Tim Brennon's (University of Sunderland Faculty of Arts) app 'Gala Manoeuvres' is available free from the Apple app store.

Durham Miners' Museum www.dmm.org.uk

Excellent virtual site relating to the North East, which also covers Cumberland and is useful for other coalmining areas too. Includes practical advice for family history research (http://www.dmm.org.uk/famhist.htm). Topics easily navigated via main menus of 'Museum', 'Mining' and 'Disasters'. 'Site Map' a good starting point, providing a list of resources and the Forum section is also useful. Also see places to visit (above).

Durham Records Online www.durhamrecordsonline.com

'International partnership of genealogists and historians'. Free search then payment. Huge database of records including mine-related examples. Useful coalmining links. Also see Search Durham Collieries (below).

Hampstead Miners Memorial Trust http://miners.b43.co.uk

Interesting site commemorating the Hampstead pit disaster of 1908.

Mining Durham's Hidden Depths

www.Durhamrecordoffice.org.uk/Pages/AdvancedSearchHiddenDepths.aspx

Durham Record Office's excellent project – via volunteers – is the creation of indexes of the Durham Miners' Association trade union records. Thousands of names in the growing searchable database. Also see Search Durham Collieries (below).

Northern Region Film & Television Archive www.nrfta.org.uk

Based at Teesside University. Explore the collection using keywords such as 'coal'.

Northumberland Communities www.communities.northumberland.gov.uk

Northumberland Archives' project. A-Z listing of places with digitised sources for local and family history research.

191

Search Durham Collieries

www.durhamrecordoffice.org.uk/Pages/AdvancedSearchDurhamCollieries.aspx

Durham Record Office's excellent database of Durham collieries, from c.1850. Search/ browse by colliery, place or map. Also see Mining Durham's Hidden Depths (above).

Tomorrow's History www.tomorrows-history.com

The regional local studies site for the North East of England. Managed by Newcastle -upon-Tyne Libraries, Information and Lifelong Learning Service. Search collection via subject (e.g. coalmining), period and keyword.

What's Your Story www.whatsyourstory.org.uk

'Discovering Family History in Tyne & Wear'. Volunteer-run site of shared information about North East ancestors, started by Tyne & Wear Archives & Museums in 2011. See Sheila Fiddler's Story, for example, on child labour in coalmining and the 1842 Report.

Useful books, film and video

Frank Atkinson, *The Great Northern Coalfield* (Durham County Historical Society/ University Tutoral Press, 1966)

Norman Emery, *The Coalminers of Durham* (The History Press, 2009)

W.R. Garside, *The Durham Miners 1919–1960* (Allen & Unwin, 1971)

Bill Griffiths, (compiler), *Pitmatic: The Talk of the North East Coalfield* (Northumbria University Press, 2005)

Mike Kirkup, *Ashington and its Mining Communities* (The History Press, 2008)

Ken and John Prestwick, *Beneath this Green and Pleasant Land. A Miner's Life* (Tyne Bridge, 2009)

Jean Smith, *The Great Northern Miners* (Tyne Bridge, 2009)

Neil Taylor, *Memories of the Northumberland Coalfields* (Countryside Books, 2009)

Les Turnbull, *Coals From Newcastle. An Introduction to the Northumberland and Durham Coalfield* (Chapman Research, 2009)

*   *   *

Brass and Banners. A History of the Great Northern Coalfield and its People (DVD: Puddle Productions)

A Tour of Westoe Colliery [South Shields] (DVD: Slipstream Productions)

Seaham Pits [Dawden, Vane Tempest etc]

The Miners' Hymns, Bill Morrison (dir) (DVD: BFI Video, 2011)

Cumberland coalfield

One of the smaller coal-bearing regions, the Cumberland coalfield was about 25 miles from north-east to south-west and about 6 miles wide at its greatest extent. The western, coastal area extended from Whitehaven to Maryport and then a further 12 miles to Wigton. There were considerable workings under the Irish Sea and Solway Firth, up to 4 miles from land.

The entrepreneurship of Sir William Lowther was important in the emergence of the area from the latter part of the seventeenth century and in the growth of Whitehaven as a coal-shipping port. The Curwen family developed their Workington area pits in the eighteenth century. In 1900, according to the *Victoria County History*, there were forty-three collieries in Cumberland, but several were quite small concerns, employing fewer than twenty hands. By 1912, the total number of persons employed and production was relatively small, 10,742 persons producing 2,133,563 tons. The coal seams were not only difficult to work due to faulting, but also contained high levels of methane gas, so explosions were always a danger. The worst disaster occurred at Wellington Pit (Whitehaven) in 1910 when there were 136 fatalities. The unfortunate Haig Colliery had explosions in 1922, 1928 and 1931, with a total loss of life of seventy-nine persons. After nationalisation, the NCB administered the coalfield from offices at Bankfield, Workington, when ten pits were still operating. Haig, with its undersea workings, was the biggest, and was the last deep mine to be worked, closing in 1986. Its site is now an interesting mining museum run by volunteers (see below).

Archives and libraries

Carlisle and Whitehaven Archives and Local Studies
Carlisle Archives Centre, Lady Gillford's House, Petteril Bank Road, Carlisle, Cumbria, CA1 3AJ
t. 01228 227 285   e. carlisle.archives@cumbria.gov.uk

Whitehaven Archives and Local Studies Centre, Scotch Street, Whitehaven, Cumbria, CA28 7NL
t. 01946 506 420   e. Whitehaven.archives@cumbria.gov.uk

The Carlisle Archive Centre's coalmining records are contained within family and estate papers: Lowther (DLONS W7: collieries; Senhouse (DSEN 5/9/2: Ellenborough and other collieries); Lawson (DLAW 1: leases include individual miners' names). CASCAT (online collection catalogue) searches through records held at all of the centres. Family history advice/information online. Keyword such as 'colliery' will reveal hundreds of results, e.g. Broughton Colliery deeds 1937–1877 (C. DX565); Roachburn disaster 1908 (C.1908); Whitehaven Colliery plans 1907–1915 (W. DH/441).; or use a colliery name such as 'Haig Colliery' for Whitehaven Coal Company records (W. DH series). See Nationalised Industries: National Coal Board summary and links to online catalogues of records: colliery plans (Broughton, Cleator, Flimby, Harrington, Whitehaven, Workington); colliery companies (Allerdale, Cumberland Coal Owners, Moresby Coal Company; Whitehaven Colliery Company (Winscales Central Mines Rescue, Cumberland District Coal Mines Scheme) and Cumberland Coalfield Records: catalogue references (and holding location) can then be accessed. Online Exhibition Gallery includes Wellington Pit Disaster 1910 and a podcast. The local studies library also has a good collection of coalmining sources including newspapers, books and maps and files.

Places to visit

Haig Pit Mining and Colliery Museum
Solway Road, Kells, Whitehaven, Cumbria, CA28 9BG
t. 01946 599 949   e. root@haigpit.com   www.haigpit.wordpress.com

Situated high on the cliffs above Whitehaven. A major 'Power House and Visitor Centre' on the site of Haig pit, which closed in 1986, which will include a new exhibition space for mining and related displays. Steam winding house and head-gear. Engines. Website has useful information on disasters, historical figures, the engines, West Cumberland Coalfield, news and events etc.

The Beacon
West Strand, Whitehaven, Cumbria, CA28 7JG
t. 01946 592 302   e. thebeacon@copelandbc.gov.uk
www.thebeacon-whitehaven.co.uk

Award-winning art gallery and museum for the Copeland area. Floor 2: Work and Play includes mining. Collections online search facility.

Family history societies
Cumbria FHS www.cumbriafhs.com

Online sources
Brayton Domain Collieries www.rumneys.co.uk

Coalmining and the people of Aspatria, Cumberland. Several images, history of the colliery, accident details, local census and directories.

Cumberland Roots www.cumberlandroots.co.uk

Cumberland family history site. Surname search. Parish records.

Useful books, film and video
J.V. Beckett, *Coal and Tobacco. The Lowthers and the Economic Redvelopment of West Cumberland 1660–1760* (Cambridge University Press, 1981 and 2008)
Ray Devlin, *Children of the Pits. Child Labour and Child Fatality in the Coal Mines of Whitehaven & District* (Friends of Whitehaven Museum, 1988 & 1999)

Yorkshire (and Nottinghamshire and Derbyshire) coalfield
This extensive area, occupying much of the old West Riding of Yorkshire, and parts of Nottinghamshire and Derbyshire, had become the most important coalfield in the UK by 1913, with more than 271,000 persons employed and an annual output of about 74 million tons. Unlike in other regions output continued to rise right through to the mid-1920s.

Accidents and disasters were commonplace throughout much of the nineteenth century, no more so than around Barnsley, communities there suffering from a huge number of fatalities in a series of dreadful explosions, most spectacularly at Lundhill (1857, 189 deaths), the Oaks (1866, 361, the worst disaster at any English coal mine) and Swaithe Main (1875, 143).

Stretching more than 60 miles from the north of Leeds to Nottingham in the south, the exposed coalfield was at its widest (c.25 miles) in its upper half, beyond Sheffield. The Barnsley seam was the most famous coal worked (often indicated in the word 'Main' after a pit's name) and the town from which it got its name was the geographic, economic and administrative centre of the old coalfield. After exhaustion of the Barnsley bed many other seams were developed via deeper workings at pits such as Cortonwood, Elsecar Main and Woolley, and at the Monckton and Manvers complexes.

A band of Magnesian Limestone overlaid the eastern edge of the coal measure rocks forming the start of a concealed coalfield. New sinkings had begun at Denaby (1864), and continued nearby at Cadeby (1889), but took off during the early years of the twentieth century at Bentley, Brodsworth, Frickley, Bullcroft, Edlington (Yorkshire Main), Askern, Hatfield, Rossington, and finally, the most awkward of all due to inrushes of water, at Thorne (1912–26). The new collieries were deep and large, employing several thousand men. Brodsworth Main, sunk by the Staveley Coal & Iron Company on the Thellusson country estate, began production from 1907, and by the 1920s (and again in the 1950s) was breaking national (in effect world) production records, referred to as the 'biggest pit in the country'. A good number of Brodsworth's c.3,500 workforce were housed in the model village of Woodlands. Two of Britain's last deep mines, at Hatfield (near Doncaster) and Thoresby (Edwinstowe, Nottinghamshire) remain in production; and, further north, Kellingley Colliery, near Knottingley, in West Yorkshire, also still operates.

During the NCB era the Yorkshire regional administrative headquarters was located in Doncaster, at Coal House.

The North Derbyshire and Nottinghamshire part of the coalfield formed part of the the NCB's East Midlands Division after 1947, administered from Sherwood Lodge, Arnold, in Nottinghamshire.

In North Yorkshire the much-heralded Selby coalfield and its complex of five 'superpits': North Selby, Riccall, Stillingfleet and Wistow (plus Gascoigne Wood drift mine) officially opened in 1976, but due to geological problems production had ceased by 2004.

Archives and libraries

Barnsley Archives & Local Studies
(Experience Barnsley Discovery Centre)
Town Hall, Church Street, Barnsley, South Yorkshire, S70 2TA
t. 01226 773 950   e. archives@barnsley.gov.uk
http://experience-barnsley.com/archives-and-discovery-centre

Online collection catalogue. Records of West Riding Miners' Permanent Relief Fund (miners and families) 1877–1988. HM Mines Inspectors' reports 1860–1979. Coalfield Community Campaign records. Houghton Main, Dearne and Darfield Coal Home Delivery services. Hundreds of mining images in photographic collection. Excellent range of printed material relating to mining. Film: *Black Diamonds* (1930s). Oral history recordings include Brian Elliott's recordings of local miners.

Brotherton Library/ University of Leeds Special Collections
University of Leeds, Leeds, West Yorkshire, LS2 9JT
t. 0113 343 5663   e. library@leeds.ac.uk   http://library.leeds.ac.uk

Online catalogue to special collection of rare books and manuscripts. Yorkshire Coal Owners' Mutual Indemnity Scheme, 1898–1902. Wentworth-Woolley Hall papers include coalmining items (Handlist 9). Newspapers and periodicals include *Leeds*

Mercury, Leeds Intelligencer, Halifax Courier, Halifax Guardian. Periodicals include *Illustrated London News* (nineteenth-century).

Chesterfield Library
New Beetwell Street, Chesterfield, Derbyshire, S40 1QN
t. 01629 533 400   e. chesterfield.library@derbyshire.gov.uk
http://derbyshire.gov.uk/leisure/libraries

Also covers North East Derbyshire. Online catalogue. Wide range of coal-related sources. Coal Collection contains technical literature. Holdings include books and pamphlets, photographs, newspaper items, NCB maps, journals (e.g. *Derbyshire Miner* 1975–83, Staveley Company magazine 1926–32), copies of HM Inspectors of Mines' reports (Midland/Yorkshire Midland District 1850–1914), HMI accident reports (Grassmoor, 1933; Markham, 1938 & 1973; Cresswell, 1950) index to abandoned mines. Barnes Collection includes eighteenth-century coalmining. Handout available on coalmining sources. Local newspapers.

County Hall Local Studies Library (Matlock)
County Hall, Matlock, Derbyshire, DE4 3AG
t. 01629 536 579   e. localstudies@derbyshire.gov.uk
http://www.derbyshire.gov.uk/leisure/local_studies/local_studies_libraries/
county_hall_local_studies/default.asp

Many Derbyshire newspapers (see http://newsplan.liem.org.uk/) and free access to British Library nineteenth-century newspaper database. Cuttings files (1960s onwards). Maps and plans. Ephemera and miscellaneous printed materials.

Derbyshire Record Office
County Hall, Matlock, Derbyshire, DE4 3AG
t. 01629 539 202   e. recordoffice@derbyshire.gov.uk
www.derbyshire.gov.uk/leisure/record_office

Online collection catalogue and record office guide. Downloadable guides include *Tracing Your Family's Roots in Derbyshire*. Collections contain many mining records e.g. NUM (Derbyshire) minutes; Sheepbridge Coal and Iron Company accident record books 1923–1957; Denby Colliery wages book 1919–1937; diary of J.F. Russ, coalminer, 1917–1929. Unlisted coalmining records references can be searched on site via index cards.

Doncaster Archives & Local Studies
Archives: King Edward Road, Balby, Doncaster, South Yorkshire, DN4 0NA
t. 01302 859 811   e. doncaster.archives@doncaster.gov.uk

Local Studies: Central Library, Waterdale, Doncaster, South Yorkshire, DN1 3JE
t. 01302 734 307   e. central.localhistory@doncaster.gov.uk
www.doncaster.gov.uk/Leisure_and_Culture/Libraries_Local_Studies

Ongoing online indexing project. Sources for Local and Family History listing includes local newspapers, monumental inscriptions and Miners' Strike Collection. Family & Local History Alphabet includes webpages on the Coal Industry (but few original records kept). Newspapers and Doncaster Family History Society. Registers of Fatal Accidents in Coal Mines (MQ?1 1914–1949 (exc. 1923/24). HM Inspectors of Mines' reports (MQ) 1885–1938 (printed). Local newspapers. McFarlane Papers (1935–85) for Cadeby Main and Denaby Main collieries.

John Goodchild Local Collection
John Goodchild, M.Univ., c/o West Yorkshire Archive Service, Registry of Deeds, Newstead Road, Wakefield, WF1 2DE
Postal enquiries preferred. t. 01924 288 929 (library) or 01924 891 871 (home)

An independent study centre containing important coalmining sources collected over many years. Original papers of colliery owners in West and South Yorkshire coalfields, c.1700–2000 and individual documents c.1330–1947. A few colliery papers from outside this area. Coal-bearing estates' records; Union records include a fine set for Lofthouse Colliery. HM Mines Inspectors' reports 1851 onwards; colliery directories and other printed material. Notes by John Goodchild, M.Univ., on individual West Riding collieries, arranged alphabetically (and also by card index); typescript notes and printed studies by Goodchild on coalmining history. Colliery plans, from eighteenth century. Biographical details of colliery owners and engineers/managers. Many Price Lists. Yorkshire Small Mines Association papers.

Hull History Centre
Worship Street, Hull, HU2 8BG
t. 01482 317 500   e. hullhistorycentre@hullcc.gov.uk
www.hullhistorycentre.org.uk

Combined material from the Hull City Archives and Local Studies Library and archives of University of Hull. Online catalogue. Family history guide: key sources and useful links, e.g. newspapers and directories. Papers of W.E. Jones 1888–1968, President of the NUM and Secretary of Yorkshire Mineworkers' Association (includes Rossington Colliery items); and papers of prolific coalmining historian Robin Page Arnot, c.1917–1976.

National Coal Mining Museum for England (see Section II, National sources)

National Union of Mineworkers Archives
Miners' Offices, 2 Huddersfield Road, Barnsley, South Yorkshire, S70 2LS
t. 01226 215 555   www.num.org.uk

The archives of the NUM contain many Yorkshire items (the building continues to be headquarters of the Yorkshire NUM, previously Yorkshire Miners' Association), photographs, ephemera, books, disaster/accident reports, union records and printed items but are uncatalogued. Access by appointment only. Also see Section II, national sources; places to visit (below); useful online sources (below).

North Yorkshire County Record Office
Malpass Road, Northallerton, North Yorkshire, DL7 8TB
t. 01609 777585   e. archives@northyorks.gov.uk
www.northyorks.gov.uk/archives

Although coalmining was less extensive in the area than lead and copper, it was important in the Colsterdale (Swinton papers) and Bowes areas (Clifton Castle archive). Online catalogue. Historic maps online. List of Mining Plans (Guide No. 9, also see Guide 1 for an overview of mining).

Nottinghamshire Archives

Castle Meadow Road, Nottingham NG2 1AG

t. 0115 958 1634   e. archives@nottscc.gov.uk

http://www.nottinghamshire.gov.uk/learning/history/archives

Online catalogue. Summary guide to holdings. Downloadable visitor guides and downloadable leaflets include Family History and the Internet and Maps and Plans. Researching your family history online guide includes sources and records. Portland MSS. Other estate and business records will contain many mining documents, for example Nottinghamshire & District Miners' Federation Union, coroner's warrants. For colliery company records prior to 1947 see the Access to Archives website at www.nationalarchives.gov.uk/a2a (SO/NCB).

Nottingham Local Studies Library

Nottingham Central Library, Angel Row, Nottingham, NG1 6HP

t. 0115 915 915 2873   e. local_studies.library@nottinghamcity.gov.uk

http://www.nottinghamcity.gov.uk/libraries

Online catalogue: 'Nelib'. Card index on site. Local maps and newspapers (cutting files on collieries), books, directories and printed items, photographic collection. Oral history recordings includes miners. Online family history guide.

Nottingham University Manuscripts and Special Collections

Kings Meadow Campus, Lenton Lane, Nottingham, NG7 2NR

t. 0115 951 4565   e. mss-library@nottingham.ac.uk

http://www.nottingham.ac.uk/manuscriptsandspecialcollections

Online catalogues. Research guide units; most useful include East Midlands Collection, D.H. Lawrence Collection and the Family and Estate Collections (Manvers, Drury-Lowe, Galway, Middleton and Thoroton Hildyard [see online guides for details]; also Portand (London) Collection, especially c.1850 onwards. Wollaton and Radford collieries shaft sinking records 1873–1905 (MS822); NCB reports 1937–1989. News-papers include a collection relating to the 1926 General Strike (MS747). East Midlands mining papers (MS649). Photographs of industrial sites including mining (MS627).

Rotherham Archives and Local Studies Library

Clifton Park Museum, Clifton Lane, Rotherham, South Yorkshire, S65 2AA

t. 01709 336 632   e. archives@rotherham.gov.uk   www.rotherham.gov.uk

Located within Clifton Museum. Online library catalogue. South Yorkshire Family History Guide (download). Business records includes mines. Use 'Local Towns and Villages' from online menu for background history of mining in local communities. Several estate records relate to mining. 'Local towns and villages' from RMBC's 'Patchwork of Parishes' includes coalmining backgrounds. Local newspapers e.g. *Rotherham Advertiser* 1858–to date. Excellent range of large-scale OS maps. Books and printed material on mining (list available). Photographic collection includes many mining images.

Sheffield Archives and Local Studies

Sheffield Archives: 52 Shoreham Street, Sheffield, South Yorkshire, S1 4SP

t. 0114 203 9395   e. archives@sheffield.gov.uk

Sheffield Local Studies Library: 1st Floor, Central Library, Surrey Street, Sheffield, South Yorkshire, S1 1XL

t. 0114 273 5009   e. localstudies.library@sheffield.gov.uk

http://www.sheffield.gov.uk/libraries/archives-and-local-studies.htlm

Online library catalogue: use keywords such as 'colliery', 'coal mine' etc for your search. Online archive collections fact sheets. Family history services. Tracing Your Ancestors in South Yorkshire download. Miners' Strike Research Guide download (with detailed sources). BBC Radio Sheffield miners' strike broadcasts (index cards). Picture Sheffield computerised image resource (see online sources below). Archives hold details relating to 126 south Yorkshire collieries (Ref: NCB). Local Studies also has a wide range of sources: printed material, local newspapers, images, periodicals e.g. *Coal News;* and oral history recordings.

Wakefield Library & Local Studies Library

Wakefield One, Wakefield Council, Burton Street, Wakefield, West Yorkshire, WF1 2EB

t. 01924 305356   e. wakefieldlibrarymuseum@wakefield.gov.uk

www.wakefield.gov.uk?CultureAndLeisure/Libraries/default.htm

Online library catalogue for book stock, which includes Ian Winstanley's 'Mining deaths in Great Britain 1850–1914' and some HM Mines Inspectors' reports. Local newspaper and ephemera collection, online index. Maps and plans. Images can be accessed via http://www.twixtaireandcalder.org.uk/default.htm.

West Yorkshire Archive Service

Morley, Leeds, West Yorkshire

2 Chapeltown Road, Sheepscar, Leeds, West Yorkshire, LS7 3AP

t. 0113 214 5814   e. leeds@wyjs.org.uk

www.archives.wyjs.org.uk/archives

Huge service has offices in Wakefield, Bradford, Calderdale (Halifax), Kirklees (Huddersfield) and Leeds. Each has some coal-related holdings but the main deposits are in Wakefield (01924 305980) and Leeds. Online catalogue and collections guides. Family history: download Use Guides 7 and 11. Local history sources. The **West Riding Registry of Deeds** at Wakefield is a superb place for family and local history research for land ownership, for personal names, properties and businesses (1704–1970) and will include houses of coal mine company owners, managers etc and related items: enquire via 01924 305 980 or research@wyjs.org.ug.

Yorkshire Archaeological Society (YAS) Library and Archives

Claremont, 23 Clarendon Road, Leeds, West Yorkshire, LS2 9NZ

t. 0113 245 7910 (library) or 0113 245 6362 (archives)

e. yas.library@googlemail.com or yas.archives@googlemail.com

www.yas.org.uk

Open to non-members (donations helpful) but by appointment only. Library contains books and journals on all aspects of Yorkshire history; also prints, photographic images, maps and aerial views. Standard family history resources also available. Catalogue searchable on site via card index or electronically. Archive has online guide, list of MI's. Relevant estate records include deeds etc relating to coalmining in Barnsley (DD164); Farnley, near Leeds (MD279); Ingelton and Bentham (MD279; Middleton Colliery (MD1098); Woolley Colliery (DD200); Bradfer-Lawrence collection (Fountains Fell, Low Side, Bierley, Oakenshaw collieries: [MD335]); Duke of Leeds collection (Barnsley coal mines). Also see family history societies and online sources (below).

Places to visit

Barnsley Main Colliery Headgear & Engine House
Oaks Lane, Barnsley, South Yorkshire
http://www.ukminingremains.co.uk/barnsley-main-colliery

Listed pithead retains one of the former headgears and engine houses of Barnsley Main Colliery, which closed in 1991. Not open to the public but can be viewed from Oaks Lane, off Pontefract Road (A628), Hoyle Mill, Barnsley. Near the site of the old Oaks Colliery where 361 men and boys lost their lives in England's worst pit disaster in 1866. Also see Experience Barnsley and Elsecar Village, Heritage Centre & Newcomen Engine (below).

Bestwood Winding Engine House & Headgear
Bestwood Country Park, Off Northern Drive, Bestwood Village,
Nottinghamshire, NG6 8XA
t. 0115 927 3674 (ranger)
http://nottinghamshire.gov.uk/enjoying/countryside/countryparks/
bestwood/winding-engine-house

Restored and open Saturday mornings, Easter–October. Last remains of Bestwood Colliery (1871–1967). Run by volunteers.

D.H. Lawrence Heritage
Durban House, Mansfield Road, Eastwood, Nottinghamshire, NG16 3DZ
t. 01773 717 353   e. culture@broxtowe.gov.uk
www.broxtowe.gov.uk/index.aspx?articleid=4654

Two visitor attractions: 1. Durban House, former headquarters of coal owners Barber, Walker & Company, now a museum featuring a permanent exhibition relating to D.H. Lawrence and has many interesting local mining items; 2. D.H. Lawrence Birthplace Museum (nearby, at 8a Victoria Street, NG16 3AW), the former home of Lawrence, where timed guided tours are available.

Elsecar Village, Heritage Centre & Newcomen Engine
Wath Road, Elsecar, Barnsley, South Yorkshire, S74 8HJ
t. 01226 740 203   e. elsecarheritagecentre@barnsley.gov.uk
www.elsecar-heritage-centre.co.uk

Located in a conservation area, excellent example of early industrial village includes miners' houses, public park and former canal. Heritage site includes restored buildings of former ironworks and colliery workshops, heritage railway, craft workshops and antique centre, exhibition centre (Building 21). On TransPennine Trail. Its gem is the Newcomen-type engine house (only surviving example on its original site in the world) of Earl Fitzwilliam's former New Elsecar Colliery, which has now undergone a major lottery-funded restoration.

Experience Barnsley Museum & Discovery Centre
Town Hall, Barnsley, South Yorkshire, S70 2TA
t. 01226 773 950   e. experiencebarnsley@barnsley.co.uk
www.experience-barnsley.gov.uk

New 'people's museum' (and archive/local studies centre) housed in Barnsley's Art Deco town hall, opened in 2013. Includes important mining exhibits and has an oral history recording studio, shop/tourist information point and educational facilities. Also see Barnsley Archives and Local Studies (above).

National Coal Mining Museum for England (see national sources)

National Union of Mineworkers Headquarters
2 Huddersfield Road, Barnsley, South Yorkshire, S70 2AS
t. 01226 215 555   www.num.org.uk

Regarded as the first purpose-built trade union headquarters in the world, its Miners' Hall/Council Chamber is a hidden gem of coalmining architecture and heritage, containing sculptures/plaques, stained-glass windows, banners and exhibits (virtual 'tour' on website). Public access is on national heritage opening days and for the annual Joe Green Lecture (second Saturday in March, check website); and also by appointment.

Nottingham Industrial Museum
Wollaton Hall, Nottingham, NG8 2AE
t. 0115 915 3900   e. online form   www.nottinghamindustrialmuseum.co.uk

The museum's collection housed in the former stable block includes coalmining items. Online article: 'My job as an under manager of a pit' (Denis Ward who worked in local mining 1947–1988). Colliery horse gin on display outside building. Steam engines. Weekend opening, check website/telephone for details.

Peak District Mining Museum
The Pavilion, South Parade, Matlock Bath, Matlock, Debyshire, DE4 3NR
t. 01629 583 834   e. mail@peakmines.co.uk   www.peakmines.co.uk

Although mainly concerning lead extraction, the museum is well worth a visit for anyone with coalmining interests as there were many common features. Guided tour of Temple Mine. Also see online sources (below).

Pleasley Colliery Mining Heritage site
Pleasley, Mansfield, Nottinghamshire, NG19 7PH
e. admin@pleasley-colliery.org.uk   www.pleasley-colliery.org.uk

A scheduled ancient monument, Pleasley Colliery functioned from 1871–1983. An excellent site for anyone interested in mining history as it includes headgears, engine houses and steam winders, plus exhibits. English Heritage award-winning restoration led by the Friends of Pleasley Pit volunteers. Open for visitors Thursdays and Sundays and on special event days/weekends: check website beforehand.

Many of the council-run museums in the region also have small collections of coal-mining artefacts, photographs and information relating to their local area, for example, Cusworth Hall and Doncaster Museum (http://www.doncaster.gov.uk/Leisure_and_Culture/Museums_and_Galleries) and Mansfield Museum (www.mansfield.gov.uk/museum).

Family history societies

Barnsley FHS   www.barnsleyfhs.co.uk
Bradford FHS   www.bradfordfhs.org.uk
Calderdale FHS   www.cfhsweb.com/web
Chesterfield & District FHS   www.cadfhs.org.uk
Derbyshire FHS   www.dfhs.org.uk
Doncaster & District FHS   www.doncasterfhs.co.uk
Huddersfield & District FHS   www.hdfhs.org.uk.
Keighley & District FHS   www.kdfhs.org.uk
Mansfield & District FHS c/o 15 Cranmer Grove, Mansfield, NG19 7RG
Morley & District FH Group   http://wakefieldfhs.org.uk/morleyfhg
Nottinghamshire FHS   www.nottsfhs.org.uk
Pontefract & District FHS   www.pontefractfhs.org.uk
Rotherham FHS   www.rotherhamfhs.co.uk
Sheffield & District FHS   www.sheffieldfhs.org.uk
Wakefield & District Family History Society   www.wdfhs.co.uk
Yorkshire Archaeological Society FH Section   www.yorkshireroots.org

Online sources

Clay Cross Geneaology www.claycross.org.uk

This site includes 'Collieries' in the main menu.

Donny Online www.donny.co.uk

Contains local history features and has a genealogy forum.

Kiveton Park & Wales History Society www.kivetonwaleshistory.co.uk

Excellent community site for the story of local pits; lives at pits; mining question and answer; oral history clips. Download: Pit ponies of Kiveton Park Barnsley Seam.

Miners' Advice www.minersadvice.co.uk

Dave Douglass's comprehensive miners' trade union advice site includes many items of Yorkshire historic interest, plus reviews and excellent links.

My Yorkshire www.myyorkshire.org

Partnership with eleven museums, including National Mining Museum for England e.g. images and audio of Life Down the Mine (Monckton/Roundwood collieries) for the Cutting Edge Heritage project.

Northern Mine Research Society www.nmrs.org.uk

Lots of mining interest for enthusiasts: also see national sources.

National Union of Mineworkers www.num.org.uk

Official website of the NUM/Yorkshire Area NUM. Menu includes history, publications, banners and miners' plates. Also see national sources.

Nottinghamshire Roots www.nottinghamshireroots.com

Tourist-style guide with family history interests.

Picture Sheffield www.picturesheffield.com

Internet version of Sheffield Local Studies Library's computerised picture collection. Searchable database has hundreds of coal-related images.

Picture the Past www.picturethepast.org.uk

North East Midland Photographic Record. Search and order prints from Derbyshire, Nottinghamshire areas. Many coalmining images.

Rotherham Web www.rotherhamweb.co.uk

Useful site for Rotherham and district local and family history, including many coalmining items: newspaper extracts, disaster reports, early mining, A-Z of local collieries, unions, welfare, strikes, photographs, plus index and easy site search.

Sheffield Indexers www.sheffieldindexers.com

Site now includes South Yorkshire Collieries and useful links.

Silverwood Colliery http://johndoxey.100freemb.com/Silverwood/

John Doxey's excellent and very detailed site about Silverwood Colliery (1900–1994), near Rotherham. Contains over 4,200 ex-miners' names.

The Magic Attic www.magicattic.org.uk

Large Swadlincote-based archive of newspapers, maps and family history information relating to south Derbyshire.

Yorkshire Film Archive www.yorkshirefilmarchive.com

Registered charity, based at the Fountains Building, York St John University. Over 16,000 film and video items. Online catalogue search. Online film clips. Many coal-related films, use keyword 'coal', 'colliery', 'miner' etc and view results.

Yorkshire Main
www.webarchive.org.uk/wayback/archive/20100407210511/
http://www.freewebs.com/yorkshiremain/

British Library's archived website. Lots of information and images about the colliery and other local pits. Also see 'Edlington Yorkshire Main' on Facebook.

Useful books, film and video
Yorkshire
Catherine Bailey, *Black Diamonds. The Rise and Fall of an English Dynasty* (Viking/ Penguin, 2007)

Ray Battye, *The Forgotten Mines of Sheffield* (Alistaire Lofthouse, 2004)

John Benson and Robert G. Neville (eds), *Studies in the Yorkshire Coal Industry* (Manchester University Press, 1976)

Brian Elliott, *Pits and Pitmen of Barnsley* (Wharncliffe, 2001)

Brian Elliott, *Yorkshire Miners* (The History Press, 2004)

Brian Elliott, *Yorkshire Mining Veterans* (Wharncliffe, 2005)

David Douglass and Joel Krieger, *A Miner's Life* [Doncaster] (Routlege, Kegan & Paul, 1983)

John Goodchild, *West Yorkshire Coalfield* (The History Press, 2000)

Alan Hill, *The South Yorkshire Coalfield. A History and Development* (Tempus/The History Press, 2001)

Robert G. Neville, *The Yorkshire Miners in Camera* (Hendon, 1976)

John Threlkeld, *A Pictorial History of Mining* (Wharncliffe, 2003)

Peter Tuffrey, *Doncaster's Collieries* (Amberley, 2011)

Peter Williams, *Images of Yorkshire Coal* (Landmark, 2005)

Derbyshire and Nottinghamshire
David Bell, *Memories of the Derbyshire Coalfields* (Countryside Books, 2006)

David Bell, *Memories of the Nottinghamshire Coalfields* (Countryside Books, 2008)

Alan Ramsey Griffin, *Mining in the East Midlands 1550–1947* (Cass, 1971)

Alan Ramsey Griffin, *The Nottinghamshire Coalfield 1881–1981* (Moorland, 1981)

Clive Hardy, *When Coal Was King* (Derbyshire Times, 2010)

Terry Judge, *The Clay Cross Calamities* (Scarthin, 1994)

Terry Judge, *Journal of a Derbyshire Pitman, 1835–1906* [Joseph Wright, a hewer] (Highedge Historical Society, 1996)

*   *   *

Kes (Film: MGM, directed by Ken Loach, 1969 and based on Barry Hines' book *Kestrel for a Knave*, set in the Barnsley area)

Portrait of a Miner [features Thoresby colliery] (NCB Archive Collection, 1966)

The Price of Coal (1977, BBC Play for Today television plays written by Barry Hines and directed by Ken Loach)

Lancashire and Cheshire coalfields
The oldest part of the coalfield had an area of 217 miles of exposed coal measures, mostly north of Manchester. Later development took place through Permian rocks further south, more than doubling the area. The Cheshire section was small,

production less than 2 per cent of the whole. An indication of the importance of the Lancashire coalfield was that 534 pits were recorded in the 1880 mine inspector's annual report and by 1911 there were over 300 collieries still working, employing 104,000 persons. Lancashire miners, like their South Wales counterparts, often worked 10-hour shifts, so the 1909 Eight Hour Act cut down production, as did the closure of many exhausted old pits. Mechanisation was also fairly slow; a good deal of coal was produced via old fashioned hand-got methods before the First World War, with associated risks to the miners.

The whole area was riddled with accidents and disasters, particularly during the 1850s and 1860s, especially around Wigan. The disasters at Wood Pit, Haydock, in 1878 (189 fatalities) and Clifton Hall seven years later (178 dead) were massive tragedies, but even these were eclipsed by the explosion at the Pretoria Pit (Over Hulton) in 1910 when 344 men and boys died in a single day.

The large number of shafts and collieries around several towns led to Atherton, Burnley, Manchester, Oldham, St Helens and Wigan being described as 'coalfields'. The thin Burnley seams meant a relatively small output and pit closures due to exhaustion of workable reserves, though sixteen collieries remained in production at nationalisation (1947). By 1970 only two, Bank Hall and Hapton Valley, still operated, closing in 1971 and 1982 respectively. In the Manchester coalfield twenty-two collieries remained at nationalisation. Mosley Common, the largest and most productive, closed in 1968. Manchester's Lancashire pits were absorbed into the NCB's Western Area and administered from its Staffordshire House offices, Berry Hill Road, Stoke-on-Trent. Oldham's pits were mostly small and closely associated with the local cotton industry. The St Helen's coalfield covered about sixty square miles, reserves in the shallow seams becoming exhausted by the 1960s, the area's output concentrated on a few large collieries such as Parkside, which functioned from 1964 to 1993 and was Lancashire's last deep mine. Wigan was probably the oldest and certainly the most intensively worked of the regional Lancashire coalfields, but there were few new collieries developed after 1900. At nationalisation just ten mines remained, Chisnall Hall being the last to finish in 1967.

Archives and libraries

Bolton Museum and Archive Service
Le Mans Crescent, Bolton, Lancashire, BL1 1SE
t. 01204 332 211   e. museum.customerservices@bolton.gov.uk
www.boltonmuseums.org/bolton-archives

Online catalogues for archives and local studies. Pretoria (Hulton) pit disaster information via menu on archives home page; also Pretoria Relief Fund. Lancs and Cheshire Miners' Federation Minutes 1920–69. Business records include Alkrington Colliery; Ladyshore Coal and Terra Cotta Company (Little Lever); Top o' th' Meadows Colliery (Darcy Lever); Westhoughton Colliery (plans) and Wingates Colliery (plans, reports etc). Estate papers contain coal mine references, especially regarding the Andrews and Bradford families. Image Collection includes coal-related pictures accessible online. Family history advice. Extensive newspaper and printed collection.

Cheshire Archives & Local Studies
Cheshire Record Office, Duke Street, Chester, Cheshire, CH1 1RL
t. 01244 973 812   e. recordoffice@cheshire.gov.uk
www.cheshire.gov.uk/recordoffice

Online catalogue allows search via archives and local studies. Mining results are mainly from estate and solicitors' collections (so limited personnel information), e.g. Shakerley Coal Company in Hulme and Somerford collection (DSS); DTO Toller family. Oakmere Hall Miners' Rehabilitation Centre, 1940s (D6078). Cheshire trade directories online. Colliery records include Astley Co., Bakestone, Hardshaw, Poynton & Worth, Shakerley Coal Co. Local studies collection also in local libraries, especially East Cheshire, Cheshire West and Chester.

Lancashire Archives/Record Office
Lancashire Record Office, Bow Lane, Preston, Lancashire, PR1 2RE
t. 01772 533 039   e. record.office@lancashire.gov.uk
www.lancashire.gov.uk/education/record_office

LANCAT online catalogue. Search via keywords 'coal', 'mine' etc for many results. Downloadable family history guide and research guides. Lancashire Lantern E-Resource (see online sources below). Main Lancashire depository for colliery records (ref NCB). Some HM Mines Inspector's reports e.g. c.1857–1870s (with gaps) and Manchester district reports e.g. 1903–04, 1906–13. Much coal industry printed material in the local studies collection.

Manchester Archives and Local Studies
Manchester Room and City Library
Elliot House, 151 Deansgate, Manchester, M3 2HN
t. 0161 234 1979   e. themanchesterroom@citylibrary

Greater Manchester County Record Office (with Manchester Archives),
56 Marshall Street, New Cross, Manchester, M4 5FU
t. 0161 832 5284   e. archiveslocalstudies@manchester.gov.uk

As from 2014 **Archives +** will operate in the refurbished Manchester Central Library in partnership with Manchester Archives and Local Studies, Greater Manchester County Record Office and other partners – see website for updates: www.manchester. gov.uk/libraries/arls. The Manchester Collection is searchable at findmypast.co.uk. For photographic images, see online sources below. Pastfinder online catalogue for Greater Manchester: use keywords such as 'coal', 'coal mine' 'colliery' and view results; or browse 'businesses' or 'family and estate papers'. Documentary Photography Archive (DPA) containing family photographs searchable via Pastfinder: enter 'DPA' in 'reference number field' when searching. HM Inspectors of Mines' reports 1851–1914 (with gaps). Estate records for coalmining (Record Office): Wilton Papers; Legh of Lyme Hall; Bagot Family and Assheton of Middleton (searchable catalogues).

People's History Museum/Archive and Study Centre – see national sources

Salford Local History Library and City Archives Centre

Salford Museum and Art Gallery, Peel Park, The Crescent, Salford, Lancashire, M5 4WU

t. 0161 778 0814   e. local.history@salford.gov.uk

www.salford.gov.uk/library

Online catalogue. Search using keywords such as 'colliery' for many results. Extensive family history sources, newspapers, photographs and printed material.

Liverpool Record Office

Central Library, William Brown Street, Liverpool, L3 8EW (from mid-2013)

t. 0151 233 5817   e. recoffice.central.library@liverpool.gov.uk

http://www.liverpool.gov.uk/libraries-and-archives/
archives-local-and-family-history

Online catalogues for archives and local studies. Liverpool in Print includes reading guides, e.g. archive sources, coroners' records, family history on the internet, family history, newspapers, photographs. Edmund Kirkby Archive: plans include Moss Colliery (Wigan) and Platts Fold (Tyldesley). Hulton Colliery disaster papers (1910) Mersey Gateway (is the image website, see online sources below).

St Helens Local History and Archives Library

Gamble Institute, Victoria Square, St Helens, Merseyside, WA10 1DY

t. 01744 676 952   e. localhistory&archivesservices@sthelens.gov.uk

www.sthelens.gov.uk/history or
http://calmview.sthelens.gov.uk/calmview (catalogue)

Online catalogue for archives, local books and collections. Many coal-related items if you use 'colliery' and 'coal mine' as keywords or use a local colliery name. Searchable index of seventy volumes of newspaper cuttings. Image gallery. Records held include Birchley Colliery collection (includes miners' wage books). Ian Winstanley's 'Mining Deaths in Great Britain' (7 vols, 1850–1914). Wood Pit/Haydock Colliery HM Inspector of Mines' report on 1878 disaster; Golborne explosion report (1979); Royal Commission on Mines (1907). Oral history collection includes Annie Nicholson, a 'pit brow lass' in 1930s; Jack Owen, James Dowd, James Knowles, John Baratt, John Boughey, John Case; Valentine Cotham coal miners/mining memories.

Wigan Heritage Services: Wigan Archives

Leigh Town Hall, Civic Square, Leigh, Wigan, Lancashire, WN7 1DY

t. 01942 404430   e. heritage@wict.org

www.wict.org/heritage-services/archives

Use online Guide to the Archives for an overview of the collections, especially business records; also occasional mining items in solicitor and and estate records. Most records deposited in Lancashire Record Office (see above) but Wigan Archives' Lancashire and Cheshire Miners' Permanent Relief Society collection is an important record of miners and their families. Maps and plans. Wigan Images Online includes many coalmining photographs (see online sources below).

Wigan Heritage Services: Museum of Wigan Life (previously The History Shop)
Library Street, Wigan, Lancashire, WN1 1NU
t. 01942 828 020 (local and family history)   e. heritage@wict.org
www.wict.org/heritage-services/museum-of-wigan-life

Extensive local and family history collections (see *A Guide to Genealogical Sources*, 3rd edition (purchasable) and 'Sources Available' on website page. Ian Winstanley's 'Mining Deaths in Great Britain' 1850–1914. Local colliery histories. Local newspapers, mainly 1830s onwards. Wigan Images Online (see online sources below).

Working Class Movement Library – see national sources

Places to visit

Astley Green Colliery Museum
Higher Green Lane, Astley Green, Tyldesley, Manchester, M29 7JB
e. info@agcm.org.uk www.agcm.org.uk

The museum is run and maintained by the Red Rose Steam Society and includes Lancashire's only surviving colliery headgear and engine house, and has the largest collection of colliery locomotives in the UK. Astley Green Colliery functioned from 1908–1970. Mining history displays. Regular openings on Sunday, Tuesday and Thursday afternoons or by arrangement.

Clifton Country Park: Wet Earth Colliery
Clifton House Road, Clifton, Salford, M27 6NG
t. 0161 793 4219   e. clifton.countrypark@salford.gov.uk (ranger)
http://www.salford.gov.uk/wetearthcolliery.htm

Industrial remains of Wet Earth Colliery, one of the first to be sunk in the Irwell valley in c.1740: engine shed (1896); Penstock arch and Wheel Chamber (both by James Brindley); Gal Pit; eighteenth-century cottage; Fletcher's folly (steam engine house) and fan house (1889). There's a visitors' centre on site.

A variety of mining artifacts and displays can also be seen at Burnley Art Gallery & Museum (Towneley Hall, www.burnley.gov.uk/towneley), the Museum of Science and Industry in Manchester (www.mosi.org.uk), and several smaller museums.

Family History Societies

Family History Society of Cheshire www.fhsc.org.uk
Manchester & Lancashire FHS www.familyhistorybolton.tk
North Cheshire FHS www.ncfhs.org.uk
St Helens Townships FHS www.sthelenstownshipsfhs.org.uk
Wigan Family & Local History Society www.wiganworld.co.uk/familyhistory

Online sources

Cheshire Memories http://blogs.chesterchronicle.co.uk/cheshire-memories
Nostalgia-type items posted, questions and answers. Search site via 'coal miner' etc.

Link4Life   w.www.link4life.org

Interesting information about coalmining in the Rochdale area: e.g. history, conditions of work, access via the Arts and Heritage section.

Images of Lancashire   http://images.manchester.gov.uk/index.php?session=pass

Manchester Local Image Collection. Over 80,000 images. Search, view and purchase high-quality A4 prints.

Lancashire Coalmining   www.jnadin1.50megs.com

Ex-miner Jack Nadin's Lancashire coalmining website. Family history name/colliery searches, a small donation welcome.

Lantern Lancashire   www.lantern.lancashire.gov.uk

Lancashire Life and Times E-Resource Network. Includes image archive, community information, local studies resources, pioneers, poetry index and library catalogue.

Northern Region Film & Television Archive   www.nrfta.org.uk

Based in Constantine Building, Teesside University, Middlesbrough. Search via 'Explore the collection' using keywords such as 'coal'.

North West Film Archive   www.nwfa.mmu.ac.uk

Based at Minshull House, Manchester Metropolitan University. Select Industry and Working Life and search for mining films using keywords such as 'coal', 'coal mine', 'colliery' etc. Limit search by date facility.

Picture Cheshire   www.picturecheshire.org.uk

Extensive photo archive (old and new images) with search, view and purchase options.

Stockport Image Archive
http://interactive.stockport.gov.uk/stockportimagearchive/searchdisplay.aspx

Coal mine/colliery items via search and view.

Wigan Images   www.wiganimages.wict.org

Wigan Leisure and Culture Trust Photographic Archive. Search, view and purchase coalmining photographs.

Wigan World   http://www.wiganworld.co.uk/stuff

Winstanley and Highfield mining communities, Park Collieries (memories of). Extensive site menu includes directories, Wigan past, Wigan dialect etc.

Useful books, film and video
Alan Davies, *Coal Mining in Lancashire and Cheshire* (Amberley, 2010)
Alan Davies, *The Atherton Collieries* (Amberley, 2009)
Alan Davies, *The Pit Brow Women of the Women Coalfield* (Tempus/The History Press, 2006/09)

Alan Davies, *The Wigan Coalfield* (Tempus, 2006)

Donald Anderson, *The Orrell Coalfield, Lancashire 1740–1850* (Moorland, 1975)

Ken Howarth, *Dark Days. Memories of the Lancashire & Cheshire Coalmining Industry* (Greater Manchester CC, 1995 edition)

H.L. Holliday, *Moston Colliery, Manchester. A Victorian Super-Pit* (Landmark, 2005)

Jack Nadin, *East Lancashire Mining Memories* (The History Press, 2008)

Geoff Simm and Ian Winstanley, *Mining Memories. An Illustrated Record of Coal Mining in St Helens* (St Helens MBC, 1990)

*   *   *

Parkside Colliery [Newton-le-Willows] *Shaft Sinking* (1959)

Oliver Wood, *West Cumberland Coal 1600–1982/3* (Cumberland & Westmorland Antiquarian and Archaeological Society, 1988)

*   *   *

Humphrey Jennings (dir), *At the Coal Face*: 40s Britain Series: featuring *The Cumberland Story* (1947) (Panamint Cinema, 2006)

The Midlands coalfields

The coalfields of the midland counties were fairly distinctive from one another and varied in size. Broadly speaking they were found in Staffordshire (north and south), Warwickshire, Leicestershire and Shropshire. A small coalfield also existed in Worcestershire but statistically it was often linked with Staffordshire. The South Staffordshire field was by far the most important in terms of extent, production and employment.

The North Staffordshire (or Potteries) field covered an area of about 100 square miles, excluding the (detached) Cheadle district, which added another 18 square miles to the total. Two smaller areas also existed: Goldsich Moss and Shaffalong. In 1874 the coal (and ironstone) mines had over 20,000 persons employed, and although many pits had closed (123 to 109 between 1851 and 1873) the surviving ones began to access reserves at deeper levels. The peak of production, over 7.5 million tons, was reached in 1939 (3.25 per cent of national output) prior to a long decline.

The larger South Staffordshire coalfield, which lay between the concealed Cannock Chase field and the Clent Hills, was about twice the size of its northern neighbour, 200 square miles in area. Reserves included the famous 30-feet 'ten-yard' or 'thick coal' seam, notably near Dudley. The seams in the Black Country were also shallow, an obvious economic advantage but countered by flooding and the awkward 'butty' system. At nationalisation over forty mines remained in Staffordshire as a whole, which became part of the NCB West Midlands Division. Baggeridge was the last south Staffordshire deep mine to close in 1967. The much-hailed Wolstanton Colliery, once the deepest mine in Europe, closed in 1985; and Littleton (1993), Hem Heath (1996) and finally Silverdale (1998) followed.

Staffordshire mining communities were badly affected by accidents and disasters, especially during the middle decades of the nineteenth century, but the most serious occurred at the Minnie Pit (Podmore Hall Colliery) in 1918 when 155 lives were lost.

The Warwickshire Coalfield covered an area of about 60 square miles between the towns of Coventry, Nuneaton and Tamworth. In the nineteenth century, there were

210

about twenty small mines. Production peaked in 1939 but by 1986 only four pits remained: Birch Coppice, Baddesley, Coventry and Daw Mill.

The oldest part of the Leicestershire Coalfield covered about 30 square miles and was centred around the town of Ashby-de-la-Zouch. It was often linked with the south Derbyshire field to the east. In 1880 there were twenty-six mines in Leicestershire. The last deep mine, Bagworth, closed in 1991. The most serious single disaster occurred at Whitwick Colliery in 1898 when thirty-five men lost their lives.

The Shropshire and Worcestershire coalfields included important areas in and around Coalbrookdale, Shrewsbury, Le Botwood, the Forest of Wyre, Dryton and Clee, in total about 98 square miles. In 1880 sixty-one mines were listed in Shropshire.

By 1913 the Midland coalfield as a whole employed 96,423 persons.

Archives and libraries
Leicestershire

Coalville Library
High Street, Coalville, Leicestershire, LE67 3EA
t. 0116 305 3565   e. coalvillelibrary@leics.gov.uk
www.leics.gov.uk/coalville_library.htm

Regional library of Leicestershire County Council – near to the Snibston colliery site and Discovery Museum – has good range of reference material about local coal-mining and sources and facilities for family history research.

The Record Office for Leicestershire, Leicester and Rutland
(and Local Studies Reference Library)
Long Street, Wigston Magna, Leicester, LE18 2AH
t. 0116 257 1080   e. recordoffice@leics.gov.uk
http://www.leics.gov.uk/record_office.htm

Online catalogue. Keywords such as 'colliery' will obtain many results for mines, ephemera, events, biographies, photographs etc. Records of the NCB in Leicester-shire c.1800–1994: business, planning, maps and plans of mines. Desford disaster. Accidents claims (Snibston). Bagworth Colliery notices of engagement 1955–1976. Purchasable family history handlists.

Snibston Discovery Museum: Mining Study Centre
Snibson, Ashby Road, Coalville, Leicestershire, LE67 3LN
t. 01530 278 444   e. snibston@leics.gov.uk
http://www.leics.gov.uk/snibston_museum

Study Centre in the old colliery office, access by appointment only. Substantial collection on Leicestershire coalfield includes technical aspects of the industry, NCB films, oral history interviews, maps, books and printed material. Online collection: start by browsing 'coal mining' to see objects relating to the Leicestershire coalfield (eg, Desford Colliery Band recording, Whitwick miner's tally) and access back-ground information via 'details' and 'resources'. Download 'mines of memory' on Snibston and Whitwick collieries and Coalville mining community via http://www.leics.gov.uk/minesofmemory.pdf. Also see places to visit, below.

University of Leicester Special Collections
David Wilson Library, University Road, Leicester, LE1 9QD
t. 0116 252 2056   e. specialcollections@le.ac.uk
www2.le.ac.uk/library/find/rarebooksandarchives/specialcollections

Special collections do not have any coal industry records but the library catalogue is worth searching via the Local History Collection (on open shelves). The 1843 commission of inquiry on employment of children in mines is SCM 06552 in the David Wilson Library.

Shropshire

Ironbridge Gorge Museum, Library & Archives
Coach Road, Coalbrookdale, Telford, TF8 7DQ
t. 01952 432 141   e. library@ironbridge.org
www.ironbridge.org.uk/about_us/libray_and_archives

The Research Library is based in the Long Warehouse, next to the Coalbrookdale Museum of Iron. The collection includes printed items on the social history of the East Shropshire Coalfield. Open weekdays by appointment.

Shropshire Archives (incorporates the former local studies library)
Castle Gates, Shrewsbury, SY1 2AQ
t. 01743 255 355   e. archives@shropshire.gov.uk
www.shropshire.gov.uk/archives

Browse online catalogue. Discovering Shropshire's History Catalogue is the most useful database, and also searches the local studies library. Link to Newsplan West Midlands website. Keywords such as 'colliery' will obtain many results eg. Madeley Court Colliery, Clee Hill Colliery, Colliers Side Colliery or search for a specific colliery; 'mine disaster' will also show several examples, e.g. Jackfield 1856, Dark Lane 1862, Madeley Wood 1910; or try searching for a named individual. Main coal records are from estate/private papers, e.g. Howard Williams, notes re Dawley and Madeley 1960s (1434) but are mostly administrative, deeds, plans; also NCB items, e.g. Highley Colliery (6277 [map]), Madeley Wood register of employees 1940–55 (6570). Shropshire Family History Society advice desk: Wed–Sat (10am–1pm). Family history and local history research guides online. Downloadable source guides include newspapers, maps, trade directories. Image service: order and purchase photographs, maps etc. Local history centres at Bridgnorth, Church Stretton, Craven Arms, Ludlow and Oswestry.

Staffordshire

Keele University Archives
The Library, Keele University, Staffordshire, ST5 5BG
t. 01782 733 237   e. h.burton@lib.keele.ac.uk
www.keele.ac.uk/library/specarc

Online catalogue. Special Collections include the papers of William Jack, formerly employed at Chaterley-Whitfield Collieries Ltd, relating to North Staffordshire mining history; also scrapbooks and minute books of the colliery (1870s–1926); and many of his photographs, an exhibition of which can be seen via the Staffordshire Past Track website (see online sources below). Family estate papers such as the Sneyd Archive also contain mining items though mainly administrative.

Stoke on Trent City Archives (SOTCA)
City Central Library, Bethesda Street, Hanley, Stoke on Trent, ST1 3RRS
t. 01782 238 420   e. stoke.archives@stoke.gov.uk

William Salt Library (WSL)
Eastgate Street, Stafford, ST16 2LZ
t. 01785 278 372   e. william.salt@staffordshire.gov.uk

The library is a registered charity supported by Staffordshire County Council, administered by an independent trust and run in close conjunction with the Staffordshire and Stoke on Trent Archive Service. 'Gateway to the Past' online catalogue also searches Stoke on Trent Archives, William Salt Library and Staffordshire Arts and Museum Service. Keywords such as 'colliery' and 'coal mine' will obtain many results: click on blue number for document details. Downloadable family history guides/sources guides include an excellent guide to colliery records (No. 6) and the relevant reference and access office, i.e. Staffordshire Record Office (SRO), William Salt Library (WSL) and Stoke on Trent City Archives (SOTCA). SRO, the main repository, holds the NCB West Midlands Division, Western Division (including Cannock Chase), Mid Staffordshire Area and North Staffordshire Area records. Individual collieries in the guide are listed according to coalfield location: Cannock Chase, North Staffordshire, South Staffordshire, Warwickshire (Staffordshire section); small items relating to other coalmining areas include Cheshire, Shropshire, Worcestershire, Yorkshire, Scotland and Wales. Trade union records for the Midland Miners' Federation/NUM Midlands Area and some NUM records (mainly minutes) are also held.

Staffordshire University Special Collections
Thompson Library, Staffordshire University, College Road, Stoke, ST4 2DE
t. 01782 294 771   e. libraryhelpdesk@staffs.ac.uk
www.staffs.ac.uk/support_depts/infoservices/library/collections/
special/list.jsp

Online catalogue. The Special Collections include the Mining Collection, which includes journals, maps, photographs, NCB records and original records from Hem Heath and Silverdale collieries – but currently uncatalogued, appointment to view required. For the Staffordshire Film Archive, formerly part of the university library collection, which includes the Sneyd Pit Disaster and *The Proud Valley* film, set in Wales, but filmed at and around Silverdale Colliery, see online sources below.

Wolverhampton Archives and Local Studies
Molineux Hotel Building, Whitmore Hill, Wolverhampton, WV1 1SF
t. 01902 552 480   e. archives@wolverhampton.gov.uk
www.wolverhampton.gov.uk/archives

Online catalogue via www.blackcountryhistory.org (also see entry for Dudley Archives below). Bilston area coal mines. Family history sources include photographs and maps, newspapers. Browse website menu under The History of Wolverhampton' (or site map) and see 'Work'; sub-list includes 'Coal Mining': Baggeridge Colliery, 'mining's legacy' and 'continue the story' through information on 'the local coalfield', 'early mining' and 'decline and closure'.

Warwickshire

Birmingham Archives and Heritage (BAH)
Central Library, Chamberlain Square, Birmingham, B3 3HQ
(BAH has moved to the new **Library of Birmingham**, Centenary Square, open from 3 September 2013: see http://www.birmingham.gov.uk/LOB for details)
t. 0121 303 4549   e. archives.heritage@birmingham.gov.uk
www.birmingham.gov.uk/archivesandheritage

Open Access Area for printed local and family history, maps and local newspapers. Archives Searchroom for archival collections, photographs, early printed material (reader's ticket needed). Online catalogue and browse types of collections (includes Public Records [e.g. coroner's inquests] and Deposited Records [e.g. estate papers, photographs and oral history recordings]). Search the catalogue (http://calmview. birmingham.gov.uk) using key words such as 'coal' and 'colliery' obtains many results. Separate catalogue for books and journals: http://www.birmingham.gov.uk/ libcat. Charles Parker Archive (MS4000) includes his BBC Radio Ballad *The Big Hewer* (1961, about miners); also see Banner Theatre of Actuality (MS1611), which includes items relating to miners' strikes (1972, 1984–5) and pit closures (1992): shows include *Collier Laddie* and *Saltley Gate*. 'Journey to your past': a guide to family history sources pack (£5).

Warwickshire County Record Office
Priory Park, Cape Road, Warwick, CV34 4JS
t. 01926 738 959   e. recordoffice@warwickshire.gov.uk
www.warwickshire.gov.uk/cro

Warwickshire Past Unlocked online catalogue (with tutorial): use appropriate keyword, e.g. 'colliery' or more precise name e.g. 'Baddesley Colliery' for results and click on 'view records' for archival details. NCB records (02942) include Coventry Colliery registers and papers re accidents (CR2468). Warwickshire Miners' Association c.1948 (CR2471/18). Warwickshire Collieries (CR2471) price lists, NUM 1902–1955. Record types include estate and family collections and business. Local newspapers, maps and plans. Also see Windows on Warwickshire (online sources below).

Warwick University Modern Records Centre
University Library, University of Warwick, Coventry, CV4 7AL
t. 024 7652 4219   e. archives@warwick.ac.uk
www2.warwick.ac.uk/services/library/mrc

Online archive search page. Use keyword such as 'coal mining' for many results, mainly twentieth century, and then access details of the full catalogue of the collection. Links to main holdings includes overview of main archives collection, which feature trade union records. 'Looking for an ancestor?' research aid, clicking on 'Miners' will reveal that some non-membership material is held (MSS.429) of the Miners' Federation of Great Britain (MFGB) and National Union of Mineworkers (NUM). Research guide: The Miners' Strike, 1984–5: Sources at the Modern Records Centre. Online exhibition web page: 'King Coal: The Turbulent Story of Coal Mining and its effect on British Life'. Papers of Lawrence Daly, former Secretary of NUM (MSS.302/11/). TUC files (MSS.292D), especially 1984–5 strike, including ephemera.

Worcestershire

Dudley Archives and Local History Service
Mount Pleasant Street, Coseley, West Midlands, WV14 9JR
(new archives and local history centre open from summer 2013 at Tipton Road site next to Black Country Living Museum).
t. 01384 812 770   e. archives.centre@dudley.gov.uk
www.dudley.gov.uk/leisure-and-culture/local-history—heritage/archive-and-local-history

Online catalogues, especially www.blackcountryhistory.org (people, places, times, subjects) searches through eight partner archives including museum services. Use keywords such as 'coal mining', 'colliery' or a colliery name for many results. Guide to sources held. 'How to' guides include family history. Dudley Web: Past and Present oral history project. 'Distinctly Black Country' network. Colliery Workmen's pay books 1848–1912 and 1848–1945. Baggeridge Colliery (e.g. R25133). The Dudley Web Oral History Project (BK04064). The Local Studies Library has an excellent range of printed material relating to coalmining. Ian Winstanley's List of Mining Deaths in Great Britain (7 vols, BK00854-65). Local newspapers and catalogued cuttings. Reports of HM Inspectors of Mines (West Midlands/Southern regions): 1911; 1952–9; 1960; 1961; 1962; 1965; 1966. Worcestershire branch of National Association of Colliery Managers (R10895). Miners' wages and the price of coal (1864–1909): R7331. Online catalogue details of company records via D6, D8, DPIt etc. The large Earls of Dudley Estate collection contains many mining references but not fully catalogued, reference DE; and other coal-industry items may not not yet be listed online.

The Hive
Worcestershire Archive and Archaeology Service
Sawmill Walk, The Butts, Worcester, WR1 3PB
t. 01905 822 866   e. archive@worcestershire.gov.uk
www.thehiveworcester.org or www.worcestershire.gov.uk/waas

New and fully integrated university [of Worcester] and [Worcester County Council] public library includes large and extensive local studies (for local and family history), archaeology and archive collections. Incorporates the former Worcester Library and History Centre. Developing online catalogue for archives. Access via keyword general search e.g. 'coal' will reveal many results, e.g. National Coal Board files 1943–48 and view; or use a more exact phrase. Archive area is on Level 2's 'Explore the Past'; public/university library is on Level 3 (download leaflet for details). Coalmining ventures into Warwickshire by Coventry family of Croome (B705:73 BA14450/233);

Forest of Dean mines (BA 9600/28vii); Abberley mines (4600/85; Baynton Colliery 1912–67 (BA 12661.Online research guides to family history, local history, oral history and community archives. Handlist to family history, microfilms, local newspapers, directory of oral history recordings (Worcestershire Sound Archive: coal mining at Worcestershire County Museum www.worcestershire.gov.uk/museum) via 'documents' menu. CARN ticket required to see original archives or bring along ID.

Places to visit
Leicestershire

Snibston Discovery Museum
t. 01530 278 444   e. snibston@leics.gov.uk
http://www.leics.gov.uk/snibston_museum

Museum on site of the former Snibston Colliery, established by George Stephenson in 1832 (pit closed 1983). Country park setting includes former garden of pit manager now the Grange Nature Reserve and landscaped pit spoil heap. Excellent coalmining displays from Tudor to modern era. Winding houses and spectacular headgears. Colliery tour with former mineworker includes engine house, lamp room, control room, medical centre etc and there is an 'underground' experience. Train ride to Coalville and old sidings via *Pitt*, the diesel locomotive, on special event days (see website for latest information). Annual miners' gala in September. Also see archives and libraries above.

Shropshire

Blist Hill Ironbridge Gorge Museums
Coach Road, Coalbrookdale,Telford, TF8 7DQ
t. 01942 580 650   e. information@ironbridge.org.uk   www.ironbridge.org

Internationally-acclaimed visitor features at Blist Hill Victorian Town include the Blist Hill Mine and winding house, fireclay mine with steel headgear, wooden headgear and ventilation furnace, adit (drift mine), candle works, mine railway and mine experience and miner's walk. Visitor Centre film show: story of the Industrial Revolution.

Staffordshire

Apedale Heritage Centre
Loomer Road, Chesterton, Newcastle-under-Lyme, Staffordshire, ST5 7JS
t. 01782 565 050   e. info@apedale.co.uk   www.apedale.co.uk

Site of Aurora/Apedale drift mine, which closed in 1998, located by Apedale Country Park. 'Mining in Apedale' online feature. Underground tours of 'authentic drift mine where the last coal was drawn in North Staffordshire': Saturdays, Sundays and Bank Holiday weekends. Museum collection has impressive collection of mining artefacts including a mine rescue van and drift mine (model). See website for sample items. Features on mine disasters, especially Minnie (1918). Miner's cottage ('bath night') and yard. Special events. Museum opens Fridays–Mondays. Also see North Staffordshire Coalfield via online sources below.

West Midlands

Black Country Living Museum
Tipton Road, Dudley, West Midlands, DY1 4SQ
t. 0121 557 9643   e. info@bclm.com   www.bclm.co.uk

One of Britain's most popular open-air museums, its collections of national and international importance, searchable online. Discover 'the world's first industrial landscape'. Guided tours of Racecourse Colliery, reconstructed over one of the Earl of Dudley's original small pits, Coneygreave Colliery No. 126, which operated from 1860 to 1902. Hear about the history of local mining. Headstocks and pulley wheel, steam-powered engine, manager's office. Brook Shaft, a reconstructed small 1930s pit is nearby, sited over an original 1840s pit worked before 1842. Canal-side village. Reconstructed full-scale replica of Thomas Newcomen's first steam engine, employed to pump water from coal mines on the Earl of Dudley estate. Working horses. Workers' Institute and Park.

Family history societies
Birmingham & Midland Society for Genealogy & Heraldry   www.bmsgh.org
Coventry FHS   www.cocfhs.org
Leicestershire & Rutland FHS   www.lrfhs.org.uk
Nuneaton & North Warwickshire FHS   www.nnwfhs.org.uk
Shropshire FHS   www.sfhs.org.uk
Warwickshire FHS   www.wfhs.org.uk

Online sources
Baddersley Colliery Disaster   www.baddersleypitexplosion.co.uk
Celia Parton's excellent website about the 1882 Baddersley (north Warwickshire) pit explosion.

Black Country Bugle   www.blackcountrybugle.co.uk
Nostalgia-type features, memories etc. Use search facility for coalmining items.

Coal Mining in North Staffordshire   www.staffspasttrack.org.uk/exhibit/coal
Multi-media archive includes audio recordings, images and information under themes such as history, safety and rescue, miners' lives, strikes, disasters, collieries.

Go Leicestershire
www.goleicestershire.com/see-and-do/industrial-heritage-nwleics-mining-tour.aspx
Includes an industrial heritage mining trail via former pit villages and towns.

Media Archive for Central England (MACE)   www.macearchive.org
Screen archive for Midlands includes former NCB archive of films collected from Chatterley Whitfield Colliery by Roy Johnson and volunteers. Free viewing. My Leicestershire Digital Archive (see separate listing below).

My Leicestershire Digital Archive
www.macearchive.org/Resource-area/My-Leicestershire.htlm

Collaboration between Midland Screen Archive and University of Leicester, East Midlands Oral History Archive (EMOHA) and local history organisations; also BBC Radio Leicester. Online repository of images, sound recordings and books, including coalmining. Searchable.

Newsplan West Midlands   http://wm.newsplan.co.uk/modules.php

Database of 1,100 newspaper titles. Includes Shropshire, Staffordshire, Warwickshire, Worcestershire and Black Country towns.

North Staffordshire Coalfield(s)   http://nsmg.apedale.co.uk/index.htm

Hosted by the Apedale Heritage Centre (see museums, heritage centres/places to visit above). Useful historical information about north Staffordshire mines and miners; also see Bob Burdon's site 'North Staffordshire Coalfields': http://myweb.tiscali.co.uk/coalface/index.htm.

Shropshire Mining   www.shropshiremining.org.uk

A history of Shropshire mining in words and images.

Staffordshire History   www.staffshistory.org

Now developed by Julian Bielewicz in Queensland, Australia. Very useful local history reference site and includes Staffordshire History Journal. Navigate website through simple click-on links.

Staffordshire Places   www.placespasttrack.org

Examples of archives (via places) deposited with the Staffordshire and Stoke on Trent Archive.

Staffordshire Past-Track   www.staffspasttrack.org.uk

Mining and quarrying theme for images and information; and search by keyword such as 'colliery'.

Windows on Warwickshire   www.windowsonwarwickshire.org.uk

Project involving Warwickshire CRO, Warwickshire libraries, museums and galleries. Browse collections by location, object and subject or use advance search for specific item. Good for images of collieries and mine-related objects.

Wolverhampton History & Heritage   www.localhistory.scit.wiv.ac.uk

This large and very useful local history site includes the Black Country and has coalmining items e.g. search Black Country and its industries; also use keyword searches.

Useful books, film and video
David Bell, *Memories of the Leicestershire Coalfields* (Countryside Books, 2007)
David Bell, *Memories of the Staffordshire Coalfields* (Countryside Books, 2010)
David Bell, *Memories of the Warwickshire Coalfields* (Countryside Books, 2011)

Harold Brown, *Most Splendid of Men. Life in a Mining Community 1917–25* [N. Staffs] (Blandford Press, 1981)

Ivor Brown, *East Shropshire Coalfields* (Tempus, 1999)

Nigel A. Chapman, *The South Staffordshire Coalfield* (Tempus/The History Press, 2005 & 2010)

Jean Caswell and Tracey Roberts, *Getting the Coal. Impressions of a Twentieth Century Mining Community* [Leicestershire: Coalville, Bagworth, Ellistown], (Mantle Oral History Project, 1992)

Paul Deakin, *Collieries of North Staffordshire Coalfield* (Landmark, 2004)

Fred Leigh, *Mining Memories. A Portrait of the Collieries of North Staffordshire* (SB Publications, 1992)

Richard Stone, *The Collieries and Coalminers of Staffordshire* (Philimore, 2007)

*　　*　　*

Miners [featuring men from Bagworth Colliery, Leicestershire] (NCB Archives [films], 1976)

Nines was Standing [Haunchwood Colliery, Warwickshire, pit consultative committee at work] (NCB Archives, 1950)

The Miner [featuring Hilton Main colliery, Wolverhampton] (NCB Archives)

The Proud Valley, Ealing Studios Collection, 1940 (2010). South Wales context but filmed at Silverdale Colliery

Sneyd Pit Disaster January 1st 1942, Staffordshire Film Archive

Bristol and Somerset/Forest of Dean (Gloucestershire) coalfields

It was conventional for official statistics to group the Bristol (and Gloucestershire) and Somerset coalfields as a single field though each had their own characteristics. The whole area covered about 240 square miles, but was important between Bristol and Bath, and especially around Radstock. The main families and companies were the Beauchamps, Bennetts, Waldegraves, Handel Cossham, Leonard Boult & Company and Egbert Spear. Working the shallow seams in probably the worst geological conditions imaginable was very demanding for the miners, who were poorly paid. Pits were small and the few disasters that took place did not result in the massive loss of life as in other coalfields, but were of course felt with an equal sense of loss. Communities associated with the Wellsway (1839), Newbury (1869) and Norton Hill collieries (1908), were affected by disasters, resulting in twelve, eleven and ten deaths respectively. Annual output of coal was quite modest, about a million tons in 1912, with 6,500 persons employed, mostly in north Somerset. In 1947 there were thirteen pits in production but reserves were low, and the mines became run down. Only six remained in 1960. A new mine, Harry Stoke (1961–63), failed and the last two collieries, Kilmersdon and Writhlington, closed in 1973.

The **Forest of Dean coalfield** was a small but thriving mining area covering about 34 square miles and had been worked from ancient times. It was peculiar because of the long association of its 'freeminers' and their defined rights to a *gale* (a lease of a defined area subject to the payment of a small royalty to the Crown). The right of sub-letting of freeminer areas (after 1838) to coal owners/companies with sufficient capital for investment and development led to a boom in production. Thus in 1880

219

the mine inspector listed seventy-one mines here in his annual report. By 1912 the number of men employed in the coalfield reached 8,524, a not inconsiderable figure. Wages, however, were low if compared with those in south Wales. At nationalisation in 1947 the Forest of Dean was exempted from state control due to its ancient and unique system of ownership and regulation. However, the NCB purchased six collieries: Arthur & Edward [Waterloo], Cannop, Eastern United, Narchard, Northern United and Princess Royal. Northern United was the last to function, closing in 1965. A few 'micro mines' continue to be worked by freeminers in this historic and attractive area.

Archives and libraries

Bristol Central Library: Local Studies
College Green, Bristol, BS1 5TL
t. 0117 903 7200   e. bristol.library.service@bristol.gov.uk
www.bristol.gov.uk/page/local-studies

Oral history collection includes several coalmining transcripts (KHP09, RO38, R081 and R102), provided by the South Gloucestershire Mines Oral History Project 2009. Dean Lane explosion, HM Mines Inspector report 1887. Local newspapers. Several published miners' memoirs.

Bristol Record Office
'B' Bond Warehouse, Smeaton Road, Bristol, BS1 6XN
t. 0117 922 4224   e. bro@bristol.gov.uk   www.bristol.gov.uk/recordoffice

Online catalogue. Use keywords such as 'colliery' for many results but mainly for eighteenth and nineteenth centuries. Click on blue numbers for details; or use a specific colliery/personal name, e.g. Bromley Colliery, Sir George White papers. Plans for mines, see 39398.

Bristol University Special Collections
Arts and Social Sciences Library, University of Bristol, Tyndall Avenue, Bristol, BS8 1TJ
t. 0117 928 8014   e. special-collections@bristol.ac.uk

Online archive catalogue. Somerset Miners' Association minutes, correspondence, 1868–1964; includes accident reports, strikes and lock-outs (DMM443).

Dean Heritage Centre: Gage Library
Camp Mill, Soudley, Forest of Dean, Gloucester GL14 2UB
t. 01594 822 170   e. gagelibrary@deanheritagecentre.com
www.deanheritagecentre.com

Registered charity. The library contains many books and printed material relating to the Forest of Dean as well as archival material, maps and images; also items relating to family history research plus access to ancestry.com. Research access by appointment or by online enquiry form. Open Wednesday afternoons. Online catalogue in progress. Also see entry in museums, heritage centres/places to visit below.

Gloucestershire Archives

Clarence Row, Alvin Street, Gloucester, GL1 3DW

t. 0152 425 295   e. archives@gloucestershire.gov.uk

www.gloucestershire.gov.uk/archives

Online catalogue (archives and/or local studies or library: use keywords such as 'coal/ coal mining', 'collieries' etc (for a quick search) for many results; then click blue 'overview of records' for details; or use a specific colliery/personal name, e.g. Forest of Dean: deeds of Collingwood Colliery. NCB 1911–1980s ([D7837] some uncatalogued/ restricted holdings): mining in Forest of Dean mainly but some South Gloucestershire/ Bristol & Somerset coal items. Forest of Dean freeminers. Genealogical database contains a name index. South Gloucestershire Resource is a guide to archive material, some of which is housed at Bristol RO (download pdf). Newspapers guide download. Researching your family history online guide to resources; sources include coroner's records from 1844.

Radstock Museum: Research Room

Waterloo Road, Radstock, Somerset, BA3 3EP

t. 01761 437 722   e. info@radstockmuseum.co.uk

North Somerset Coalfield items. The research room is open Tuesdays by appointment, when the archives can be consulted. Useful for family history mining ancestry research. Excellent photographic collection is viewable at www.radstockmuseum photos.blogspot.com. Also see museums, heritage centres/places to visit below.

Somerset Heritage Service: Archives and Local Studies

Somerset Heritage Centre, Brunel Way, Langford Mead, Norton Fitzwarren, Taunton, TA2 6SF

t. 01823 337 600   e. archives@somerset.gov.uk

www.somerset.gov.uk/archives

Online archive catalogue. Keywords such as 'coal' and 'colliery' will obtain many results (click on blue number for details of record) e.g. 32: nominal roll Kilmerston and Writhlington collieries (ref': A/BDM/15/2/7). Try searching more specifically via 'Somerset coalfield' or a colliery name; or use the surname search facility. NCB records re Somerset mines (DD/NCB) and British Coal Corporation records (A/BDM). Some Somerset Miners' Association (1912) and Bristol Miners' Association (1889–94) records. Library catalogue (new window). Research/holdings guides include researching your Somerset family, coroner's records (pdf), maps, newspapers, estate and manorial records, pictures and photographs (including Frith and excellent postcard by browsing locations and locations/images), printed sources. Online OS maps complete set of 1:10,560 for Somerset (c.1885 & c.1903). Somerset Voices Oral History Archive (new window) includes several ex-miners.

Places to visit

Dean Heritage Centre

Camp Mill, Soudley, Forest of Dean, Gloucestershire, GL14 2UB

t. 01594 822 170   e. online form   www.deanheritagecentre.com

Forest of Dean Heritage Centre includes a museum and educational/research facility. History of the forest including coalmining information and displays (in Gallery 3). Visit a replica of a traditional hillside mine used by the freeminers.

Hopewell Colliery Museum
Speech House Road, Cannop Hill, Coleford, Gloucestershire, GL16 7JP
t. 01559 810 706

Seasonally-working Forest of Dean drift mine with small museum. Underground tour. Summer opening but check for details before visiting.

M-Shed
Princess Wharf, Wapping Road, Bristol, BS1 4RN
t. 0117 352 6600   e. info@mshed   www.mshed.org

Former dockside industrial museum now transformed into a modern and major visitor attraction exploring Bristol's history. Local mining information in Places Gallery and via online site: 'explore and contribute' has useful background on the Bristol coalfield. Radstock pithead head gear is in store.

Radstock Museum
Waterloo Road, Radstock, BA3 3EP
t. 01761 437 722   e. info@radstockmuseum.co.uk
www.radstockmuseum.co.uk

The many interesting mining exhibits and displays include a replica coal face, miner's cottage, two-decker cage, artefacts etc. Mine disaster information. *Five Arches Journal* (Radstock & Midsomer Norton & District Museum Society). Shop and tearoom.

Ram Hill Colliery site
Coalpit Heath Westerleigh, South Gloucestershire
http://www.southglos.gov.uk/LeisureCulture/MuseumsHeritage/RamHill.htm

Nineteenth-century colliery remains (OS ref: ST679802) include engine house, horse gin, dramway. Scheduled ancient monument. Friends Group.

Family history societies
Bristol & Avon FHS www.bafhs.org.uk
Gloucestershire FHS www.gfhs.org.uk
Somerset & Dorset FHS www.sdfhs.org

Online sources
Bath in Time www.bathintime.co.uk

Searchable image library. Shops and Industry menu includes 'Working Life'. Many coal-related items.

Bristol Stories www.bristolstories.org
Watershed digital story project in partnership with M-Shed (see museums, heritage centrtes/places to visit above) and Bristol Museums, Galleries and Archive Service.

Integrated sound and image collection includes Dean Lane Pit 100-year commemoration; mining in Bedminster.

Bristol Past: The Changing Face of Bristol   www.bristolpast.co.uk

Photographic archive of Bristol includes coalmining: view images and captions. Image database can be searched via flckr. Message Forum for family/local history research.

Clutton (north Somerset)   www.clutton.org.uk

Somerset village had three local pits: Burchells, Fry's Bottom and Greyfield, historical details and background.

The Colliers Way   www.colliersway.co.uk

Interesting coalmining details via Heritage menu near and along the recreational path linking Dundas, Radstock and Frome.

Frampton Cotterell Mining (Coalpit Heath, South Gloucestershire)
http://www.framptoncott.co.uk/mining.htm

History of mining at Coalpit Heath by local historian Trevor Thompson.

Forest of Dean Local History Society
http://79.170.40.163/forestofdeanhistory.org.uk

CD of mine fatalities and freeminers listing available. Research guides. Events programme.

Gloucestershire Revealed   www.gloucestershirerevealed.co.uk

Guide to local museums, galleries and heritage.

Nailsea and District Local History Society   www.ndlhs.org.uk

Includes a history of mining in the locality. DVD: Nailsea Bottle Green and Coal Black.

Somersetshire Coal Canal Society (SCCS)   www.coalcanal.org

The canal carried coal from the Paulton and Radstock areas to the Kennet and Avon Canal. Images, maps, history and features.

South Gloucestershire Mines Research Group   www.sgmrg.co.uk

Useful site with many interesting items relating to mining. Includes local publications e.g. *Bristol's Forgotten Coalfield – Bedminster* (2012); *Frog Lane Colliery* (2009); *Kingwood Coal* (2008); *The Bristol Coal Industry* (2003). Open days at Oldwood Pits, during annual national Heritage Open Days.

Useful Books, film and video

Beth Anstis and Ralph Anstis, *Diary of a Working Man, 1872–1873. Bill Williams* [of Trafalgar Colliery] *in the Forest of Dean* (Sutton, 1994)

Ralph Anstis, *Blood on Coal. The 1926 General Strike and Miners' Lockout in the Forest of Dean* (Black Dwarf Publications, 1999)

John Cornwall, *Collieries of Somerset & Bristol* (Landmark, 2005)

John Cornwall, *The Bristol Coalfield* (Landmark, 2003)

C.G. Down and A.J. Warrington, *The History of the Somerset Coalfield* (David & Charles, 1971, reprinted by Radstock Museum, 2005)

Fred Flower, *Somerset Coalmining Life* (Millstream, 1990)

Ken Griffiths, *Miners' Memories of the South Bristol Coalfield* (Fiducia Press, 2011)

Cyril Hart, *The Free Miners of the Forest of Dean and Hundred of St Briavels* (Black Dwarf Lightmoor Press, 2002 [revised edition])

A.J. Parfitt, *My Life as a Somerset Miner* (Radstock Museum, 2005 [first published 1932])

*   *   *

Nailsea Bottle Green and Coal Black (DVD: 1st Take)

Somerset Mining Memories. A History of Coal Mining in Somerset told by the Men and Women who Lived it (DVD: Radstock Museum, 2005)

Kent coalfield

This entirely concealed field, only an hour or so from London by rail, was not discovered until 1890, Kent Collieries Limited developing the Shakespeare (Dover) mine in 1905–15. Kent Coal Concessions Limited also sank several pits. The great depths needed for shafts and inundations of water made development very difficult, with lots of stops, starts and abandonments. The survivors were Tilmanstone (1906–86), Chislet (1918–69), Snowdown (1908–86) and the largest, Bettshanger (1924–89), famously the last pit to return to work after the 1984/85 miners' strike (and the last to close). Many miners from the old coalfield regions of south Wales, the Midlands and northern England found work in one or more of the four big pits of Kent, and new communities emerged at places such as Aylesham, Elvington, Hersden and Mill Hill.

Archives and libraries

Kent History and Library Centre (KHLC),
James Whatman Way, Maidstone, Kent, ME14 1LQ
t. 08458 247 200   e. historyandlibrarycentre@kent.gov.uk
www.kentarchives.org.uk

New centre replaces Centre for Kent Studies, East Kent Archives Centre and several libraries. Online catalogue searches material at the KHLC and Canterbury Archives. Using keywords such as 'colliery' will result in references to Bettshanger, Chislet, Dover, Snowdown, Tilmanstone and Guilford collieries. NACODS East Kent branch records 1937–1990. Maps and plans. Photographs and aerial views. Online family history reference resources. Explore Kent's Past project (see online sources below). The book collection cane be searched via the online Kent Libraries catalogue. Some local libraries have coal industry items such as news cutting files, images, maps and newspapers.

Dover Museum
Market Square, Dover, Kent, CT16 1PB
t. 01304 201 066   e. museumenquiries@dover.gov.uk
www.doverdc.co.uk/museum

224

Mining artefacts, oral history collection and a large database of photographs in the museum collection. Online information on Kent coalfield and Miners' Way Trail via CHIK (Coalfield Heritage Initiative Kent – see online sources below). Rich Seam walks pack (purchasable).

Family history societies

Kent FHS   www.kfhs.org.uk

Online sources

Coalfields Heritage Initiative Kent (CHIK)   www.dover.gov.uk/kentcoal

Excellent site on the Kent coalfields with lots of useful information in the form of text, images and oral histories. Started by Dover District Council and led by Dover Museum and the White Cliffs Countryside Project. Includes the Miners' Way Trail.

Dover History Scrapbook   http://doversociety.homestead.com/collieries.html

Interesting site includes Dover (Shakespeare) Colliery information and images.

East Kent Local History Pages   www.eastkent.freeuk.com

Use menu to access 'Mining' ('A brief history of mining in East Kent . . .').

Exploring Kent's Past   www.kent.gov.ExploringKentsPast

Search the Kent Historic Environment Record for colliery-related items: sites, buildings and finds.

Here's History Kent   www.hereshistorykent

Search Kent History and Kent place-names for pictures and articles.

Kent History Forum   www.kenthistoryforum.co.uk

Very useful forum for family history research/contacts. Try searching for recent comments on Kent collieries, e.g. Bettshanger or place your own request online.

Useful books

J.P. Hollingsworth, *Those Dirty Miners. A History of the Kent Coalfield* (Stenlake, 2010)
Ross Llewellyn, *Hersden. Chislet Colliery Village* (K H McIntosh, 2003)
A.E. Ritchie, *The Kent Coalfield, its evolution and development* (Nabus Press [digital reprint of original 1923 edition], 2010)

WALES

Regional Welsh coalmining records that survive are well scattered amongst many former coalfield archives and libraries, but the South Wales Coalfield Collection, held partly at the University of Swansea's Singleton campus and at the South Wales Miners' Library, is a resource of international importance. An overview of archival holdings can also be seen via the Welsh Archive Network, referred to below. There are also several excellent museums that are well worth visiting, including **The Big Pit** and **National Waterfront Museum**, both included in Section II, national sources.

North Wales Coalfield

Often overlooked but with a proud mining heritage, this small coalfield covered about 103 square miles and was concentrated in the counties of Denbigh, Flint and a small part of the island of Anglesey. Faults and inclined seams always hampered mining. In the early 1900s production gradually increased to a peak of c.3.1 million tons with 16,000 persons employed, coal closely allied to the local iron industry. The decline of the area led to a migration of some miners, for instance from Mostyn to Carlton, near Barnsley, where the Welsh formed their own distinctive community. At nationalisation in 1947 the NCB managed six deep mines: Gresford, Llay Main, Point of Ayr, Bersham, Hafod and Ifton, part of its North Western Division, with Area headquarters at Llay, near Wrexham. By 1974 only Bersham and Point of Ayr remained, the latter closing in 1996. Although north Wales was not noted for major disasters, the terrible explosion and fire at Gresford in 1934 killed 266 men, the highest number of fatalities at a British colliery in the modern, post-First World war era.

Archives and libraries

Flintshire Record Office

The Old Rectory, Rectory Lane, Hawarden, Flintshire, CH5 3NR

t. 01244 532 364   e. website enquiry form   www.flintshire.gov.uk/archives

Online index to records. User guides (downloadable) include family history (No. 3). Source guides include Coroner's Records (No. 12). Personal/subject name indexes. Records from medieval to modern times include businesses and industries, families and estates e.g. Mostyn of Talacre Estate MSS (mines in Picton, Gwespyr and Holywell [D/Mt/94-96]; Hawarden coalmining accounts, 1739 (D?Bj/358) and coal-mining deeds for Mold collieries, 1868–1927 (D/DM/292/2-7). Browse Subject Index for document reference numbers e.g. accidents: list of subscribers to Gresford Disaster Fund 1934 PC70/17; collieries/coalmining: Point of Ayr photograph of two miners 1957 D?DM?1300/1. Holdings also include a large collection of NUM North Wales Area records (D/NM). Gresford Colliery Disaster Relief Fund MSS (GB0208 D/GF). Large compensation claim files by individuals re industrial disease c.1930–1970: indexed in the search room but part restricted under Data Protection Act: access/ application via the Freedom of Information Office, Flintshire County Council. Downloadable lists include coalmining records (contains general, place and named collieries, including Gresford disaster (1934)); local newspapers; photographs (arranged by parish). Coleshill Colliery Handbill (purchasable). Quarterly news-letter: *The Hourglass* (download) e.g. Spring 2012 includes 'A Hawarden Colliery Accident 1784'. Archive (images) Gallery.

Flintshire Libraries
Library Headquarters, County Hall, Mold, CH7 6NW

t. 01352 704 411   e. libraries@flintshire.gov.uk   www.flintshire.gov.uk

Search the online catalogue and browse online reference sources. A good community network of local and family history research facilities. For information access 'History and Heritage at Your Library' from the menu of Leisure and Culture. The @answers centre at Mold has a major local history collection. It's Flintshire Memories oral history recordings includes an interview with ex-miner Tom Jones aka 'Tom Spain', who served in the Spanish Civil War, an active trade unionist. Tom worked in Rhos, near Wrexham and recalls the Gresford disaster and Bersham Colliery. Mining in the old Clwyd area of Flintshire.

University of Bangor: Archives and Special Collections
College Road, Bangor, Gwynedd, LL57 2DG
t. 01248 382 983   e. library@bangor.ac.uk
www.Bangor.ac.uk/library/archive

Online catalogue. Archive collection includes estate and family papers from medieval times to present day. Plas Gwyn Papers. Welsh Library collection. Colliery records available include Berw Uchaf, Glantraeth, Penrhyn Mawr.

Wrexham Archives and Local Studies Collection: A.N. Palmer Centre
Wrexham County Museum and Archives, Regent Street, Wrexham, LL11 1RB
t. 01978 297 480   e. localstudies@wrexham.gov.uk or e. archives@wrexham.gov.uk
www.wrexham.gov.uk/english/heritage/archives

Online catalogues. Searching museums, archives and local studies catalogue using key words such as 'colliery' will give many results. Books and printed material. Maps and plans. Local newspapers: holdings downloads. Photographic collection. Sources for family history research. Picture Wrexham (see online sources below). Websites for family historians.

Places to visit
Bersham Colliery Mining Museum
Bersham Heritage Centre, Bersham, Wrexham, LL14 4HT
t. 01978 318 970   e. bershamheritage@wrexham.gov.uk
http://www.wrexham.gov.uk/english/heritage/bersham_colliery-visitors.htm

Scheduled ancient monument in the care of Wrexham CBC and Bersham Colliery Trust. Open by prior appointment and on open days. 'Former engine house and the last headgear still standing in the North Wales coalfield', Bersham Colliery's history began with its sinking by the Barnes family from Liverpool in 1868 and was the last working pit in the Denbighshire coalfield, closing in 1986. The current metal headgear, from nearby Gatewen Colliery, replaced a timber-framed version destroyed by fire in 1930. The adjacent coal-tip/muckstack is now also preserved following a campaign/protest by Cadw (Welsh historic monuments agency) in 2007 when the shale spoil was threatened with sale and removal.

Mold Museum/Flintshire Museums Service
Earl Road, Mold, Flintshire, CH7 1AP
t. 01352 754791   www.flintshire.gov.uk

Daniel Owen (1836–1895) came from a local mining family; his father and two brothers were killed in a flooding accident at Argoed Colliery. Apprenticed as a tailor, against all the odds he became one of Wales's greatest writers, famous for novels such as *Rhys Lewis* (1885) and *Enoc Huws* (1891). On display is a reconstruction of Owen's study and shop; the collection also has items relating to Buckley and Mold

227

collieries, available by appointment. Flintshire museums main coalmining collection relates to the Point of Ayr Colliery.

Gresford Colliery Disaster Memorial
(Near Gresford Colliery Club, Bluebell Lane, Pandy, Wrexham, LL12 8EE, off A483)

Commemorates one of Britain's worst pit disasters when an explosion and subsequent fire caused the deaths of 266 miners. Erected in 1982, comprising two tapering stone piers supporting one of the winding sheaves from the colliery. In 2000 the names of all those who lost their lives were added to the memorial.

Flintshire Museums
www.flitshire.gov.uk

Mining collection relates to Point of Ayr Colliery; smaller items concerning Buckley and Mold mines at Mold museum.

Family History Societies
Clwyd FHS   www.clwydfhs.org

Online sources
North East Wales History (BBC)
http://www.bbc.co.uk/wales/northeast/sites/history/pages/pits.shtml

Useful pages on pit names, personal nicknames (Wrexham link), family history; Gresford disaster also featured on www.bbc.co.uk/wales/northeast/sites/wrexham/pages/gresford_disaster.shtml.

North Wales Miners Association Trust   www.northwalesminers.com

Bersham Colliery mine site charity trust. Working life in the coal mines, Gresford disaster, news items and lots of useful information about mine sites, colliery lists etc and useful links.

Picture Wrexham   www.wrexhamimagebank.org.uk

Digital images from Wrexham Archives and Local Studies Service. Search and buy mining prints.

Useful books, film and video
Ithel Kelly, *North Wales Coalfield. A Collection of Pictures.* Vol. 1 (Bridge Books, 1990)
The Terrible Price. Gresford 1934 (DVD: Panamint Cinema)

South Wales Coalfield
At the eve of the First World War the South Wales Coalfield was the largest and most important in Britain, and one of the biggest in the world, covering a huge area of almost 1,000 square miles, from Pontypool in the west to St Brides Bay in Pembrokeshire. In 1912 it produced a quarter of all UK coal output from 649 mines and had 221,000 employees, a small number of them women. Glamorgan was by

far the most important county (398 mines), followed by Monmouth (122 mines) and Carmarthen (71). A small number of mines were also located in Brecon (25) and Pembroke (6). The quality of the coal – bituminous, steam and anthracite – was exceptional, and the black gold of South Wales was sold worldwide from the ports of Cardiff, Newport, Swansea, Port Talbot and Barry.

The demand contributed to the relatively higher wages of Welsh miners but this was also due to the great efforts of the unions, its leaders and men constantly protesting for their rights at pit and district levels. The miners also worked in the most dangerous coalfield in Britain where seams were fiery and deep. Accidents were commonplace. Between 1850 and 1920 about one in three of all mining fatalities were in south Wales. The average annual death rate for the years 1901–10 was 1.78 per thousand employees, worse than any other coalfield, some 70 per cent higher than in Yorkshire, which was by no means a safe area. Disasters at Llanerch (176 dead) and Morfa, Glamorgan (87) in 1890 were soon followed by Great Western (63) and Combs (139) in 1893; and the huge (290-fatality) disaster at Albion in 1894. About half of the major disasters in Britain from 1890 to 1920 were in south Wales. The terrible tragedy at Senghenydd (Glamorgan) in 1913 when 439 miners were killed remains Britain's worst mining disaster.

The South Wales coalfield fared badly during the 1920s and 1930s, losing almost half of its collieries. At nationalisation in 1947 135 collieries remained and the NCB sank new mines, for instance Cynheidre in 1954–56. But decline accelerated through the 1960s. In 1984, at the start of the miners' strike, fewer than thirty mines remained. The last deep mine, Tower Colliery (at Hirwaun), closed by British Coal in 1994, was the subject of an heroic buyout by Welsh miners and continued to function until 2008. A resurgence of interest in high-quality coal has resulted in the redevelopment of the Unity and Aberpergwm drift mines in the Neath Valley and anthracite will be extracted by opencast methods around Tower Colliery. Gleision Colliery in the Swansea valley, one of a handful of very small private pits still working in south Wales, attracted worldwide media attention when four miners lost their lives there following an inrush of water from old workings in 2011.

Archives and libraries

Cardiff Central Library Local Studies Department
The Hayes, Cardiff, CF10 1FL
t. 029 2038 2116   e. centrallibrary@cardiff.gov.uk
www.cardiff.gov.uk

Online catalogue. Local newspaper collection. *Colliery Guardian* 1861–1976*. Mines & Quarries Inspectors' Reports 1921–75*; HM Inspectors of Mines Disaster Reports (mostly S. Wales region, with in-house index); List of Mines 1893–1950*; *South Wales Coal Annual* 1903–1937*; Mon & S Wales Miners' Permanent Provident Society Annual Reports 1881–1920. 25 inch OS maps, South Wales coalfield maps 1873–1924. Ian Winstanley's Mining Deaths in Great Britain 1850–1914 [7 vols]. *South Wales Coalfield Directory* [2 vols, compiled by Ray Lawrence, 1998]. Some MS material, see MS catalogue http://apps.cardiff.gov.uk/WebCat Images/PDF/PDF055.pdf (* = with gaps).

Carmarthenshire Archive Service
Parc Myrddin, Richmond Terrace, Carmarthen, SA31 1HQ
t. 01267 228 232   e. archives@carmarthenshire.gov.uk
www. archives.carmarthenshire.gov.uk

Downloadable holdings include family and estate papers, business papers: records of Emlyn Colliery is the main item relating to the coal industry.

Glamorgan Archives
Clos Parc Morgannwg, Leckwith, Cardiff, CF11 8AW
t. 029 2087 2200   e. glamro@cardiff.gov.uk   www.glamarchives.gov.uk

Online catalogue: htttp://calmview.cardiff.gov.uk/calmview/. Using keywords such as 'colliery' will obtain many results e.g. Cardiff Collieries Ltd, Llanbradach Records; Universal Colliery Explosion, Senghenydd, Coroner's Report and so on: but very few employment records; also please note that not all colliery records are accessible via the online catalogue. General description of former NCB (South Wales Area) records can be seen on the online catalogue (general reference DNCB); more detailed cataloging pending. Pay books and accident compensation registers for a small number of collieries. Patchy coverage of mines inspectors' reports (DNCB 67): copies for some districts e.g. South Wales, Cardiff and Newport; annual reports (DNCB/67/2) from 1888 and explosion/disaster reports from 1885 (DNCB/67/3). Tynewydd disaster account written by miners who were buried underground and later rescued (DX557/1). Powell Duffryn Ltd (DPD) records are catalogued and online.

Gwent Archives (formerly Gwent County Record Office)
Steelworks Road, Ebbw Vale, Blaenau Gwent, NP23 6DN
t. 01495 353 363   e. enquiries@gwentarchives
www.gwentarchives.gov.uk

Holdings include many coalmining records. Subject Index under 'Miners' contains a list of names of miners mentioned in records, mainly deeds; and under 'Mining Disasters' there are items such as 'Trust Funds after colliery explosions' and 'Death Rolls' (these often provide name lists). Accident Compensation Registers (D3491) c.1920–c.1951 (some closed due to data protection). *And they worked us to Death*: three booklets by Ben Fieldhouse listing victims of multiple-death pit disasters. Wages sheets from Big Pit c.1950s (not yet indexed: D2732/ACC3072). Guide to research No. 3: *The Coal and Iron Industries*, lists main resources held, e.g. Report of Inspection of Coal Mines 1856; maps and plans; coal company records e.g. Blaenavon Iron & Coal, Brynmawr Iron & Coal, Guest Keen & Nettlefolds, Nantyglo & Blaina Iron & Coal, Partridge Jones & John Paton; nationalisation papers, NUM (South Wales)/ Miners Federation of Great Britain Lodge records c.1890s–c.1960s; Area records 1907–1974. Useful for reference: *The South Wales Coalfield Directory* by Ray Lawrence.

West Glamorgan Archive Service
Civic Centre, Oystermouth Road, Swansea, SA1 3SN
Archives: t. 01792 636 589   e. westglam.archives@swansea.gov.uk
www.swansea.gov.uk/westglamorganarchives

Archives: a joint service for the councils of the City and County of Swansea and Neath Port Talbot Borough. There are also Service Points in Neath and Port Talbot (see website for details). Archive Search Room, Family History Centre and Shop are housed in Swansea Civic Centre (formerly the County Hall). Tracing your family history printed guide. Comprehensive download 'Sources available in the Family History Centre ...' includes 'Glamorgan colliery disasters': index of victims at Senghenydd and Wattstown, 1901–1913 (fiche); Penallta Colliery workmen's register, 1915–1919 (fiche); Tracing your Family History and related downloads. Online archive catalogue. Relevant records in business (Ynyscedwyn Iron, Coal and Steel Co [D/D YISC]; Main Colliery company[D/D MC]; Glenavon Garw Colliery Company [D/D TDN]; estate and family papers; also Women Archive of Wales: [WAW 1; WAW 4; WAW 11] for 1984/85 miners' strike/support groups. Browse catalogue e.g. business records or conduct a general search using online catalogue. Keywords such as 'coal', 'colliery' will generate many results. The oral history archive includes several recordings of former mineworkers and women talking about local mining/ mining communities: browse to see basic details of colliery names, personal names and places.

Swansea Central Library
Central Library, Civic Centre, Oystermouth Road, Swanse, SA1 3SN
Local Studies: t. 01792 636 464   e. libraryline@swansea.gov.uk
www.swansea.gov.uk/libraries

The Local Studies collection contains an excellent range of resources suitable for family and local history research; and online use of the Cambrian Index (see online sources below). Online library catalogue. Local newspapers e.g. the *South Wales Daily/Evening Post* (1893–to date), the *Western Mail* (1869–to date). Newspaper cuttings file. Maps and plans. Photographs and other illustrations.

National Waterfront Museum – see national sources

Newport Reference Library & Local Studies Library
Central Library, John Frost Square, Newport, NP20 1PA
t. 01633 656 656   e. reference.library@newport.gov.uk   www.opac.gov.uk

Covers former county of Monmouthshire. Online library catalogue. Local newspapers: *South Wales Argos* (1892–to date); *Monmouthshire Merlin* (1829–1891). Local Studies card catalogue e.g. South Wales Mining Company Prospectus (1925); List of Abandoned Mine Plans for Monmouth Division (1929); Reports of HM Inspectors of Mines (1947).

Pembrokeshire Record Office
The Castle, Haverfordwest, SA61 2EF
t. 01437 763 707   e. record.office@pembrokeshire.gov.uk
www.pembrokeshire.gov.uk

Online summary of main collections download; also family history and useful Coal Mining in Pembrokeshire downloads (accessible via Topic Lists on main website). Also browse index via Archives Wales http://arcw.llgc.org.uk/anw/browse_repository. php?inst_id=32?&L=0. Private collections (Business) include items re coalmining at

Hook, Sandersfoot, Nolton and Roch. Local newspapers e.g. *Western Telegraph* 1854– to date. Pembrokeshire section of the 1842 Employment of Children report (HDX/ 159/43). Indices at the record office under 'coal' headings. Maps and plans. Books on the Pembrokeshire coalfield.

Rhondda Cynon Taf Library Service (RCTLS)
www.rctcbc.gov.uk

Reference and family history sources at **Aberdare** (Green Street, Aberdare, CF44 7AG; t. 01685 880 050; e. Aberdare.Library@rhondda-cynon-taff.gov.uk)**:** Price Collection, for Powell Duffryn); **Treorchy** (Station Road, Treorchy, CF42 6NN; t. 01443 773 204; e. Treorchy@rhondda-cynon-taff.gov.uk): Ferndale Relief Fund Minute Books now on CD Rom; HM Inspector of Mines Reports; and **Pontypridd** (Library Road, Pontypridd, CF37 2DY; t. 01443 493 258; e. Pontypridd.Library@rhondda-cynon-cynon-taff.gov.uk). The RCTLS Photographic Archive enables search and purchase of many images (see online sources below). Many local newspapers e.g. *Rhondda Leader* 1899–1902. Winstanley Mining Deaths in Great Britain 1850–1914.

Swansea University Richard Burton Archives
Library and Information Centre, Singleton Park, Swansea, SA2 8PP
t. 01792 295 021   e. archives@swansea.ac.uk
http://www.swan.ac.uk/lis/historicalcollections/archives

Holds the **South Wales Coalfield Collection** (SWCC), a huge resource that includes records of the South Wales Miners' Federation (later the NUM South Wales Area) and its individual lodges; also records from miners' institutes, co-operative societies and individuals connected to the mining industry; books, pamphlets, posters, etc. There is an online catalogue for the SWCC at www.agor.org.uk/cwm (archives, photographs, audio tapes, video, banners and printed material. Documents and photographs (over 4,000 images) are held at Singleton Park and the 'media' collection (banners, audio/video tapes, books etc) at the **South Wales Miners' Library** (SWML: see below). Leaflets: The South Wales Coalfield Collection; The Richard Burton Archives.

South Wales Miners' Library (SWML)
Information Services & Systems, Swansea University Henrefoelan Campus,
Gower Road, Swansea, SA2 7NB
t. 01792 518 603   e. miners@swansea.ac.uk   www.swansea.ac.uk/iss/swml

Part of the South Wales Coalfield Collection (see above), an exceptionally important library of coalmining history, especially for the coalfield valleys, with excellent facilities, open to all researchers as well as university students and staff. Online library catalogue: http://ifinddiscover.swan.ac. Pamphlets, posters, oral history and video collections, newspaper cuttings, miners' banners and books. Some HM Mines Inspectors' and Mine Disaster reports. Leaflets: South Wales Miners' library; Lest We Forget: Banners of the South Wales Miners. Banners can be viewed at www.agor.uk/ cwm/banners.

Places to visit

Aber Valley Heritage Centre and Museum

Senghenydd Community Centre, Senghenydd, Caerphilly, CF83 4HA
t. 02920 830 4445   e. senghen.heritage@btconnect.com
http://www.your.caerphilly.gov.uk/abervalleyheritage

Established by the Aber Valley Heritage Group, the museum commemorates the explosions at the Universal Colliery, especially the 1913 disaster. Wider aspects of mining and community history are also displayed, including the Windsor Colliery. Contains artefacts, memorabilia, photographs and film archive. Cabinet displays and two touch-screens. BBC audio recording of William Vizard who survived the 1913 disaster; also the award-winning *Mourning of the Valley* YouTube film. Mon–Sat openings, 11am-2pm normally. Heritage Trail nearby. Also see online sources below.

Big Pit Mining Museum – see national sources

Cefn Coed Colliery Museum

Neath Road, Creunant, Neath, SA10 8SN
t. 01639 750 556   e. colliery@btconnect.com   www.npt.gov.uk

Was the deepest anthracite coal mine in the world when sunk in 1913, also unaffectionately known as 'the Slaughterhouse' because of the dangerous working conditions. Former steam winding engine is now electrified but remains impressive. Engine House, headframes, drams and displays. Excellent online audio tour (down-loadable) by ex-Blaenant Colliery Deputy and tour guide. Summer opening only, 28 May to 1 Oct (check website or phone museum).

Cwm Colliery & Abernant Tunnel

t. 01685 727 474   e. tic@merthyr.gov.uk   www.visitmerthyr.co.uk

Opposite Merthyr Tydfil Leisure Village. Remains of the old colliery (1845–1910) and associated buildings, once part of William Crawshay's Cyfartha Works. The tunnel, completed in 1863, took the Vale of Neath railway from Merthyr to Abernant Halt (Aberdare) and Hirwaun Junction. It closed in 1963. Also see Cyfartha Castle Museum & Art Gallery below.

Cyfartha Castle Museum & Art Gallery

Brecon Road, Merthyr Tydfil, CF47 8RE
t. 01685 727 371   e. museum@merthyr.gov.uk   www.visitmerthyr.co.uk

Industrialist William Crawshay's house, now a museum. Collection includes several coalmining artifacts and equipment. Also see Cwm Colliery & Abernant Tunnel above.

Fforest Uchaf Pit Pony Sanctuary

Maendy Road, Penycoedcae, Pontypridd, Rhondda, CF47 1PS
t. 01443 480 327   e. info@pitponies.co.uk   www.pitponies.co.uk

Last few retired pit ponies/horses at Uchaf Fforest Farm Pony Rehabilitation Centre and Pit Pony Sanctuary. Excellent online videos on the charity website include the last Welsh pit ponies. Information via 'modern pit ponies' menu. Open May–October (Monday–Friday & Sunday).

Kidwelly Industrial Museum
Broadford, Kidwelly, SA17 4LW
t. 01554 891 078   e. Info@kidwellyindustrialmuseum.co.uk
www.carmarthenshire.gov.uk and www.kidwellyindustrialmuseum.co.uk

Site of one of Britain's oldest tinplates works but coalmining exhibits include colliery headframe, steam winding and Morlais coal complex.

National Waterfront Museum – see national sources

Newbridge Colliery Beam Engine
University of Glamorgan, Pontypridd, CF37 1DL

Although not in situ, this restored steam winding engine, often regarded as the first of its kind in the Rhondda, is well worth seeing. Located across the road from a car park, the engine appears as an almost sculptural as well as engineering campus feature. By Varteg Iron Company, dating from 1844, it was installed at Newbridge/ Gelliwion Colliery in 1844 by the coalmaster John Calvert and functioned until 1919. It was re-erected here shortly afterwards, an impressive open-air showpiece and exhibit for the then South Wales School of Mines. The engine's latest restoration was by the University in 1996.

Pontypool Museum
Park Buildings, Pontypool, Torfaen, NP4 6JH
t. 01495 752 036   e. pontypoolmuseum@hotmail.com
www.pntypoolmuseum.org.uk

The museum's local industry collection includes mining items (closed Mondays). The Dobell-Moseley Library and Archive has ephemera and printed material, photographs, maps and plans and local books: by appointment only, Wednesday and Thursday mornings.

Rhondda Heritage Park
Lewis Merthyr Colliery, Coed Cae Road, Trehafod, Pontypridd, CF37 2NP
t. 01433 687 420   e. reception@rhonddaheritagepark.com
www.rhonddaheritagepark.com

Based at Lewis Merthyr Colliery, which functioned c.1862–1983. Visitors' Centre includes art gallery, shop and cafe; and Village Street, which includes Tyneydd mine disaster exhibition. Black Gold Tour well worth experiencing, guided by an ex-miner (see miner profiles on website); includes pit-head buildings such as engine house, lamp room and realistic 'underground' visit. Check website for events and opening/ tour times.

South Wales Miners' Library (banners) – see archives etc above

234

South Wales Miners' Museum
Afan Forest Park, Cynonville, Port Talbot, SA13 3HG
t. 01639 851 833   e. southwalesminers@btconnect.com
www.southwalesminersmuseum.co.uk

In pleasant country park setting, outside exhibits include blacksmith shop, lamp room, pulley wheel, engine and drams. Tour guide. Many interior exhibits and displays. Cafe and gift shop. Small library. Open Easter–October daily; Tuesday–Sunday winter.

St Fagans National History Museum
Cardiff, CF5 6XB
t. 029 2057 3500   e. use web contact form
www.Museumswales.ac.uk/en/stfagans

'Wales' most popular heritage attraction'. Open-air museum in grounds of St Fagans Castle and gardens. Reconstructed buildings include The Workmen's (Oakdale) Institute; and there is a reconstructed miner's home interior.

The Winding House/Elliot Colliery
Cross Street, New Tredegar, NP24 6EG
t. 01143 822 666   e. windinghouse@caerphilly.gov.uk
www.windinghouse.co.uk

Built on the site of the former Elliot Colliery, its centrepiece being the original Victorian winding engine, which is demonstrated on Bank Holidays and event days (check website for running days). Online History of Elliot Colliery, which functioned from 1888 to 1967. New museum opened in 2008 by Caerphilly County Borough Council (open Tues–Sun and Bank Holiday Mondays, 10–5) incorporating the Elliot attraction. Has coalmining displays and a Heritage Research Centre. Searching online 'Our Collection' via 'Explore History' menu using keywords such as 'colliery' will reveal many results relaying to objects, documents and photographs.

University Colliery Mining Disaster Memorial
Nant-Y-Parc Primary School, Caerphilly, Mid Glamorgan, CF83 4GY
GR: ST1139591033

Aber Valley memorial to the 1901 and 1913 disasters at Senghenydd, which accounted for 81 and 439 deaths of men and boy miners. Colliery headframe set on raised brick platform was erected in 1981 near the site of the pit and next to a primary school. An attached bronze plaque commemorates the disasters. A new Memorial Wall has now been funded to commemorate the disasters, to be officially unveiled to mark the centenary of the 1913 event. Also see Senghenydd Heritage Centre above and Aber Valley Heritage online source below.

Family history societies

Dyfed FHS   www.dyfedfhs.org.uk

Glamorgan FHS   www.glamfhs.orh

Gwent FHS   www.gwentfhs.info

Online sources

Aber Valley Heritage   http://your.caerphilly.gov.uk/abervalleyheritage

Site of Aber Valley Heritage Group, heritage centre and museum. Also see places to visit above.

Agor   www.agor.org.uk

University of Wales Swansea's site includes many very useful items relating to coal mining in South Wales: photographs, videos, audio recordings and information. Also see **Coalfield Web Materials**, below.

Cambrian Index Online   www.swansea.gov.uk/index.cfm?articleid=5673

Index of the *Cambrian*, the first English-language newspaper to be published in Wales, 1804–1930. Also see West Glamorgan Archives above.

Coal House   www.bbc.co.uk/wales/coalhouse2/index.shtml

Interesting BBC Wales series (2007/08) filmed at Bleaenavon replicating the lifestyle of a family living in a coalmining town. First series set in 1927 and second in 1944, the latter including conscripted Bevin Boys. Also see extracts on YouTube.

Coalfield Web Materials   www.agor.org.uk/cwm

Based on the South Wales Coalfield Collection at the University of Wales Swansea (see above). Explore video clips, audio recordings and photographs. Also see archives, libraries and local studies centres above.

Senghenydd   http://www.senghenydd.net/senghenydd_explosion_octobe/

Simon Barnett's US site is a photographic record of the 1913 Senghenydd disaster. 'Explosion Gallery' is a collection of postcards by Benton showing aftermath of the disaster.

Senghenydd Pit Disaster BBC Wales History Blog
http://www.bbc.co.uk/blogs/waleshistory/2011/10/
the_senghenydd_pit_disaster_html

BBC Wales History blog featuring Phil Carradice's comments on the Senghenydd pit disaster of 1913. Includes audio of William Vizard who survived the disaster.

The Winding House Collection
http://yourcaerphilly.gov.uk/windinghouse/explore-history/our-collections

Explore collection of The Winding House/Elliot Colliery site, research centre, events etc. Also see museums, heritage centres and places to visit above.

Wallace the Pit Pony   www.youtube.com/watch?v=dlcD8tS3rmE

Life of a pit pony short film 'as sung by Wallace the adorable animated pony and his mates'. For primary school consumption but useful generally. Part of Film Encounters heritage education programme. More pit pony clips can be seen on YouTube.

Useful books, film and video

David Barnes, *Black Mountains. The Recollections of a South Wales Miner* (Y Lofta Cyf, 2002)

A.J. Booth, *Small Mines of South Wales* (Industrial Railway Society, 1995)

M.R. Connop-Price, *Pembrokeshire. The Forgotten Coalfield* (Landmark, 2004)

B.L. Coombes, *These Poor Hands. The Autobiography of a Miner in South Wales* (Victor Gollancz, 1939)

John Cornwall, *Collieries from Aberdare to Ebbw Vale* (Landmark, 2009)

John Cornwall, *Rhondda Cynon Taff Collieries* (Landmark, 2008)

John Cornwall, *Collieries of Blaenavon & the Eastern Valleys* (Landmark, 2009

John Cornwall, *Collieries of South Wales* (Landmark, 2001, 2002)

Sharon Ford, Ceri Thompson and Peter Walker, *The Big Pit* [guide]. National Coal Museum (National Museum of Wales, 2005)

Bill Jones and Beth Thomas, *Coal's Domain* (National Museum of Wales, 1993)

David Lewis, *The Coal Industry in the Llynfi Valley* (Tempus/The History Press, 2006)

John O'Sullivan. *A Photographic History of Mining in South Wales* (Sutton/The History Press, 2001/10)

David Owen, *South Wales Collieries* (six vols) (Tempus/The History Press, 2001–05)

Leslie M. Shore, *Peerless Powell Duffryn of the South Wales Coalfield* (Black Dwarf Lightmoor Press, 2012)

W. Gerwyn Thomas, *Welsh Coal Mines* (National Museum of Wales, 1979)

Ceri Thompson, *Harnessed. Colliery Horses in Wales* (National Museum of Wales, 2008)

Ceri Thompson, *Miniature Miners* [child labour in mines] (National Museum of Wales, forthcoming)

*   *   *

Blue Scar (film directed by Jill Craigie), post-nationalisation drama includes underground scenes at Llanharan Colliery, Abergwynfi, Outlook films, 1949

How Green Was My Valley (film starring Walter Pidgeon and Maureen O'Hara, based on Richard Llewellyn's classic novel), Twentieth Century Fox, 1941

The Proud Valley (film starring Paul Robeson) Ealing Studios, 1940

The Welsh Miner. A Hard Life. The History of Miners and Mining in Wales (DVD: Artsmagic, 2007)

The Welsh Miner. The Bitter End. The History of Miners and Mining in Wales (DVD: Artsmagic, 2007)

Chapter 10

NATIONAL SOURCES

Making the most of local and regional sources makes a great deal of sense but many national collections contain information not available elsewhere. Much can be achieved online via their respective websites but there is no substitute for a personal visit. Providing you are well prepared (and websites and/or curators/librarians/ archivists will advise you on what is required) much can be achieved in one or a few sessions. In most cases you will need to make an appointment and/or register but this process is very straightforward. You can also keep up to date through respective social media sites, blogs, flickr (images) and by obtaining email/newsletter updates and apps.

You will certainly gain both information and experience from a visit to one or more of our excellent national mining museums. Other national museums and art galleries, with their gallery displays, website images and audio collections, should not be overlooked.

As we have seen, personal records of miners are hard to come by, but the facility to obtain official state-owned information about our more recent mining ancestors is available by request from the Iron Mountain document storage (and retrieval) service – a facility that is well known by solicitors working on miners' compensation scheme claims; and the Coal Authority's Mining Heritage Centre in Mansfield is worth visiting in order to access old mine plans and many thousands of digitised photographs.

The separate selections of online sources listed here, by no means exhaustive, should help with both researching background information and specific items of interest.

Moving image collections provide us with some of the most compelling insights into the life and times of miners, families and communities. They really should be viewed. The footage is twentieth century, of course, but often the images hark back to earlier periods. Alongside oral history archives, film is the most underrated of sources on coalmining history.

SCOTLAND
National Mining Museum Scotland

> Lady Victoria Colliery, Newtongrange, Midlothian, EH22 4QN
> t. 0131 663 7519   e. enquiries@nationalminingmuseum.com
> e. keeper@nationalminingmuseum.com (for collections/library)
> www.nationalminingmuseum.com

The museum, created in 1984, is based at the former Lady Victoria Colliery, which functioned from 1895 until closure in 1981. Exceptionally, most of the old surface buildings remain. Guided pit-head tours by ex-miners and self-guided audio tours. 'Big Stuff' machinery tour (Wed/Sun). The Old Power House is now a function room but contains original features. The 'processing area' : Tippler Floor, Picking Tables, Elevator Shed and Undercroft can be seen; and also the magnificent former steam winding engine (now electrically powered) and towering headstocks. Miles Oglethorpe's article (from his excellent *Scottish Collieries* [RCAHM Scotland] book) about the colliery can be downloaded as a pdf file via the About the Colliery menu. The major exhibition themes are The Story of Coal and A Race Apart. Cafe and shop (some products available to purchase online). For museum entry fees see 'Visiting' menu of website.

For research, the **Archives and Reference Library** holds mining books, journals, trade catalogues, HM Inspector of Mines' reports (1855, 1873, 1881, 1883, 1884, 1888, 1891–94, 1896–1906 and all years from 1910–1938 (and the single wartime volume covering 1939–1946); also some Scottish regional and special disaster reports 1850s-1880s and 1907 (copy). Records of the Lothian Coal Company, former owners of Lady Victoria Colliery also available. A useful family history/'mining ancestors' information/research guide. There is a large and extensive image/picture collection. The library is open to researchers by appointment on Thursdays (for enquiries see contact details above).

Access the museum collection online is via the Collection menu under broad themes such as 'photo collection' (via mining equipment, coal industry, collieries, communities, underground scenes, unions, workers), 'object collection' (mining equipment and social history)'; and you can also get information relating to oral histories, exhibitions, new acquisitions, online exhibitions, the library, research papers etc. As well as sample images and information you can also search using keywords. Under the Learning menu, downloads, see: 1984 Miners' Strike; Qualifications; Women and Mining Communities; Women and Children pre-1842; Early Mining; Housing; Mines Rescue; and Ponies. Also useful is the download information pack about Bevin Boys.

National Records of Scotland (NRS)
The new official body following the merger of National Archives of Scotland (NAS) and General Register Office for Scotland (GROS). Also incorporates ScotlandsPeople Centre for family history research.*

HM General Register House, 2 Princess Street, Edinburgh, EH1 3YY
t. 0131 535 1314   e. enquiries@nas.gov.uk   www.nas.gov.uk

Historic Search Room (HSR)
t. 0131535 1334   www.nrscotland.gov.uk

ScotlandsPeople Centre
Room 28, New Register House, 3 West Register Street, Edinburgh, EH1 3YT
t. 0131 314 4300   e. enquiries@scotlandspeoplehub.gov.uk (or online enquiry form)
www.Scotlandspeoplehub.gov.uk

NRS holds the main historical records relating to coalmining in Scotland. A very useful research guide is available online (http://www.nas.gov.uk/guides/coalmining.asp) and there is an online public catalogue.

A major resource is their holdings of the National Coal Board records (CB), mainly from mid-twentieth century, but some pre-nationalisation (pre-1946) records of earlier coal companies (a dated list is shown on the guide referred to above) are available. Documents such as wage, pay and output books may be worth consulting for named workers and some of these may also be found within private (GD) collections. The latter will also include rules and regulations governing a pit, bonds binding colliers and their families to the mines. A source list of mining material found in private papers is available in the search rooms.

For HM Mines Inspectorate reports search the catalogue by entering 'Inspectorate' in the *Search for* box and 'CB' in the *Reference* box, but the post-NCB era reports have limited family history value.

Eminent mining engineer Robert Bald's reports on various collieries (CB27) may be useful if your ancestor was a miner c.1800–25.

Other 'family history' mining sources include those relating to Court of Session (CS) cases where coal companies appeared before the court, therefore some will relate to names in wage books and daybooks (and certainly concern colliery owners). Sheriff court records may also have personnel information relating to miners. The names of more than 200 mineworkers from Stirlingshire, for example, were recorded by the coal owners in Stirling sheriff court (SC67/63/6).

Friendly Society records (FS), especially the mineworker operated examples such as Kilmarnock Coal Cutters Society (FS1/2/41) and Carfin Colliery Friendly Society (FS1/16/29), are also held.

Coalmining plans (RHP) may also be useful for a particular colliery where your ancestor worked (see online guide to this source: topographical, architectural and engineering plans). Plans are mainly accessed (digitally) in the Historical Search Room (HRR), though some may be seen remotely on the ScotlandsPeople website. Certain plans may only be available by appointment with the HRR at Thompson House, for example those that are fragile or technically difficult to reproduce electronically.

Another useful online research guide concerns Fatal Accident Inquiries (FAI). Between 1861–1895 persons involved in mine accidents should be recorded in the Procedure Books in the Lord Advocate's records (AD12/19-21) and also be included in the sheriff court (SC) accident inquiries and/or workmen's compensation series; but there will be gaps.

Post-1855 death records can be viewed from the ScotlandsPeople website at a reasonable cost (full certificates only for deaths more than fifty years ago) and you can order an official extract (i.e. statutory register entry).

A large illustrated booklet, *The Coalminers* (1983), published by the former Scottish Record Office, is still valid for background information on Scottish mining and miners. It can be obtained from the ScotlandsPeople Centre shop (in person, email or post). Tristram Clarke's *Tracing Your Scottish Ancestors* is the NCM's official guide and is also available as an e-book. For coalminers see part 28, pp. 194–5. Try to obtain at least the latest, currently 6th revised, edition.

[*ScotlandsPeople allows you to view digital images of many NRS/Office of the Lord Lyon records either via pay-to-view (online) or by visiting the centre. Personal visits will be possible regionally when the SP resources become available in local family history centres around Scotland.]

The National Library of Scotland (NLS)

George IV Bridge, Edinburgh, EH1 1EW

t. 0131 623 3700   e. enquiries@nls.uk; or use *Ask a Librarian* online service.

Department email addresses include ils@nls.uk (document supply);
manuscripts@nls.uk; maps@nls.uk; modernscottish@nls.uk (post-1900 publications);
newsplanscotland@nls.uk (newspapers).

www.nls.uk

Online catalogue: very many results for keywords such as 'colliery', 'mine disaster', mine explosions etc or use a colliery name, colliery owner/company; event, person, coal-related subject etc. Helpfully, a selection of related names e.g. 'collier', 'strike', 'lockout' etc will also appear in the *Discover* menu.

The NLS manuscript collections include the Scottish Area National Union of Mineworkers (NUM) records (NRAS 4081); also items relating to several mine-workers' associations e.g. Ayrshire, Fife & Kinross: see Trade Unions and co-operative societies (Scottish labour history collections: mineworkers' listings) via http://www.nls.uk/catalogues/labour-history/1. Papers of individuals connected to the mining industry include William Small, the Lanarkshire miners' leader; and the miscellaneous papers of the Scottish labour history collections include 'mining life', transcripts from tapes of interviews with miners working in Lady Victoria Colliery (now National Mining Museum Scotland) and other Scottish pits (10801/ 37), though some are classified as restricted.

Online family history help includes 'frequently asked questions' (http://www. nls.uk/family-history/questions) and a menu of genealogical guides. *Maps of Scotland* images are via http://maps.nls.uk. The *Licensed Digital Collections* (LDCs) can be browsed by subject e.g. History, Biography and Genealogy; Newspapers; Pictures and Images (for **Scottish Screen Archive**, see below). LDCs can be freely consulted in the NLS library (register online) and many remotely if you live in Scotland. View examples of digitised material via the *Digital Gallery*. Very usefully, the NLS holds a complete run of the HM Mines Inspectorate reports from c.1854 onwards: try searching the catalogue under 'mines inspection' and/or consult a librarian for availability of particular reports.

Also very useful is the NLS's *Scottish Bibliographies Online*, a huge database which allows you to search via a subject (e.g. coal miner), author, journal, keyword, and so on. Another outstanding source is the library's searchable *Scottish Post Office Directories* – over 700 digitised examples (1773–1911). Search for coal companies/ collieries, pit managers, agents, mining engineers etc by name and you can view pages and download; and see histories of places, lists of trades, businesses, shops and services in mining communities over time.

Scottish Screen Archive (SSA)

National Library of Scotland, 39–41 Montrose Avenue, Hillington Park,
Glasgow, G52 4LA

t. 0845 366 4600   e. ssaenquiries@nls.uk   www.ssa.nls.uk

The national moving image collection, part of the National Library of Scotland. A general search via the online catalogue using 'coal', 'coal mining', 'colliery' will find results, some will have viewable film clips and full videos, alongside a detailed description; others description only. Examples include: *Coalmining in Central Scotland* (ref. 3942 [1930s]); *Industrial Stirlingshire* (1956 [1950]; *Scottish Coalmining* (0496 [1953]); *Hewers of Coal* (2381 [1939]); *New Day* (Glenrothes New Town) (0307 [1959]); *The New Mine* (Comrie Colliery, Fife) (0297 [1945]); and *Scottish Miners' Gala Day* (Edinburgh) (2022 [1953]). Wonderful footage here, well worth viewing. Subject to the usual copyright conditions you can buy or hire many of the films in a variety of formats, and view requested copies through the NLS's General Reading Room at St George's Bridge, Edinburgh (or by appointment on site at the SSA).

National Museums Scotland

National Museum of Scotland (NSM), Chambers Street, Edinburgh, EH1 1JF
t. 0300 123 6789   e. info@nms.ac.uk   www.nms.ac.uk

Museum collections can be searched online. Image library: see http://www.nms. ac.uk/about_us/about_us/collections_reearch/picture_library.aspx, or enquire via 0131 247 4236/4026. The Scottish Life Archive is accessible via *scran* (see below). Coalmining forms a part of Trade and Industry gallery in the museum. There is also a waterwheel-driven pump and working Newcomen pumping engine, formerly used at Caprington Colliery, Ayrshire.

The **Research Library** (RL) at the NMS (Level 3) has many printed items and archives, searchable via the online catalogue. Use of generic keywords such as 'coal', 'coal mining', 'colliery' will generate many results; or try a more specific name search. Contact the RL on 0131 247 4137 or library@nms.ac.uk to enquire/arrange a visit.

Royal Commission on the Ancient and Historical Monuments of Scotland (RCAHMS)

John Sinclair House, 16 Bernard Terrace, Edinburgh EH8 9NX
t. 0131 662 1456 e. enquiry form
www.rcahms.gov.uk

Massive archive of photographs, maps, drawings about Scottish buildings and landscapes, browsable, copied or purchased online or in person. Search for digital images via *Canmore* or use the National Collection of Aerial Photography facility: http://aerial.rcahms.gov.uk/ for colliery sites. Related publication: *Scottish Collieries*, Miles Oglethorpe (RCAHMS, 2006).

Scottish Genealogy Society

15 Victoria Terrace, Edinburgh, EH1 2JL
t. 0131 220 3677   e. enquiries@scotsgenealogy.com
www.scotsgenealogy.com

Provides volunteer-led help on Scottish family and local history, plus events/ courses/talks. Library and Family History Centre with many useful resources and internet access.

Online sources

ASGRA (The Association of Scottish Genealogists and Researchers in Archives)
www.asgra.co.uk

Includes a list of professional researchers.

Ask Scotland   www.askscotland.org.uk

Online information service provided by Scotland's libraries. Customized response to any email request.

Gateway to Scotland   www.geo.ed.ac.uk

Very useful introduction/starting point of internet information on Scotland.

Gazetteer for Scotland   www.scottish-places.info

Online encyclopaedia featuring towns and villages. Search via maps and places or history timeline or pages. Check featured events, e.g. Udston pit disaster.

Genuki   www.genuki.org.uk/big/sct/

Genealogical information relating to Scotland via county and subject and sources. Many useful links.

Scottish Archive Network (SCAN)   www.scan.org

Online catalogue enables you to obtain contact details for Scottish archives and related organisations (and take a virtual tour of some); and search holdings of more than fifty Scottish archives. Digitisation programme of historic records ongoing: check website for latest information.

(BBC) Scotland on Film   http://www.bbc.co.uk/scotland/history/scotlandonfilm/

Sound and vision archive with clips from historic film, television and radio programmes. Forum. Use 'work' theme and then 'The Mines' to access video and radio clips. Check the Forum for related posted comments.

Scottish Coal Collections   www.coalcollections.org

This useful website provides an overview of Scotland's coalmining collections held in museums, libraries and archives: names the collection, institution where held and provides a brief description of the records. Search the entire collection or via a subject menu or by location.

Scottish Mining Website   www.scottishmining.co.uk

Excellent website containing a great deal of information on collieries, accidents and disasters, housing, strikes, official reports, unions, with useful FAQs and links. Indexes to fatal and non-fatal accidents. Barrowman's glossary of Scottish mining terms. Site search facility. Also see Chapter 2.

Scran   www.scran.ac.uk

Online learning resource base containing over 360,000 images and media items from museums, galleries and archives. Buy images or subscribe. There may be free access via a public library.

ENGLAND (& UK-WIDE)
National Mining Museum for England (NCM)

Caphouse Colliery, New Road, Overton, Wakefield, West Yorkshire, WF4 4RH

t. 01924 848 806   e. use online contact form for general enquiries

www.ncm.org.uk

Based on the former Caphouse Colliery site, the museum opened in 1988 as the Yorkshire Mining Museum, at a time when many local pits had recently closed, Caphouse itself having closed three years earlier. The British Coal Collection was absorbed into its collections in 1995 and the museum's status and function became national. Surface buildings to see include the steam winding engine house, headgear, pithead baths, medical centre and administration block, lamp room, stables; and also the buildings associated with the adjacent Hope Pit complex. Underground tour (book on arrival) led by ex-miners includes 140m descent/ascent in the cage, after being kitted out with hard hat and battery lamp, to discover aspects of mining through the ages. The museum galleries contain wide-ranging exhibits, audio and visual displays and there are regular special exhibitions (see What's On web menu). Shop and cafe. Online collection summaries include Paintings and Pictures, Lives and Voices and Tools of the Trade. Digitisation of the collection is ongoing: search via keywords or via menu e.g. 'Accident & Recovery', 'Unions and Societies', 'Social History', 'Colliery Professions' (http://ww.ncm-collection.org.uk). Useful 'Starting Point' printable guides: Statistics (1), Mining Words (2), Tracing Your Mining family History (3) and Bevin Boys. Entry is free to the NCM.

The library contains many printed items including rare books and journals. There is a full run of HM Mines Inspectors' Reports for 1878–1987 and 1992–1993; and whole/part reports for 1855 and 1871–1877. *Coal News* (from 1961), *Mining Journal* (from 1835), *Colliery Guardian* (c.1878s onwards), *Guide to the Coalfields* (Colliery Guardian, 1948 onwards [not 1950]), Mining Year Books (annual), Transactions of the Institute of Mining Engineers; and the now digitised NCB magazine *Coal* (later published as *Coal News* [see above]) can be searched online (1947–1956) via www.ncmonline.org.uk. This is very useful for family historians as keywords such as a colliery name or event or personal name will obtain results. You can print and save or download extracts. Also available is Ian Winstanley's 7-volume Mining Deaths in Great Britain (1850–1914) and parliamentary select committees' reports, most notably the 1842 'women and children in mines' (Employment Commission) report. Information lists include recipients of colliery manager qualifications; Albert, Edward and Empire medal recipients and Order of Industrial Heroism awardees; and students at Royal School of Mines, 1851–1920, 1947, 1958, 1960. Online library catalogue: http://lib.ncm.org.uk/liberty/libraryHome.do. The museum's excellent oral history collection can also be accessed via the library. Extensive photographic and picture collection. The library is open Wednesdays (1–4pm), Thurs/Fri (10am–12.30pm & 1–4pm (and first full weekend in every month: times as per Thurs/Fri). Book beforehand or enquire via 01924 848806 or curatorial.librarian@ncm.org.uk.

The British Library (BL)

St Pancras, 96 Euston Road, London, NW1 2DB

t. 0843 2081144 (switchboard) e. Customer-Services@bl.uk www.bl.uk

A vast amount of mainly background information relating to coalmining is available. You will need to register and obtain a reader pass, then references, information and many images can be viewed online.

The long-established and world famous newspaper library based at Colindale is likely to be closed by 2014, most of the collection accessed via microfilm and digitally in a new News Reading Room at St Pancras (and increasingly digitally online). Hard copies of newspapers will be stored in the new Newspaper Storage Building (NSB) at the BL's Boston Spa site. For the latest information contact newspapers@bl.uk or see the BL's Collection Moves News Bulletin.

It is best to familiarise yourself with the main website via the *Quick Links* menu in order to search for information. The *Contact Us* link provides a detailed list of telephone/email contacts. The most useful research areas are British Printed Collections; Moving Image; Picture Library and Images Online; Prints, Drawings and Photographs; Social Science, Law and Official Publications; Newspapers: and Sound Archive.

Online catalogues include main catalogues (search the British Library, but excludes archives/manuscripts); manuscript catalogues; other catalogues of printed materials; photographic catalogues and union catalogues. Using general keywords such as 'colliery', 'coal mine' etc will obtain many thousands of results via the main catalogue. Using more specific words and places will narrow your search, e.g. 'Oaks Colliery, Barnsley' will obtain just three hits. The searchable *Sound and Moving Image* catalogue includes recordings of coalminers and interviewees whose fathers or grandfathers were miners. There are content summaries, e.g. for Joe Wills (1938–), last member of the National Miners' Union, who recalls his work in North Staffordshire mines. The online image Learning facility is very good, for example 'Drawing of a child miner, 1842' under 'Dickens in Context'.

Help for researchers includes a useful 'coal mining bibliography' that you can download as a PDF file, a Social Science Collection Guide (http://www.bl.uk/ reshelpsubject/socsci/topbib/coal/coal.html); and you can email 'ask the reference team' online. Genealogical reference sources are in the Humanities reading room and a select list plus guide can be seen online under Help for Researchers (Genealogy: reference sources).

Use the Online Gallery to search and print many thousands of items such as colliery ephemera, adverts, views etc.

The Coal Authority (Mining Heritage Centre [MHC])

200 Lichfield Lane, Mansfield, Nottinghamshire, NG18 4RG
t. 0845 762 6848   e. online form
http://coal.decc.gov.uk/en/coal/cms/services/records/records/records.aspx

Government organisation now part of the **Department of Energy & Climate Change**. No personnel records are held but the MHC holds two very useful major types of historical coalmining records. There are over 100,000 **Coal Abandonment Plans** and they can be digitally viewed on site; and prints or digital copies can be purchased. Viewing is free (for half a day a week), by appointment: 01623 637 255; or you can pay for a search. Plans were required to be deposited from 1872. This, therefore, may be a very relevant family history resource if you wish to see a plan of a particular colliery where your ancestor worked. But bear in mind that many earlier plans are lost or deposited in other archives.

The other important source is the MHC's huge **Photographic Collection,** c.120,000 images from the former NCB/British Coal Corporation, which are now fully digitised and available for purchase. Again, these can be viewed free of charge on site by appointment (t. 01623 637 235). You can search via a colliery name or activity e.g. 'working on the coal face' or 'pit top' or by machine name, etc; staff will advise.

The Coal Authority produces a useful downloadable 'mining records brochure' in a pdf format and there is a small onsite library.

Institution of Mechanical Engineers (IMechE)

1 Birdcage Walk, Westminster, London, SW1H 9JJ
t. 020 7973 1274 (library)   e. library@imech.org or archive@imech.org
www.imech.org

If your ancestor was a mining engineer the library at ImechE may well be a useful source for general background, and possibly specific information, as it is one of the most extensive of its kind in the UK. Open to the public, it houses the papers of many engineers. Online library catalogue and archive 'historical records' catalogue (http://www.imeche.org.uk/ils/catalogues.asp). Virtual library for members. Search the archive for specific events e.g. Hartley Colliery disaster will obtain results, or try a place-name or personal name.

Iron Mountain (UK) Limited

Central Enquiry Service, PO Box 3238, Stafford, ST16 9LS
t. 0844 2641 486   e. onlineform or britishcoalrecords@ironmountain.co.uk
www.ironmountain.co.uk

Staffordshire-based Iron Mountain manages personnel records of former National Coal Board (NCB) and British Coal (BC) employees, on behalf of the Government (for the Department of Energy & Climate Change). If your relative worked for one or both of the nationalised mining industries (post-1946) you can request a form in order to access their employment records. For a deceased person you will need to include full name, date of birth and ideally the National Insurance Number and name of last colliery. There is scope to provide additional information, which will always assist document retrieval. You can also access an accident report if relevant (so include the month/year if possible). For a living person two pieces of evidence of your identity are required and you need to obtain a covering letter from the individual concerned giving permission for you to access his/her records. The form and procedure is not complicated and is a free service. You can request either a printed or electronic 'record pack'. The access to miners' employment records facility originated following the process of the miners' compensation scheme and associated claims by individuals and solictors after 2003, but of course will continue to be valuable for family history research. For background information see http://www.ironmountain.co.uk/resource/casestudies/berr-case-study.pdf and/or http://www.ironmountain.co.uk/resource/casestudies/DepartmentofTradeandIndustry.pdf.

The National Archives (TNA)

Kew, Richmond, Surrey, TW9 4DU

t. 020 8876 3444   e. online contact form and Live Chat www.nationalarchives.gov.uk

Using generic keywords such as 'coal mine' in the 'all collections' in the 'discover our collections' catalogue will result in many thousands of hits; but a much more manageable number will appear in the growing 'online collections' option. Use more specific keywords to narrow your search and take note of the comments set out below.

Don't be daunted. The best starting point is TNA's guide **Mines and mining** (http: www.nationalarchives.gov.uk/records/research-guides/mines-and-mining.htm). This will take you through the main sources and their references from medieval to modern times. This includes industrial diseases and accidents, colliery records and NCB/British Coal records. Do bear in mind that there are no personnel records (see Iron Mountain, above and/or regional former coalfield record offices and libraries, referred to in Part I). The guide is not exhaustive – you will still be able find other mine-related items via the collections as well.

Another tip is to make use of one or more of the **Information Sheets** that you can pick up on site or by request. The most useful examples under 'Domestic Records Information' are No11 (Family History in England & Wales); No. 30 (Coroners' Inquests); No. 35 (Coal Mining Records in The National Archives); and No. 131 (An Inventory of Photographic Series). Although somewhat out of date, but still quite relevant for its overview of coalmining records and appendix of POWE class records (Ministry of Fuel & Power, formerly Home Office and Board of Trade records), try 'Your Archives' at http:yourarchives.gov.uk/index.php?title=Coal_and_Coal_Mining.

For images, TNA's photographic collections include Rev. F.W. Cobb's photographs (mainly Nottinghamshire): COAL 13 and a very useful collection of NCB/British Coal photographs, c.1890–1990. The latter – arranged in albums – include buildings and people (but also see the Coal Authority's own and far greater photographic collection, above).

You can now use TNA's 'looking for a person' online guide, though unfortunately the 'workers and employees' menu does not yet include mineworkers.

When using the TNA's website it is easy to set up a 'MyPage' facility so that you can park document references etc for future use.

You will need a reader's ticket before consulting original documents; otherwise access to the reading rooms is free and there is no need to book. Full details are shown via the *Before you visit* menu.

National Register of Archives – see Archon in online section, below

National Union of Mineworkers

2 Huddersfield Road, Barnsley, South Yorkshire, S70 2LS

t. 01226 284006   www.num.org.uk

Official headquarters and website of the Britain's main mining union. Regional NUM officials and contact details are also posted on the site under *Contacts*. The union records, mainly post-1947 printed material, books, photographs and ephemera, are not yet catalogued. The most useful family history source is the NUM's collections of annual HM Mines Inspectors' reports and special disaster reports. Earlier miners' association (union) records are held at the national and regional archives identified in this research section. For research enquiries contact the head office in Barnsley in the first instance.

Working Class Movement Library (WCML)

Jubilee House, 51 The Crescent, Salford, Lancashire, M5 4WX
t.0161 736 3601   e. enquiries@wcml.org.uk   www.wcml.org.uk

Based on the collection of Ruth and Edmund Frow, the WCML holds a huge collection of material (from 1760s) relating to the lives of ordinary men and women, particularly their trades, trade unions, politics (Labour & Communist parties), working-class leaders, co-operative movement, art and culture, some of which will include items of coalmining interest.

The WCML online collections catalogue: search via keywords such as 'colliery', 'pit disaster' etc for results. There is also a separate online library catalogue. Click on 'family history' menu via the main *Our collection* heading for very useful background information and many links. The 'protest' menu includes items on Chartism, Communism, Lancashire Women Against Pit Closures and the Pit and Factory papers.

Of particular family history interest are the WCML's holdings of the Lancashire and Cheshire Miners' Federation annual reports c.1896 onwards; South Wales miners' minutes, Yorkshire Miners' Association (1916, 1917, 1935–40; Northumberland Mineworkers' Federation reports 1935; Miners' Federation of GB annual reports 1893, 1895, 1898, 1900–17, 1920 onwards. Lodge books include William Pit Lodge Rooms minute book 1890–96; Maestreg (S. Wales Miners' Fed) minute book 1944–51; Llynfr Valley Free Church Federation Council minute book 1944–51. Individuals will be mentioned in specific circumstances, e.g. accident facilities, compensation claims.

The display galleries are located on the ground floor and there are online samples of banners, trade union emblems, posters.

Admission to the WCML is free but book an appointment beforehand in order to access research material; opening hours and visitor facilities are posted online.

Online

Adit Now   www.aditnow.co.uk

Very user-friendly and useful site relating to mine exploration, also containing a huge photographic (searchable) database, reference articles and historical document resource. Free registration. Forum. Lists of collieries and OS map locations. Events and meets.

ARCHON   http://www.nationalarchives.gov.uk/archon/

Contact details for record repositories in the UK (and overseas) which have substantial manuscript collections under the **National Register of Archives** indexes. Browse A-Z by region/country.

Archive Images   www.archive-images.co.uk

High quality scans to purchase or download. Under industrial search for collieries e.g. Kent Coalfield section will show images of surface workings, buildings, screens, underground scenes, groups of miners etc.

BBC Nation on Film   http://www.bbc.co.uk/nationonfilm/topics/coal-mining/

'King Coal', film clips of mining and mining life, especially in North East England.

BBC Film Archive: Coal Mining in Britain   www.bbc.co.uk/archive/mining/

Includes interesting viewable film clips relating to coalmining.

Britain From Above   www.britainfromabove.org.uk

Growing (over 20,000) digital (and zoomable) archive of historic aerial images from 1919 to 1950s, taken mainly from the Aerofilms Ltd collection. A search by place-name, map or year will reveal some very useful pit village/town and colliery site images. Online guide. Memory sharing. Best to keep checking site for new images.

British Film Institute   www.bfi.org.uk

Includes the National Archive of film and television collections. Also useful is the BFI screenonline (www.screenonline.org.uk) online encyclopaedia. Many mining clips and films. Also see Search Your Film Archives, below.

British Pathé   www.britishpathe.com

Film clips of mining can be accessed and purchased via the search facility. View clips and stills on line. Footage includes several disasters, e.g. Bickershaw (1932), Cresswell (1950), Knockshinnock (1950). This is an excellent site that enables you to view rare coalmining films.

Coal Mining History Resource Centre   www.cmhrc.uk

Excellent extensive and detailed site originated and developed by the former Lancashire miner and teacher Ian Winstanley over many years. The site is now owned by Raleys, the Barnsley-based solicitors, long associated with miners' compensation and the NUM.

Main menu includes history of mining disasters in the UK, national database of mining deaths in Great Britain (compiled by Ian Winstanley), mines location maps, mining poems, 1842 Royal Commission reports, colliery scrapbook; and day in the life of Tommy Shotton, a Greenside, near Newcastle, miner in 1939. Literary features also include books on mining history, glossary of mining terms and women and coal mining. The photo gallery is also well worth visiting. The accidents and deaths database is searchable (by surname/colliery) and disaster reports can be down-loaded: also see Chapter 2.

Durham Mining Museum   www.dmm.org.uk

Although the site is based on northern England, there is some information on other mining regions and a very handy links section. Also see Part I of this guide.

English Heritage Archive www.english-heritage.org.uk

Search the archive collection, *Britain from Above* (see separate entry, above) and Library for coal-related images and information. Formerly part of the National Monuments Record. Searching regionally, via a relevant county, should obtain many results: colliery sites and monuments especially; or try using a keyword such as a colliery name. Obtain reference number, see or print the reference image and order online or by phone: 0870 333 1181. *Viewfinder* will also let you search through historic photographs of England dating from the 1850s; and also useful is *Images of England* for listed colliery buildings and/or *The National Heritage List for England* database. For queries use the online form via the *About Us/Contact Us* facility or try customers@ english-heritage.org.uk.

Gettyimages www.gettyimages.co.uk

Searching the archive by mining area place-name or coal-related theme (or via their keyword guide) will obtain some results from this world-famous commercial picture archive. Costly but some superb images.

Mine Explorer www.mine-explorer.co.uk

This site is excellent for anyone interesting in visiting and exploring old mine sites throughout Great Britain. Discussion forum. Free registration provides access to photographs/documents.

Heroes of Mine www.heroes-of-mine.co.uk

Philip Clifford's informative site relating to mines rescue, accidents and disasters, awards and medals,

Miners' Advice www.minersadvice.co.uk

Ex-Durham and Yorkshire (Hatfield) miner, NUM branch representative and author Dave Douglass's ('Danny the Red') excellent site to help miners/former miners regarding their compensation claims and rights also includes a great deal of useful historical information. Book reviews and further reading list. News. Photographs. 1984/85 miners' strike. Colliers of Wales. Guestbook may be useful for family history requests.

Mining History Network http://projects.exeter.ac.uk/mhn/

An information resource for mining historians by Professor Roger Burt (of Exeter University), the site contains much useful bibliographical as well as background/ contextual information; and there's a discussion forum.

My Learning www.mylearning.org

Website created to allow access to free leaning resources from museums, libraries and archives. Although targeted at schools, the subject menu includes family history, local studies and oral history. Search the site using 'coal mining' for many interesting and useful items, e.g. glossary of mining words, Victorian mining, women in mining (mainly from resources of **National Coal Mining Museum for England** (see above).

National Association of Mining History Organisations (NAMHO)
www.vmine.net

The national body for mining associations in the UK and Ireland. Online newsletter and useful links. Forum.

National Mining Memorabilia Association   www.mining-memorabilia.co.uk

UK-wide site for collectors of mining memorabilia contains information on items such as pit checks, tokens, medals and awards, badges and mine lamps; and commemorative items; useful mining articles arranged by region.

Northern Mine Research Society (NMRS)   www.nmrs.org

Its records relate to most coalfield regions. Publishes *Memoirs* and *Monographs* under its 'British Mining' imprint that can be ordered or accessed via membership subscription (online form). Run by enthusiasts. Field meetings. Newsletter (quarterly) and library. Online site search facility.

Old UK Photos   www.oldukphotos.com

Free-to-view site, which displays old photographs of places and people throughout the UK. Contains many family history and coalmining images, e.g. Senghenydd disaster images.

Oral History Society   www.oralhistory.org

The national organisation for oral history research, guidance and projects. Regional network contacts. Handbook and bibliography listings. Regular training courses. Online membership subscription facility. Journal.

Pitwork   www.dmm-pitwork.org.uk

Ex-miner Bill Riley's very useful and informative site, hosted by the Durham Mining Museum (see above). Browse Bill's menu for disasters, heroes, history, stories, pictures, memories, songs/poems, jokes etc. Contains a great deal of mining information and links. Well worth visiting.

Search Your Film Archives   http://unionsearch.bfi.org.uk

This very useful site enables you to do a UK-wide search for coalmining films via the British Film Institute (BFI) and regional film archives.

Subterranea Britannica   www.subbrit.org.uk

'Sub Brit' is a specialist and enthusiasts' site which includes a UK directory of 250 UK mine sites open to the public, along with background information.

Trade Union (TUC) Library Collections
http://www.londonmet.ac.uk/sas/library-services/tuc/

London Metropolitan University/TUC site on working lives. Also see The Union Makes Us Strong (http://www.unionhistory.info/index.php) and Chapter 2.

WALES

National Museum Wales

Comprises several museum sites, some of which are of interest for mining family history research (see below). The main website (www.museumwales.ac.uk) also contains useful background information and the collections can be browsed and searched via **Rhagor** (Welsh for 'more' (also see below)).

(1) Big Pit : National Coal Museum

Big Pit, Blaenafon, Torfaen, South Wales, NP4 9XP
t. 029 2057 3650   e. use online form   www.museumwales.ac.uk/en/bigpit

Opened in 1983 as Big Pit Mining Museum (after NCB closed Big Pit), but was taken over by the National Museum of Wales in 2001 and re-named Big Pit: National Coal Museum. Since then has undergone much redevelopment, winning the prestigious Gulbenkian Prize for Museum of the Year in 2005. Entry is free.

The old mine has a complex history but the former Kearsley Pit was renamed Big Pit following shaft widening and deepening in 1880. Surface buildings include headstocks, winding house, fan house, tram circuit, lamp room, medical centre, pithead baths, blacksmiths' shop, explosives magazine, canteen etc, but the highlight for most visitors is the realistic underground tour in the care of a former miner-guide. The mining galleries include simulated underground workings and a multimedia presentation not to be missed. Exhibition spaces in the pithead baths include children in mines, health and welfare and life and work of the miner; also information and exhibits relating to trade unions and nationalisation, along with mining memorabilia. Cafe and shop. For events check the What's On menu on the National Museum Wales website.

Excellent published visitors' guide to Big Pit includes much background information on Welsh mining. Also very useful is the 'people's history' magazine *GLO*, containing information on Welsh miners and mining life.

Big Pit provides a wonderful experience for anyone with mining ancestry, mining and social history interests and is a superb educational resource; but family history researchers should (apart from the local and regional archives and libraries described in Part I of this research guide) use the **National Waterfront Museum** and other national sources referred to below.

(2) National Waterfront Museum (NWM)

Oystermouth Road, Maritime Quarter, Swansea, SA1 3RD
t. 029 2057 3602   e. via website   www.museumwales.ac.uk/en/swansea

This modern museum, located in the historic maritime quarter of Swansea, close to Swansea city centre, opened in 2005 and is devoted to the story of industry and innovation in Wales. There are limited coalmining exhibits and information on display; and related items, for example Truck shops, though the main in situ interpretation by the National Museum of Wales is at **Big Pit** (see above).

The **Industry Reference Library** (http://www.museumwales.ac.uk/en/205) at the NWM contains a very large and extensive range of books and periodicals relating to the Welsh industry and transport, including c.3,000 relating to coalmining.

Amongst the most important for family history research are their complete holdings of Welsh (and many English and Scottish) HM Inspectorate of Mines annual reports from 1856–1914, as well as the earlier reports (1851–1855). (For background and more detailed information see Chapter 2.) The later, less useful (post-1914) statistical reports are also available. Almost all Welsh (and many English and Scottish) special reports relating to specific colliery disasters are also held.

Lists of working coal mines in Wales can be accessed via the library's incomplete run of Hunt's Mineral Statistics (1854, 1856, 1858–60 1860, 1861, 1863–65, 1869–81) and in HM Inspector of Mines annual reports 1872–82 (referred to above), continued in the complete run of of Mining and Mineral Statistics 1883–87, incomplete run of List of Mines and partial run of Colliery Yearbook & Coal Directory, near complete run of Guide to the Coalfields (Colliery Guardian publications); and complete for the recent era (post-1997) International Guide to the Coalfields and British Geological Survey Directory of Mines and Quarries (1984 onwards).

There is also a very large picture collection which includes c.10,000 coal-related images, searchable via a geographical card index.

The Reference Library and photographic collection are open to the public by appointment weekdays only. Contact information: 029 2057 3602 or email by website.

(3) National Museum Cardiff

Cathays Park, Cardiff, CF10 3NP
t. 029 2057 3500   e. use online form   www.museumwales.ac.uk/en/cardiff

An outstanding part of Cardiff's civic complex, Wales's national museum is open Tuesdays–Sundays. It is well worth visiting, to see at first hand coalmining-related paintings in the art collection.

The collections of **National Museum Wales** can be searched online through *Rhagor* (htttp://www.museumwales.ac.uk/en/rhagor) and particularly useful is the *Images of Industry* theme, where you can browse the 'Coal Industry' category. Information is also provided on 'coal miners' badges' and there is a related article about the 1984 miners' strike; and features on the Senghenydd and Tynewydd disasters.

For **St Fagans National History Museum** see the Coalfield Regions (South Wales) reference section above.

National Library of Wales (NLW)

Aberystwyth, Ceredigion, SY23 3BU
t. 01970 632 800 e. enquiry@llgc.org.uk w. www.llgc.org.uk

Family history research facilities in the South Reading Room. Online guide. Searchable online databases via the main website include 'genealogical source' headings for maps; pictures, photographs, sound and moving image; estate and personal. The library's excellent *Digital Mirror* contains e-copies of books, manuscripts, pictures, photographs etc and this resource can be used remotely if you register as a reader. It includes Welsh Biography (searchable). Ongoing digitisation projects e.g. journals, historic newspapers.

Searching online using general terms such as 'coal mining' will result in very many results and a window will also open with suggested related keywords such as disaster, accident, strike, miner, colliery and lockout. Try searching using a more specific word such as a colliery name, event or personal name. Archives collections mainly available through their ISYS:web (http://isys.llgc.org.uk/)

The NLW houses the national collection (over 800,000) of mainly Welsh photographs.

Enquire via online form, email or instant chat service. Also see the National Screen and Sound Archive of Wales (below). Remote access to some e-resources may have rersidential (Wales) restrictions.

National Screen and Sound Archive of Wales (NSSAW)

t. 01970 632 828   e. online enquiry form   www.archif.com

Part of the NLW (address as above). The national collection of film, television programmes, videos, sound recordings and music. Search the entire database using general or specific mine-related terms. A search using 'coal miner' under 'film' included twenty-seven items with detailed content summaries. You can save your search and request the item (using your reader number/password), allowing 24 hours notice. Remote access to e-resources may have residential (Wales) restrictions.

Online sources

Archives Wales   www.archivesnetworkwales.info

Online catalogue/database enables you to search through historical records in the holdings of twenty-one archives in Wales. Part of the National Archives Network.

BBC Wales History Archive   http://www.bbc.co.uk/wales/history

Contains many interesting coalmining features. Use online index for specific coal-mine related items; or themes (e.g. nineteenth and twentieth century mining, dangers of coalmining, miners' strike); or conduct a keyword search. History blog. Family history advice.

Cadw   www.cadw.wales.gov.uk

Welsh government's historic environment service. Includes conservation areas, monuments and listed buildings. Photographic library: Blaenavon Industrial Landscape. Also see RCHM below.

Gathering the Jewels   http://www.gtj.org.uk

Features of over 30,000 images of objects, books, letters, aerial photographs and other items from museums, archives and libraries throughout Wales.

Library Wales   www.librarywales.org

Useful online resources for Welsh libraries. Many features including *Newsbank* which allows you to search popular local and national newspapers for past/present articles; Ask a librarian service. Free online resources if registered with a Welsh public library.

Royal Commission on the Ancient and Historical Monuments of Wales (RCHMW)
www.rcahmw.gov.uk

Investigation body and national archive for the historic environment of Wales. The National Monuments Record of Wales (NMRW), which includes many images (drawings, photographs, aerial views, maps) can be searched online via their Coflein database: either by the mapping facility or a text search. Search using text, for example 'colliery' for many results or define by a colliery name, e.g. Abernant Colliery. There is a growing digital archive. Also see **Cadw**, monument and listed building database, above.

Welsh Coal Mines   www.welshcoalmines.co.uk

Excellent site run by a former miner and covers the whole of Wales. Browse menu for Introduction, Collieries, Poems and Stories, Glossary, Web Links and use the Forum.

Welsh Mines Society   www.welshmines.org

Mining enthusiasts' site containing many interesting features.

Welsh People's History Society (Llafur)   www.llafur.org

Llafur (journal), 1972 onwards, includes many excellent mine-related items, contents viewable online and some back copies purchasable. Online newsletter. Events. Downloadable membership form.

INDEX

A N Palmer Centre – see Wrexham
  Archives
Aber Valley Heritage Centre & Museum
  (Senghenydd) 233
Ablett, Noah (miners' leader) 84
accidents (fatal), records for Scotland 67
Acts of Parliament
  1842 Mines Act 10, 50, 51, 106–8
  1872 Coal Mines Regulation 85
  1885 Coal Mines Regulation 104
  1909 Eight Hours 205
  1911 Coal Mines 10, 19, 42, 52, 73, 84, 104
  1912 Coal Mines Minimum Wage 36
  1916 Eight Hours 121
  1916 Military Services 121
  1918 Education Act (Fisher) 10
  1918 (miners' disability) Act 44
  1944 Education Act (Butler) 10
Adamson, Rev J 106
Airdrie Library Discovery Room 178
Albert Medal 75, 76, 80
Alexander, William (mines inspector) 46
Allinson, Sydney (author) 123
Apedale Heritage Centre 216
archives (national) – see separate entries
archives (regional) – see separate entries
Arksey 130
Ashington 3, 166
Ashley, Lord 106, 113
Astley Green Colliery Museum 208
Atkinson, John (mines inspector) 46
Attlee, Clem (Labour leader) 90
awards, bravery 163–4
Ayrshire Archives 175
Ayton, Richard 114

badges, strike/ union & association 154–6
Bailey, John 15
Banks, Tony 153
banners (union) xi, 90
Bantams (regiment) 123, 124
Bargoed 15

Barnsley 3, 13, 22, 32, 34, 40, 42, 57, 70, 72,
  77, 84, 85, 86, 88, 92, 93, 100, 101, 107,
  114, 158
Barnsley Archives/Discovery Centre 195
Barnsley Main (pithead remains) 200
Bates, Denise (author) 113, 114, 116
bathing/baths 16, 26–27, 28
Baxter, Walter 142, 143
Beafort 107
Beamish 59
Beamish Museum (and archives) 185, 189
Beith, William 76
Bellingham Heritage Centre 189
Benton, W (postcard publisher) 70
Bersham Colliery Mining Museum 227
Bestwood Winding Engine House 200
Beverley, Frank 37
Bevin Boys 118, 120, 132, 134–8, 182, 236,
  239
Bevin, Ernest (MP) 134
Bewdley 142
Big Pit – see National Coal Museum (Wales)
Bigland, Alfred (MP) 123
Biram, Joshua (mine engineer) 52
Birkinshaw, James 39
Birmingham Archives and Heritage 214
Bishop family 146, 148
Black Country Living Museum 217
Blackwell, John (mines inspector) 46
Blaenavon 107
Blaina 107
Blyth (Notts) 127
Blyth Library (Northumberland) 185
Bold, Robert 113
Bolsterstone 5
Bolton Museum & Archive Service 205
bond (miner's) 36
Booth, Gerald 37
Booth, Mary 107
Bowes Railway 190
breathing apparatus 74
Brighton 146

British Coal Corporation (BCC) 2, 166, 229, 246, 247
British Geological Survey (BGS) 167
Bristol 54
Bristol Central Library 220
Bristol Record Office 220
Bristol University Special Collections 220
British Library, The 63, 64, 71, 244–5
Brotherton Library (University of Leeds) 195–6
Brough, Lionel (mines inspector) 46
Broughton, John 145
Bryan, Thomas (miner-VC) 130
burial registers 45
Burns Monument Centre 175, 176
Busby, Mick 129
butty system 36

Cardiff 85
Cardiff Central Library 229
Cardwell, John 50–2, 65
Carlisle & Workington Archives 193
Carlton (S.Yorks) 13, 72, 226
Carmarthenshire Archive Service 230
Carnegie Hero Fund Medal 79
Carr, Matlida 112
Castleford 129
CEAG (lighting company) 17, 157
Cefn Coed Colliery Museum 233
census (how to use) 140–51
Chandler, Robert (Edward Medal) 77–78
Charles Close Society (maps) 169
checks (pit) 152, 154
checkweighmen 36–7, 91
Cheshire Archives and Local Studies 206
Chesterfield Library 196
child miners 106–112
Children's Employment Commission 108–16
civil registration 45
Clackmannanshire Archives & Local Studies 176
Clamp, John 17
Clarke, Robert Couldwell 115
Clarke, Tristram (author) 240
Clarke, William 127, 128
Clay Cross 58
Clayton, Arthur 15–16, 17, 21
Clayton, W (photographer) 96, 105
Cleveland FHS 191
Clifton Country Park (Wet Earth Colliery) 208
Clydach 107

Clifford, Philip 74
clothes (miner's) 16, 17, 18
Coal Authority, The 166, 170, 245–6, 247
Coal Mine History Resource Centre (website) 65–6, 113, 167, 249
coal mines – see collieries
Coalville Library 211
Cobb, Rev F W (photographs) 247
collieries
  Aberaman 162
  Aldwarke Main 129
  Apedale 216
  Arthur & Edward 220
  Askern Main 134, 161, 195
  Baddesley 211, 214
  Baggeridge 210, 214, 215
  Bagworth 211
  Balaclava 170
  Bank Hall 205
  Barnburgh Main 12, 13
  Barrow 155
  Baynton 216
  Beamish 58
  Bentley 69, 195
  Bersham 226, 227, 228
  Bettshanger 224
  Bilston Glen 175
  Birch Coppice 211
  Blaenavon 107
  Bottom Place 103
  Brodsworth Main 6, 14, 195
  Bromley 220
  Broughton 193
  Bullcroft 195
  Burgh 107
  Bwllfa 54
  Cadeby Main 82, 133, 195, 197
  California 170
  Cannop 220
  Caphouse 32, 107, 244
  Cardowen 181
  Castlebridge 175
  Chatterley Whitfield 212
  Chislett 224
  Chisnall Hall 205
  Clee Hill 212
  Cleland 179
  Coleshill 226
  Colliers Side 212
  Collingwood 221
  Comrie 154
  Cortonwood 92, 119, 127, 128, 195
  Coventry 211

Cwm 132
Darfield Main 92, 135
Daw Mill 43, 211
Deep Navigation 154
Denaby Main 41, 42, 84, 87, 125, 133, 195, 197
Desford 211
Dinnington Main 33, 155
Dodworth 44
Dover 224
Dryden 108
Dry Clough 58
Easington 184
Eastern 54
Eastern United 220
Edlington Main 12, 14
Edmunds Main 59
Ellington 184–5
Elliot 235, 236
Elsecar Main 195
Emley Moor 23
Emlyn 230
Frickley 195
Gardrum 7
Gascoigne Wood 195
Gawber 51
Gleision 43, 229
Grange 30
Greencroft Tower Drift 170
Gresford 226
Grimethorpe 43
Hafod 226
Haig 96
Hapton Valley 205
Harry Stoke 219
Hatfield Main 154, 195
Hem Heath 210
Highley 212
Hopwood's 114–5
Horden 184
Houghton Main 43
Howgill 99
Hoyland Silkstone 77
Ifton 226
Ince Hall 47
Intake 112
Isabella 170
Kellingley 43, 195
Kilmerston 221
Killoch 175
Kilmersdon 219
Kilnhurst 166
Kinneil 180

Kiveton Park 157
Lady Victoria 238–9
Lewis Merthyr 234
Littleton 210
Llay Main 226
Lofthouse 153
Longannet 175
Low Elsecar 50
Madeley Wood 212
Maltby 43, 195
Manor 153
Manvers Main/complex 79, 135, 136, 195
Marine 130
Middleton 200
Mitchell's Main 129
Monckton Main/complex 44, 122, 154, 195
Monktonhall 175
Monkwearmouth 123, 184
Moreton 107
Mosley Common 205
Narchard 220
New Oaks 82
North Gawber 12
North Selby 195
Northern United 220
Oaks 32, 57, 200
Orgreave 143
Parkside 205
Penallta 78, 138, 231
Percy Main 123
Pleasley 201–2
Point of Ayr 226
Princes Royal 220
Racecourse 217
Riccall 195
Rockingham 161
Rossington 195, 197
Rothes 175
Ryhope 184
Seafield 175
Seaham 184
Silverdale 210, 213
Skellington 60
Snibston 91, 216
Snowdown 224
South Hetton 184
South Kirkby 22
Stillingfleet 195
Swaithe Main 158
Swannington 91
Swinton 121, 129
Thorne 35, 195
Thorseby 195

Thurcroft 143
Thrybergh Hall (Kilnhurst) 121, 129, 166
Tilmanstone 224
Tower 229
Townhill 50
Treeton 141, 142, 143, 145–6
Tylorstown 58
Universal 57, 120
Victoria (Yorks) 34
Wallsend 190
Washington F 189
Wath Main 129
Welbeck 43
Wellington 193
Wharncliffe Woodmoor, 1,2&3 4, 42, 160
Whitehaven 193
Whitwick 211
Wistow 195
Wolstanton 210
Woodhorn 190
Woolley 27, 195, 200
Writhlington 219, 221
Yorkshire/Edlington Main 195
colliers 23–26
Collins, Eddie 82–3
Collins, Thomas (Pte) 125
Commonwealth War Graves 128
Communist Party of Great Britain 84
compensation (miners') 44, 68
Cook, A J (miners' leader) 83, 84, 90
Coombes, B L (miner-author) 3, 26, 132
Cooper, John (photographer) 101
Cooper, Samuel Joshua (philanthropist) 75
coroners' records 67
County Hall (Matlock) Local Studies Library
  196
Court, Vince 138
Crabtree, Eric 30
Culhare, William 99
Cwm Colliery & Abernant Tunnel 233

D.H. Lawrence Heritage 200
Daley, Lawrence (miners' leader) 90, 215
Dalton 129
Darfield 15
Darlington Library 186
datallers (day-wage men) 22
Davies, Alan (author) 99, 106
Davies, Ivor 138
Davis, Mary 111–2
Davis, Sir Robert (Siebe-Gorman) 74
Day, Elizabeth 114–5
Day, Mary 115

Dean Heritage Centre 220, 221
Deepcar 5
deputies 28–30
Derby 32
Derbyshire Record Office 196
Dibnah, Fred (broadcaster) 34
Dickinson, Joseph (mines inspector) 46, 47,
  48
Dinnington 33, 128
disasters (mine)
  Abercam 75
  Albion 229
  Barrow 70
  Bentley 72
  Bickershaw 249
  Blantyre 174, 179
  Cadder Valley 177
  Cadeby 41–2, 52, 75
  Clifton Hall 205
  Combs 229
  Cresswell 196, 249
  Dark Lane 212
  Diglake 62
  Golborne 207
  Grassmoor 196
  Great Western 229
  Gresford 92, 226, 227
  Haig 193
  Hampstead 70
  Haswell 184
  Haydock 205, 207
  Herbertshire 180
  Hoyland Silkstone 70
  Hulton 207
  Huskar 39, 115
  Jackfield 212
  Knockshinnoch 176, 249
  Llanerch 229
  Lofthouse 43, 153
  Lundhill 92, 194
  Markham (Derbys) 196
  Mauricewood 174
  Madeley Wood 212
  Maypole 52, 70
  Midsomer Norton 70
  Minnie 210, 216
  Montague 188, 189
  Morfa 229
  New Hartley 184, 189, 190
  Newbury 219
  Nitshill 174
  Norton Hill 219
  Oaks 1, 32, 39, 40, 75, 194, 200

Podmore 52
Pretoria 52, 205
Redding 180
Seaham 61, 184
Senghenydd 52, 57, 70, 229, 230, 231, 233, 235, 236
Sneyd
Stanrigg 179
Swaithe Main 75, 194
Thorne 35
Tyneydd 76, 234
Udsen 174
Wallsend 184
Washington 70
Wattsdown 231
Wellington 52, 193
Wellsway 219
West Stanley 70
Wharncliffe Silkstone 70
Wharncliffe Woodmoor 72
Whitwick 211
Woodhorn 188
diseases (miners') 43–44
Ditchburn, Ray 70–71
Dodds, Harriet 128
Doncaster 35, 41
Doncaster Archives & Local Studies 196
Doon Valley Museum 181
Douglass, Dave (author) 202
Dover Museum 224
drawers – see trammers
Dudley 149
Dudley Archives & Local History Service 215
Dugdale, T D (photographer) 101
Dundonald, Lord 113
Dunfermline Carnegie Library 177
Dunn, Mathias (mines inspector) 46
Durham Clayport Library 186
Durham County Record Office 186
Durham Light Infantry 123
Durham Miners' Gala 90, 191
Durham Mining Museum 65, 167–8, 190–91
Durham University Library Archives 186

East Ayrshire Libraries 176
East Dunbartonshire Libraries and Archives 177
Eastwood, George 43
Ecclesfield 32
Edinburgh 90
Edinburgh Central Library & City Archives 180–1

Edlington 29
Edward VII 77–8
Edward Medal 75, 76–7
Elliott family 1, 2, 4, 5, 10, 36, 41, 42–43, 44 133, 160
Ellis, Joseph 107
Elsecar 13, 50–1
Elsecar Heritage 200–01
Embleton, Thomas William 75
Emms, Tom 12, 29
Empire Gallantry Medal 78
engine winders 35
engineers 30, 31–32
ephemera (mining) 69, 160–1
Evans, Thomas (mines inspector) 46
Everson, Henry (Edward Medal) 77–8
evictions (by coal owners/companies) 84, 87
Experience Barnsley (museum) & Discovery Centre 201
Ezra, Derek (NCB chairman) 31

Falkirk Community Trust Libraries & Archives 180
Fairhurst, Sarah 103
Faulkes, Sebastian (author) 118, 125
'Featherstone Massacre' (1893) 87
female miners 37, 47, 50, 92–3, 96–116
Fence (Rotherham) 141
Fergusan, Annie 96
Ferriday, John 99
Fforest Uchaf Pit Pony Sanctuary 233
first aid 74
First World War 10, 21, 35, 92, 104, 118–131, 163, 174, 185, 205
Fisher, Richard 100
fitters 22
Fitzwilliam, Earl (aristocratic landowner) 13, 50, 51, 65, 201
Flintshire Libraries 226
Flintshire Museums 228
Flintshire Record Office 226
flying pickets 88
Foers, Martha 145
Franks (sub-commissioner) 109, 111–2
Fynne, Mark 70

galas and demonstrations 89–90
gallantry awards 75–80, 127
Gallery of English Costume 106
Gateshead Library 187
Gaunt, William 57
General Strike (1926) 83, 89
George Cross 76, 78, 79

George Medal 79
Gill, Eric (artist) 79
Glamorgan Archives 230
Glasgow 60
Gloucestershire Archives 221
Goddard, Bernard 13, 30–1
Gomersall, Mike (author) 129
Gooder, Sarah 51
Gormley, Joe (miners' leader) 31
Gothard, Warner (postcards) 70
Grantham 143
Great War – see First World War
Gresford Colliery Disaster Memorial 228
Grey, Sir George (Home Sec) 45
Grounds, Ellen 103
Gwent Archives 230

Hackett, William (miner-VC) 125, 126
Haig Pit Mining & Colliery Museum 96,
    193–4
Haldane, John Scott (mining safety
    equipment inventor) 74
Hall, Joe (miners' leader) 92
Hall, Lee (playwright) 3
Hardie, Keir (labour/miners' leader) 84, 90,
    176
Hargreaves, John 107
Harris, Betty 114
Harris, John 75–76
Harris, Lewis 75
Harris, Mel 137
Hart, Tommy 21
Hartley, Joe 134–5, 136, 137
haulage 9, 16
Healey, Philip 66, 74
Heath, Edward (Prime Minister) 88, 88
Hedley, John (mines inspector) 46
Hedonsford 142, 143
Helliwell, Jane 107
Henwood, Tom 25
Hepburn, Tommy (miners' leader) 90
Herbert, Thomas 75
hewers 41, 100
Higson, Peter (mines inspector) 46
Hiley, Michael (author) 106
Hinds, Annie 129
Hines, Barry (author) 3, 43
Hive, The – see Worcestershire Archive
Holmes, George 58
Home Front 118
Home Guard 118, 133
Hopewell Colliery Museum 222
Hopkinson, Tom 72, 73

Horner, Arthur (miners' leader) 90, 131, 132
Howell, John 76
Hughes, William John 58
Houfton, Percy Bond (architect) 14
housing 13, 14
Hudd, Mark 54–5
Hull History Centre 197
Hunter, George 32
Hunts Mineral Statistics 167, 253
hurriers – see trammers
Hyde, Sarah 40
Hyde, Thomas 40
Hyndley, Lord (NCB chairman) 165

Imperial War Museum 138
Institute of Mechanical Engineers (ImechE)
    246
Ironbridge Gorge Museum, Library &
    Archives 212, 216
Iron Mountain (UK) Ltd 3, 246–7

Jackson, Colin (author) 168
Jeffcock, Parkin (mine engineer) 32, 75
Jevons, H Stanley (author) 184
John Goodchild Collection 197
John Gray Centre (East Lothian) 177
John, Martha 107
Johnson family 145
Johnson, Frank 37
Johnson, Patrick 60
Jolly, Elizabeth 47
Jones, Bill 3
Jones, Sir Fred John 143

Kaye, Ernest 17, 89
Keel University Archives 212
Keep, John Howard 143
Kemp, George 13, 25–6
Kennedy (sub-commissioner) 114
Kent History & Library Centre 224
Kenworthy, Reuben 23, 24
Kerr, Jane 108–9
Kidwelly Industrial Museum 234
Kilner, Roy 12–13
Kings Own Yorkshire Light Infantry
    (KOYLI) 123
Kirkaldy Central Library 178
Kitchen, Doris 72
Kyte family 145

lamp carriers 16–17
Lanark Library 179
Lancashire Archives/Record Office 206

Lancashire Fusiliers 127
Lancashire Library Service 64
Lancaster, William (mines inspector) 46
Lee, Peter (miners' leader) 90
Leeds 123
Leicester & Rutland Record Office & Library 211
Leveston, Margaret 111
Lewis, Richard 85
libraries – see separate entries
lighting 16–17
Little, Robert (photographer) 101, 103
Lindley family 145
Lindley, George 51
Liverpool Record Office 207
Llanelli 71
Lloyd George, David (MP, PM) 11, 120
Londonderry, Lord 51
Lonsdale, Lord 114
Lovett, Levi (miners' leader) 91
Lowther family 98
Lowther, Sir William 192, 193

McCarron, Hannah 96
McDonald, Alexander (miners' leader) 85, 90
McFarlane, Jim (author) 41
McGregor, Ian (NCB chairman) 89
McKone, Thomas 69
M-Shed (Bristol) 222
Mackworth, Herbert (mines inspector) 46
Madge, 'Sal' 98
Maerdy Women's Support Group 89
Mallinder family 145
managers (colliery) 13, 30
Manchester Archives & Local Studies 206
Mansfield 170
Mammatt, John Edward 75
Martin, Michael 66
Marx Memorial Library 132
Matlock Local Studies Library – see County Hall (Matlock)
Meko-Briggs (mine safety equipment: also see Proto) 74
Mercer, Thomas 145
Merthyr Tydfil 83, 84, 85
Midlothian Libraries & Archives 179
Mitchell Library (Glasgow) 178
Millard, Louisa (photographer) 101
Miners' Association of Great Britain 143
Miners' Welfare Scheme 140
miners' leaders 91–92
miners' strike (1984–85) 86, 87, 88, 89

mines inspectors (and their reports) 39, 41, 45–55, 99, 167, 176, 177–8, 186, 188, 189, 195, 196, 197, 199, 206, 229, 231, 239, 240, 253
mine(s) rescue 71–75, 79, 80, 163, 164
Mineworkers' Pension Scheme 160
Mining and Mineral Statistics 167
Mining Deaths in Great Britain (database) – see Winstanley, Ian
mining memorabilia 152–64
Mitchell, Joseph 158
Modern Records Centre 93
Mold Museum 227
monuments (mining) 68–69
Moore, Robert 58
Morley (Derbys) 99
Morton, Charles (mines inspector) 46, 50, 51
Mortomley 32
Moseley, Miles 75
Moss, Jane 107
Mostyn 226
Moxon, Fred 12
Munby, Arthur 102, 103–4, 105, 106
museums (national) – see separate entries
museums (regional) – see separate entries

Nantyglo 107
National Archives – see The National Archives
National Archives of Scotland 67
National Coal Board (NCB) 2, 14, 59, 86, 88, 143, 154, 160, 161, 164, 165, 174, 185, 193, 195, 205, 210, 211, 220, 240, 246, 247
National Coal Museum (National Museum Wales: Big Pit) 138, 168, 225, 252
National Library of Scotland 63, 93, 241
National Library of Wales 63, 93, 253
National Mining Museum for England 20, 32, 67, 107, 112, 244
National Mining Museum Scotland 109, 171, 238–9
National Museum Cardiff 253
National Museums Scotland 242
National Museum Wales 252–3
National Records of Scotland 239–40
National Screen and Sound Archive of Wales 254
National Union of Mineworkers (NUM: archives) 197, 201, 203, 247–8
National Waterfront Museum (National Museum Wales) 225, 252
nationalisation (coal, 1947) 43, 154, 165–6, 174

Newbridge Colliery Beam Engine 234
Newcastle City Library 187
Newcastle University (Robinson) Library
    187
New Edlington 14
Newcomen engines 201, 217
Newport Reference Library 231
newspapers
    Ardrossan & Saltcoats Herald 176
    Ayrshire Post 176
    Barnsley Chronicle 100
    Barnsley Record 50, 57, 58, 59, 57, 58, 59
    Bristol Mercury 56
    Consett Chronicle 59
    Daily Herald 72, 79
    Dalkeith Advertiser 179
    Darlington & Stockton Times 186
    Derby Mercury 56
    Durham Chronicle 56, 186
    Durham County Advertiser 56, 186
    Examiner (London) 58
    Falkirk Herald 180
    Guardian, The 75
    Halifax Courier 196
    Halifax Guardian 196
    Kirkintilloch Herald 177
    Leeds Intelligencer 196
    Leeds Mercury 195–6
    Manchester Guardian 104
    Milngavie & Bearsden Herald 177
    Monmouthshire Merlin 231
    Motherwell Times 179
    Northern Echo 186
    Observer, The 64
    Rhondda Leader 54, 58, 232
    Rotherham Advertiser 141, 198
    South Wales Argos 231
    South Wales Daily/Evening Post 231
    South Yorkshire Times 127
    Stirling Journal & Advertiser 179
    Times, The 58, 64
    Wellington Journal 99
    West Lothian Courier 180
    Western Mail 231
    Western Telegraph 232
NCB – see National Coal Board
Newton, Sarah 39, 115
Newton Aycliffe FHS 191
Nixon, Arthur 12
Normanson, John (miners' leader) 158
North Ayrshire Archives 176
North East England Mining Archive &
    Research Centre (NEEMARC) 187

North Lanarkshire Heritage Centre 178–9
North Tyneside Central Library 188
North of England Institute of Mining &
    Mechanical Engineers (NEIMME)
    Library 187–8
North Yorkshire County Record Office
    197–8
Northern Institute of Mining & Mechanical
    Engineers 113
Northumberland Archives at Woodburn
    188
Northumberland Fusiliers 129
Northumberland Libraries 188
Northumberland Miners' Picnic 90
Nottingham Local Studies Library 198
Nottingham University Manuscripts &
    Special Collections 198
Nottingham Industrial Museum 201
Nottinghamshire Archives 198
nurses (pit) 41

Oglethorpe, M A (author) 168
Order of Industrial Heroism 72, 79
Orgreave 141
Orwell, George (author) 3, 107, 108, 132
Otley 123

Palmer, Ron 72
Pals battalions 121–2
Parkes, Harry 138
Patterson, Margaret 50
pay (miners') 35–37, 84, 104–5, 133, 161
Paynter, Will (miners' leader) 131, 132
Peak District Mining Museum 168, 201
Penrith 98
People's History Museum 94, 206–7
Pembrokeshire Record Office 231
periodicals and magazines
    Coal/Coal News 186, 188, 199, 244
    Colliery Guardian 65, 186, 188, 229, 244,
        253
    Colliery Yearbook & Coal Directory 253
    Derbyshire Miner 196
    Graphic, The 60, 64, 65
    Guardian, The 64
    Guide to Coalfields 253
    Illustrated London News 60, 61, 65, 196
    Illustrated Police News 60, 62, 64
    Illustrated Times 60
    Iron & Coal Trade Review 188
    London Gazette 75
    Mining Journal 188, 244
    Penny Illustrated 63, 64

Pictorial Times 60
Picture Post 132
Pike, E Royston (author) 108, 113, 115
pit brow women – see female miners
pithead baths – see bathing
pit lasses 163
pitman painters 3
pit sinkers 33–5
Pleasley Colliery Mining Heritage 201–2
Poar, Jeff (NCB photographer) 23
Pontypool Museum 234
pony drivers 19–20, 21–22
Potter, Henry 58
Potter, Stan 14, 17, 37
Preen, Charles 75
Prestongrange Industrial Heritage Museum 181
price lists 36, 161
Pride, Isaac 76
Proto (mines safety equipment) 74, 126
Putney 32

Radstock Museum 221, 222
Ralph, Mary Ann 100–01
Raleys – see Coal Mining History Resource Centre
Ram Hill Colliery 222
Ratcliffe, Thomas 59
Rawmarsh 129
Rawson, George 16, 21, 25
relief funds 36
Rennison, Norman 22
Reeves, James 18
Rhondda, the 54, 76
Rhondda Cynon Taf Library Service 232
Rhondda Heritage Park 234
Riley, Bill 79
Robens, Lord (NCB chairman) 86
Rokicki, Marion 24
Rotherham 65, 129, 140
Rotherham Archives & Local Studies Library 198
Rotherham Mines Rescue Station 164
Rothervale Colliery Company 141, 143, 149
Royal Antediluvian Order of Buffaloes Medal 80
Royal Army Medical Corp (RAMC) 118
Royal Commission on Ancient & Historical Monuments 168, 242, 255
Royal Engineers 120
Royal Humane Society Medal 79
Royston (Yorks) 130

St Fagans Natural History Museum 235
St Helens Local History & Archives Library 207
St John's Ambulance (first aid) 118
St John's Life Saving Medal 79
safety lamps (miners') 156–7
Salford Local History Library & City Archives Centre 207
Saltley Gate 88
Sankey Commission 37
Saville, John 112
Scargill, Arthur (miners' leader) 88, 89, 90
Scottish Genealogy Society 242
Scottish mining galas 90
Scottish Mining Museum 171, 238–9
Scottish Screen Archive 241–2
screens (pit-top) 14, 15, 16, 96
Second World War 118, 120, 132–8
Segedunum Roman Fort, Baths & Museum 190
Selby mine complex 153
Sheffield 5, 37, 141
Sheffield Archives & Local Studies 199
Sheffield Indexers 203
Shepherd, Albert (miner-VC) 130
Shropshire Archives 212
Siebe-Gorman (mine safety equipment) 74
Silkstone 112, 115
Simons, William 75
Smith, Herbert (miners' leader) 90, 92
Smith, Robert 107
Snibston Discovery Museum & Mining Study Centre 211, 216
Somerset Heritage Service 221
Somme (battlefield) 123, 129, 130
Sorbie Family (Lanarkshire Mining) 183
South Ayrshire Libraries 175–6
South Tyneside Central Library 189
South Wales Borderers 130, 131
South Wales Coalfield Collection 232
South Wales Miners' Library 90, 232
South Wales Miners' Museum 235
souvenirs (disaster) 158–9
Spanish Civil War 118, 131–2, 227
snap (food consumed underground) 17, 23, 159
Staffordshire University Special Collections 213
Steer, Jack 16–17, 37
Stephenson, George (engineer) 190
Stirling Libraries & Archives 179
Stoke on Trent City Archives 213
Summerlee Museum of Industrial Life 181

Sunderland City Library & Arts Centre 189
surveyors (mine) 22
Swadlincote 40
Swansea Central Library 231
Swansea University Richard Burton
    Archives 232
Symons, M V (author) 71
Symonds (sub-commissioner) 112, 115

Taberner, Maggie 103
Tankersely 70, 73
Taylor, Fionn 66
Taylor, Thomas (photographer) 101
Territorial Army (TA) 120
Thatcher, Margaret (Prime Minister) 89
The Beacon (museum, Whitehaven) 194
The National Archives (TNA) 93, 112–3,
    138, 247
Thomas, Daniel 76
Thomas, Jenkin 54
tobacco/twist tins 159
Ton Pentre 54
Tonypandy 159
trade unions – see unions (trade) and
    associations
Tredegar 96, 105
Treeton 140–51
Trent Archive Service 213
Tinkler, Alexander 145
Tremenheere, Hugh Seymour (first mines
    inspector) 107
trammers 10, 16–17, 110
transport (to work) 13, 14
trappers (ventilation door operators) 16, 17,
    18, 50– 1, 52
tunnellers (miners as, in the First World
    War) 123–4, 125, 126, 127
Tunnicliffe, Ernest 145
Tyne & Wear Archives 189

UK Coal 184
under managers 30, 31
unions (miners') history of 82–85
union records & where to find them 93–5
unions (trade) and associations
    Bristol Miners' Association 221
    Coalville & District Miners' Association
        91
    Cumberland Miners' Union 104
    Durham Miners' Association 85, 155, 186
    Lancashire & Cheshire Miners' Federation
        205
    Lancashire Miners County Union 104

Leicestershire Miners' Association 91
Midland Miners' Federation 213
Miners' Association of Great Britain &
    Ireland 85
Miners' Federation of Great Britain 37,
    84, 85, 91, 92, 131
Miners' National Union 85, 245
National Association of Colliery Managers
    30, 215
National Association Colliery Overmen,
    Deputies & Shotfirers 187
National Union of Mineworkers 82, 84,
    85, 86, 88, 92, 93, 155, 158, 241
National Union of Winding & General
    Enginemen 35
North Staffordshire Miners Federation
    155
Somerset Miners' Association 221
South Wales Miners' Federation ('The
    Fed') 85, 131, 232, 248
South Yorkshire Miners' Association
    89–90
'Spencer Union' (breakaway,
    Nottinghamshire) 85, 88
West Yorkshire Miners' Association 90
Yorkshire Miners' Association 92, 155,
    248
Universal Colliery (Senghenydd) Mining
    Disaster Memorial 235
University of Bangor Archives & Special
    Collections 227
University of Leicester Special Collections
    212
University of Glasgow Library & Archives
    178

Vardy, Thomas S 163
Victoria, Queen 110, 115
Victoria County Histories 166–7
viewers – see mining engineers

wages – see pay
Wakefield 85, 153
Wakefield One Library & Local Studies
    Library 199
Walters, William 75
war memorials 119, 128, 129
Wardell, Frank (mines inspector) 46–47
Warwick University Modern Records Centre
    214
Warwickshire County Record Office 214
Washington F Pit Museum 190
Washington, William 75

Waters, T (Corp) 133, 134
Wentworth 13
West Dunbartonshire Libraries & Archives 177
West Glamorgan Archive Service 230–1
West Lothian Libraries & Archives 180
West Yorkshire Archive Service 199
West Yorkshire Coal Owners' Association 123
Whitehaven 41, 96, 98, 192
Wigan 3, 47, 101, 102, 103, 107
Wigan Heritage Services & Archives 207
Wigan Life, Museum of 208
Wilberforce, Lord 88
Wilson, Harold (Labour leader & PM) 88, 90
William Salt Library 213
Williams, Barbara 89
Williams, Chris 3
Williams, Elizabeth 99
Williams, John Henry (miner-VC) 130–1
Williams, Robert (mines inspector) 46, 49, 50
Williamson, John 12–13, 17
Winding House, The (Elliot Colliery) 235

Winstanley, Ian (author) 39, 67, 113, 180, 186, 207, 208, 215, 229, 232
Wolverhampton Archives & Local Studies 213
Wombwell 82, 92, 128
women's work (home) 26–27
women and girl miners – see female miners
Woodhorn Colliery Museum 90, 190–1
Woodlands (model village, Doncaster) 14
Woofinden, Thomas 59
Worcestershire Archive & Archaeology Service (The Hive) 215
Working Class Movement Library 94, 208, 248
Workington 192
Wragg, Herbert (photographer) 101
Wrexham Archives (A N Palmer Centre) 227
Wroe, Patience 107
Wynne, Thomas (mines inspector) 46, 47

Yorkshire Archaeological Society Library & Archives 199–200
Yorkshire Film Archive 203
Ystrad 54

Discover Your History

Ancestors • Heritage • Memories

Each issue of *Discover Your History* presents special features and regular articles on a huge variety of topics about our social history and heritage – such as our ancestors, childhood memories, military history, British culinary traditions, transport history, our rural and industrial past, health, houses, fashions, pastimes and leisure ... and much more.

Historic pictures show how we and our ancestors have lived and the changing shape of our towns, villages and landscape in Britain and beyond.

Special tips and links help you discover more about researching family and local history. Spotlights on fascinating museums, history blogs and history societies also offer plenty of scope to become more involved.

Keep up to date with news and events that celebrate our history, and reviews of the latest books and media releases.

Discover Your History presents aspects of the past partly through the eyes and voices of those who were there.

FREE BOOK
WHEN YOU SUBSCRIBE TO
Discover Your History

UK only

Discover Your History is in all good newsagents and also available on subscription for six or twelve issues. For more details on how to take out a subscription and how to choose your free book, call 01778 392013 or visit **www.discoveryourhistory.net**